Islam and Revolution in the Middle East

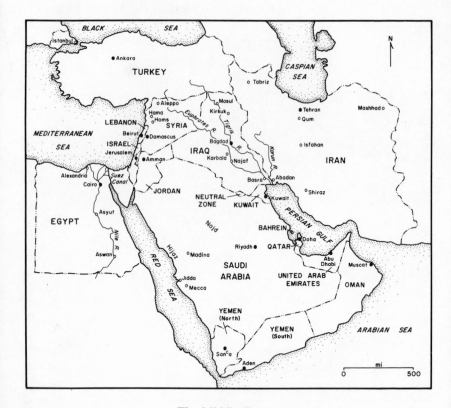

The Middle East

Islam
AND
Revolution
IN THE
Middle East

HENRY MUNSON, JR.

Yale University Press
NEW HAVEN AND LONDON

To Leila, John, Michael, and Nadia

Designed by James J. Johnson
and set in Times Roman types by
Brevis Press, Bethany, Connecticut.
Printed in the United States of America by
Vail-Ballou Press, Binghamton, New York.

Library of Congress Cataloging-in-Publication Data

Munson, Henry, 1946–
  Islam and revolution in the Middle East.

  Bibliography: p. 159.
  Includes index.
  1. Islam and politics—Middle East.   2. Middle East
—Politics and government.   3. Revolutions—Religious
aspects—Islam.   4. Shī'ah—Iran.   I. Title.
BP63.A4N426   1988   322'.1'0956   87–21531
ISBN 0–300–04127–6 (cloth)
     0–300–04604–9 (pbk.)

The paper in this book meets the guidelines for
permanence and durability of the Committee on
Production Guidelines for Book Longevity of the
Council on Library Resources.

10   9   8   7   6   5

Contents

Contents

Preface

Why did an "Islamic revolution" occur only in Iran? Why have Muslim "fundamentalists" elsewhere been incapable of emulating their Iranian counterparts? The principal purpose of this study is to answer these questions. At the same time, however, I have tried to provide an overview of the social and religious origins of the principal Middle Eastern Islamic movements of the twentieth century—with particular attention to the 1970s and 1980s.

The book is divided into three parts entitled "Islam as Religion and Ideology," "Islam and Politics since the Late Nineteenth Century," and "Explanations." Part I focuses on the comparison of Sunni and Shi'i Islam and on the contrast between popular religious belief and fundamentalist ideology in both. (The Sunni-Shi'i dichotomy is of particular significance in the context of this work since Iran is the only large country with an overwhelmingly Shi'i population.) Part II consists of narrative histories of the political role of Islam in Iran, Saudi Arabia, Egypt, and Syria since the late nineteenth century, with a concluding chapter comparing the social bases of the Islamic movements in these countries (and others) during the 1970s and 1980s. Part III consists of an appraisal and a synthesis of various explanations of Iran's unique revolution, some of which are linked to more general theories of revolution.

I have focused primarily upon Iran, and secondarily upon Saudi Arabia, Egypt, and Syria, for several reasons. To begin with, these countries all experienced some form of Islamic revolt in the late 1970s or early 1980s. But only in Iran was there a full-fledged revolution. Second, some familiarity with the twentieth-century histories of these countries is essential to anyone seeking to understand the fundamentalist movements of the seventies and eighties in the Middle East generally.

I have said virtually nothing about Libya because, contrary to popular belief in the United States, Qaddafi had little impact on the Islamic movements of the seventies and eighties. Shi'i fundamentalists blame him for the death of the Lebanese Shi'i leader Imam Musa al-Sadr, and Sunni fundamentalists condemn his idiosyncratic interpretations of Islam. (See the articles by Lisa Anderson and Augustus Richard Norton listed in the Bibliography.)

I have also said relatively little about Morocco, where I have done most of my own research. This is partly because Morocco's Islamic movement in the seventies and eighties was insignificant when compared with those discussed here. Second, I am writing another book about the relationship between Islam and politics in Morocco. And third, I have tried to narrow the scope of this study so as to avoid saying too little about too much. I do, however, frequently refer to Morocco in the notes.

With respect to the term *revolution*, I use it to refer to the overthrow of a government and a social order by large numbers of people. In the Middle East, as in the third world generally, every time a few officers stage a successful coup, they call what they have done a revolution. This is perfectly natural. It is easy to speak of a revolution as "glorious" or "great" in that it conjures up images of an oppressed people overthrowing a corrupt and despotic regime. Somehow the term *glorious coup* does not have quite the same ring to it. But not being in the position of having to worry about such matters, I refer to coups as coups and to revolutions as revolutions.

I have attempted to demonstrate that the widely held view that the Iranian Revolution was the result of overly rapid modernization is egregiously inadequate. Nationalistic resentment of foreign domination was a much more important cause of the Iranian Revolution, just as it has been a major cause of the Marxist revolutions of the third world. But resentment of foreign domination, like many of the other grievances that led to Iran's revolution, has existed for a long time in most Muslim countries (and most third world countries) without engendering revolutions of any kind.

Revolutions occur only in countries where there is widespread discontent. But they do not *inevitably* occur wherever there is such discontent. Usually, they are successful only when the ancien régime has been somehow crippled and where there exist opposition forces capable of articulating popular grievances and mobilizing political action. Such a situation existed in Iran in the late seventies primarily because of the following factors: the charismatic authority of Khomeini, the alliance of the principal "modern" and "traditional" opposition groups made possible by the writings of Dr. 'Ali Shari'ati, and the impact of the Carter administration's human rights policy. The shah's cancer was also a factor that aggravated his government's weakness in 1978–79.

The shah's ties to the United States, it is argued, were both his greatest liability and his greatest asset. Politically conscious Iranians had condemned him as an American puppet ever since the CIA returned him to his throne in 1953. And the expansion of education in the sixties and seventies greatly increased the number of such politically conscious people. But at the same time, virtually all Iranians viewed the shah as invulnerable so long as he enjoyed American support. The Carter administration's human rights policy, and the shah's vacillating and superficial attempts to conform to it, convinced both the secular and the religious opposition that the Pahlavi regime was no longer invulnerable. Khomeini was able to exploit this perceived weakness thanks to his charismatic authority, both institutional and personal, and thanks to Shari'ati's Islamic version of liberation theology, which induced the educated young to join forces with men they had once dismissed as reactionaries.

The Carter human rights policy precipitated the shah's downfall, as it did that of Somoza in Nicaragua. This does not mean, however, that the United States should not push for democratization and respect for basic human rights in the third world. On the contrary, it must. Failure to do so ultimately strengthens Muslim fundamentalist as well as Marxist movements. But such pressure must be exerted discreetly and at the proper time. There is no point in hastening the overthrow of a dictator unless there is a strong democratic opposition to replace him.

The biases of an author inevitably shape a book dealing with religious and political matters, and some of my own are probably already fairly clear. With respect to fundamentalist movements, I have no sympathy for anyone who seeks to force a society to conform to sacred

scripture, be it the Ayatollah Khomeini, the Reverend Falwell, or
Rabbi Kahane. But the purpose of this book is not to condemn. It is
to explain. And to explain the successes and failures of the Middle
Eastern Islamic movements in the 1970s and 1980s, it is necessary to
understand how the people who participated in them perceive the
world and why they perceive the world as they do.

I have written this book for the general reader as well as for scholars
specializing in the study of the Islamic world. Therefore I cover a lot
of material with which specialists are thoroughly familiar, especially
in the narrative histories and some sections dealing with Islam in
part I. But this is not intended to be an anodyne textbook reducing
the scholarship of others to pap. In chapters 4 ("The Ulama, Popular
Religion, and Fundamentalist Ideology in Sunni and Shi'i Islam") and
9 ("Social Bases"), as well as in most of part III ("Explanations"), I
have taken issue with some widely accepted misconceptions about Islam and Islamic movements, such as the notion that there is no distinction between religion and politics in Islam and the idea that Islamic
fundamentalists are often people whose lives have been disrupted by
rural-urban migration.

I have tried to avoid social science jargon. And I have tried to limit
the number of notes but at the same time provide adequate documentation. All sources for a given paragraph are usually in one note at
the paragraph's end—except for quotations and situations where this
might cause confusion. References are given in short form in the notes
and in long form in the Bibliography.

I have used a simplified system of transliteration with no diacritics.
' represents the Arabic 'ayn, made by pressing the root of the tongue
against the back of the throat. ' represents the hamza, or glottal stop—
a quick closure of the vocal cords. *Q* represents a k-like sound produced farther back in the mouth. And *kh* represents the voiceless
vibration of the uvula, similar to the final sound in *Bach*. In translit-
erating Persian words, I have generally remained faithful to their written Arabic forms. But I have used the common anglicized
transliterations of well-known names, such as *Khomeini*.

The translations of Quranic verses are my own. I refer to Quranic
chapters according to the standard enumeration.

Some readers may be puzzled by the fact that the Shi'i holiday of
'Ashura occurred in June of 1963 but in December of 1978. The reason
for this is that the Islamic calendar is lunar rather than solar. In other

words, the Islamic year consists of twelve months as counted from new moon to new moon, with twenty-nine or thirty days in each. This lunar year is about eleven days shorter than the solar year upon which the Western calendar is based. There is therefore no fixed relationship between the Islamic year and the Western one. Over time, a particular Islamic holiday, such as 'Ashura, travels around the solar year.

I would like to thank the following institutions for fellowships that made it possible to write this book: the Center for Arabic Study Abroad at the American University in Cairo, the Social Science Research Council, the Fulbright-Hays program of the Office of Education, the National Endowment for the Humanities, and the Summer Faculty Fellowship Program at the University of Maine. I would also like to thank the Center for Middle Eastern Studies at Harvard University for inviting me to present an earlier version of chapter 9 ("Social Bases") in March of 1986.

I am indebted to Jean-François Clément, Dale Eickelman, Patrick D. Gaffney, Alex Grab, and George Joffé for their comments on earlier versions of several chapters and to Bahman Bakhtiari, Mary Hegland, Nikki R. Keddie, and Bruce B. Lawrence for their comments on the manuscript as a whole. These scholars should not be held responsible for my views. (This is, of course, also true of the institutions mentioned above.) I thank Steve Bicknell of the University of Maine for drawing the maps. And I thank Ellen Graham, Cecile Watters, and Laura Dooley of Yale University Press for helping to transform my manuscript into a book.

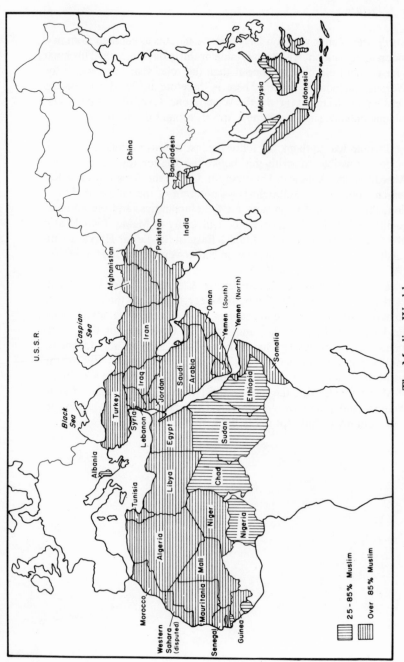

The Muslim World

(There are also important Muslim minorities in India and the Soviet Union.)

25 – 85% Muslim

Over 85% Muslim

PART I

Islam as Religion and Ideology

Principal Muslim Countries of the Middle East: Selected Social and Economic Features at the Time of the Iranian Revolution of 1978–79

Country	Population Millions (1977)	Percent Muslim (1977)	GNP per Capita $ (1977)	Percent Adult Literacy[a] (1977)	Percent Labor Force in Industry[b]		
					(1960)	(1980)	Percent Increase
Egypt	38	90	340	44	12	30	150
Iran	35	98	1,600[c]	38	23	34	48
Iraq	12	97	1,570	30	18	26	44
Jordan	3	92	940	68	26	20	−23
Libya	3	97	6,520	50	17	28	65
Saudi Arabia	6	100	7,230	22	10	14	40
Sudan	17	73	330	22	6	10	67
Syria	8	86	860	56	19	31	63
Turkey	42	99	1,110	60	11	13	18

a. Estimates based on nearest years for which rates are given in the *World Development Report 1983*.

b. "Industry" is understood to include mining, construction, and utilities as well as manufacturing.

c. 1976.

SOURCES: World Bank, *World Tables,* 2nd ed.; *World Development Report 1983*; and various country studies. There are no census data for Saudi Arabia, and estimates vary.

1

Introduction

Characterizing the Islamic movements that advocate strictly Islamic states and societies as *fundamentalist* poses a number of problems. First of all, the doctrines of some of these movements are more reminiscent of liberation theology in Latin America than they are of Christian fundamentalism in the United States. For example, a leaflet published in 1977 by the Organization of Iranian Moslem Students in Wilmette, Illinois, concluded with the following phrase printed in large boldface capital letters: "VICTORY TO THE JUST STRUGGLE OF THE WRETCHED OF THE EARTH AGAINST IMPERIALISM, ZIONISM, AND REACTION IN THE WAY OF CONSTRUCTING A FREE, MONOTHEISTIC, AND CLASSLESS SOCIETY."[1] And on September 24, 1979, Khomeini told the Muslims making the pilgrimage to Mecca:

> My Muslim brothers and sisters! You are aware that the superpowers of East and West are plundering all our material and other resources, and have placed us in a situation of political, economic, cultural, and military dependence. Come to your senses; rediscover your Islamic identity! Endure oppression no longer, and vigilantly expose the criminal plans of the international bandits, headed by America![2]

Such references to "the wretched of the earth," "imperialism," "oppression," and "identity" pervade much of the Islamic fundamentalist literature of the late seventies and early eighties, whereas they do not usually figure prominently in the homilies of twentieth-century Christian fundamentalists. It would, for example, be difficult to imagine the Reverend Jerry Falwell exhorting his congregation to support "the just struggle of the wretched of the earth against imperialism, Zionism, and reaction in the way of constructing a free, monotheistic, and classless society."

On the other hand, however, fundamentalist Protestant movements—that is, movements advocating a society in accordance with sacred Scripture—have often had a radical egalitarian orientation in past centuries. One thinks, for example, of the peasant revolts in sixteenth-century Germany and of the Levellers, Diggers, and Fifth Monarchy Men in seventeenth-century England.[3]

Another problem with the term *fundamentalist* is that it is of Protestant rather than Muslim provenance. Some Muslims regard its usage in the Islamic context as a form of Western intellectual imperialism. The people referred to as "Muslim fundamentalists" in the West do not characterize themselves this way. They usually speak of themselves either as "Muslims" (the implication being that those Muslims who do not share their views are not really Muslims at all) or, more recently, as "Islamists" (*Islamiyyun* in Arabic).[4]

Despite these various problems, I have decided to retain the term *fundamentalist* in this work for the following reasons. For one thing, I cannot think of an adequate alternative term to characterize those Muslims who advocate a strictly Islamic policy. The term *Islamist* strikes me as a clumsy neologism. As for the term Islamic *militant*, which I have used on occasion, it is not applicable to the moderate fundamentalists who generally shun violence. Moreover, it says nothing about the specific goals of Islamic movements that distinguish their members from Muslims in general.

In addition to the absence of a satisfactory alternative, I would also argue that the concept of *fundamentalism* has transcended its origins much as *puritanism* and *zealotry* have transcended theirs. In scholarly as well as ordinary usage, the term has come to refer to anyone who insists that all aspects of life, including the social and the political, should conform to a set of sacred scriptures believed to be inerrant and immutable. It is in this sense that S. Zalman Abramov speaks of Jewish fundamentalism in Israel.[5] And it is in this sense that we can speak of Islamic fundamentalism in the Muslim world.

RADICALS AND REFORMISTS

But if we are going to characterize people striving to create a strictly Islamic state and society as Muslim fundamentalists, we must not assume that all such people understand this goal in the same way. Some Islamic movements—for example, that of Khomeini in Iran—are radical in the sense that the people in them seek to overthrow the governments of their countries and initiate fundamental political, social, and economic transformations. Others, however, such as Pakistan's *Jama'at-i Islami* (the Society of Islam) and the Egyptian Muslim Brotherhood of the 1970s and 1980s, are more reformist in character.

It is a basic (and common) mistake to assume that all Islamic movements demanding a strictly Islamic polity have identical ideological orientations. For example, a basic goal of the Ayatollah Khomeini and his closest associates was the elimination of all forms of American domination. But in Pakistan, the Islamic movement that led to General Zia al-Haqq's coup of 1977 and the subsequent Islamicization of Pakistani public life did not have the salient nationalistic character of its Iranian counterpart. And whereas the relationship between the United States and Iran's Islamic Republic was one of overt hostility during the late seventies and early eighties, Zia al-Haqq's Islamicized Pakistan continued to receive billions of dollars in American aid during this period.[6]

Even within individual countries, Islamic movements are usually internally divided into radical and reformist wings, with these tendencies themselves further fragmented. In Egypt, the reformist Muslim Brotherhood is challenged by a number of more radical and militant groups, including the one that assassinated Anwar Sadat in October 1981. In Pakistan, many radical Islamic activists condemn the leaders of the Jama'at-i Islami for their lack of revolutionary zeal. And in Iran, the Islamic Republic has had to suppress the opposition of the radical Islamic *Mujahidin* (Holy Warriors). Similar conflicts can be found in all the Islamic movements of the seventies and eighties.[7]

The conflict between the Khomeini regime and the radical Mujahidin of Iran demonstrates that even among Islamic revolutionaries, we find both radicals and moderates, just as among reformists, we find some people more radical than others. What we find, in effect, is a continuum of political orientations among Islamic movements that sometimes makes it difficult to classify them as radical or reformist, especially since ostensibly reformist rhetoric may sometimes reflect fear of repression rather than a nonrevolutionary orientation.

However, in addition to the obvious criterion of explicit commitment to fundamental political, social, and economic change, there are several other useful indices of where the advocates of strictly Islamic politics stand with respect to the radical-reformist distinction. The revolutionaries tend to emphasize (by acts as well as words) their opposition to foreign economic, political, and cultural domination, whereas the reformists place less stress on such themes and more on conformity to Islamic law. The radicals constantly excoriate "American imperialism," whereas the reformists often have good relations with the United States, as in the case of the governments of Pakistan and Saudi Arabia. The most radical Islamic revolutionaries tend to be hostile to private property and free enterprise, whereas the reformists tend to favor both. And since 1979, the radicals outside Iran have usually been supported by Iran's Islamic Republic, whereas the reformists have usually been supported by Saudi Arabia.[8]

In practice, the radical-reformist dichotomy is often also complicated by sectarian and nationalistic tensions, although fundamentalists insist that Islam transcends such divisions. Thus although the Khomeini regime has encouraged revolutionary Islamic movements all over the world, it has had much closer ties with Shiʻi movements than it has with Sunni ones. Conversely, the movements supported by Saudi Arabia are invariably Sunni as well as nonrevolutionary.[9]

In short, then, the various movements advocating a strictly Islamic state are by no means homogeneous. Nor are they in any sense united.

2

Islamic Sacred History in Popular Religion and Fundamentalist Ideology: The Common Core

If we wish to understand the political role of a religion, we need to try to understand it as it is understood by the believer—by the various kinds of believer. And this entails that we examine its sacred history. If we look only at the explicitly political facets of a religion, as enshrined in tracts, laws, and institutions, we overlook the meaning of that religion as it is experienced by "ordinary people" during the course of their everyday lives. And we are thereby prevented from understanding or explaining the crucial relationship between religion as it is understood by the ordinary believer and religion as it is depicted in fundamentalist ideology.[1]

All religions have *sacred histories*—that is, stories about primordial beginnings that are understood by the believer to explain the human condition. Sacred history narrates events in the lives of extraordinary people in the distant past who are seen by the believer as exemplars to be emulated in the present. Such history is thus a form of *myth*— as this term is generally used by anthropologists and students of comparative religion. In this sense, rather than being illusory, myths are models of what is most real—from the believer's point of view. The question of whether the events described in myth actually occurred is irrelevant insofar as we are concerned with the impact of myth upon the believer's apprehension of the world.[2]

Myth shapes the believer's conception of history. But history in turn shapes the believer's conception of myth. Martin Luther King's

7

reference to the black American's exodus "from the midnight of Egyptian captivity to the glittering light of Canaan freedom" suggests that he interpreted the plight of the black American in terms of the bondage of the Israelites much as he interpreted the bondage of the Israelites in terms of the plight of the black American.[3] His pharaoh was not the pharaoh of Menachem Begin nor that of Jerry Falwell because, like everyone else, he interpreted his myths in the context of his history, and vice versa. Muslims are no different, which means that in order to understand how Muslims interpret their history, we need to know their myths. And to understand how they interpret their myths, we need to know their history. We begin with their myths.

IN THE BEGINNING

Muslims believe that after creating the heavens and the earth in six days, God (*Allah*) created Adam and Eve and placed them in a garden in which the fruit of one tree was forbidden. When Satan (*al-Shaytan*) tempted them to eat the fruit of this tree, God banished them from the garden. Then Adam "received words" from God, who forgave him and said he would send a series of prophets to guide "the children of Adam." Among the most prominent of these emissaries of God were Noah, Abraham, Moses, Jesus, and the ultimate prophet, Muhammad. The Quran repeatedly emphasizes that God punishes those who reject the prophets sent them.[4]

Muslims regard the sacred Scriptures of Judaism and Christianity as incomplete versions of God's revelations to the early prophets, whereas the Quran is regarded as the literal and inerrant text of God's word as revealed to the final and greatest prophet, Muhammad. Like the Quran, the Scriptures of Judaism and Christianity are said to emanate from a divine and eternal book in heaven, which is why Jews and Christians are referred to as "the people of the Book" (*ahl al-kitab*).[5]

THE PROPHET MUHAMMAD AS EXEMPLAR

At the core of Islamic sacred history is the life of the prophet Muhammad, who has come to serve as the principal model of how Muslims (especially Sunnis) ought to act. The story of Muhammad's life is told in the Quran, in the thousands of *hadiths* (reports) concerning the prophet's words and acts, and in a number of biographies, the most influential of which was written by Ibn Ishaq in the eighth century. The *Sunna* (customary practice) of the prophet Muhammad, as embodied in the hadiths, is the second most important source of Islamic law after the Quran.[6]

The following summary of Muhammad's life focuses on the best-known events that have had a particularly powerful impact on the Islamic imagination. These events are perceived in different ways by different kinds of Muslims. In popular Islam, the prophet Muhammad is generally perceived as an ethereal being who intercedes on behalf of all believers on the day of reckoning as well as at times of imminent danger in this world. But in the fundamentalist literature of the late twentieth century, Muhammad is often portrayed as a great revolutionary who led "the oppressed" (*al-mustad'afun*) in a social as well as spiritual revolution.[7]

FROM BIRTH TO THE FIRST REVELATION ON THE MOUNTAIN

Muhammad was born in Mecca in about A.D. 570. His father died before he was born and his mother died when he was six. After the death of his paternal grandfather two years later, Muhammad was raised by his paternal uncle Abu Talib, whose son 'Ali was to become one of the most revered figures in Islam (especially in Shi'i Islam). As a young man, Muhammad went to work for a wealthy widow named Khadija. Although she was fifteen years older than he was, Khadija and Muhammad were soon married and she bore him two sons and four daughters, the two boys dying in infancy. By the time he was forty, Muhammad was a respected and well-established merchant. But he was spiritually troubled and would frequently go to a mountain outside Mecca to pray and meditate.

One night as he slept in a cave on this mountain, the angel Gabriel appeared to him and told him to recite the following words written on a silk cloth:

> Recite in the name of your Lord who created—
> Who created man from a clot of congealed blood
> Recite and your Lord is the most kind
> He who taught by the pen
> Taught man what he knew not.[8]

These are believed to have been the first words of the Quran (Recitation) revealed to Muhammad. Muhammad was frightened by this vision, but then he heard the angel Gabriel say, "O Muhammad, thou art the apostle of God and I am Gabriel."[9]

THE LYRICAL REVELATIONS OF MECCA

After a brief period during which the prophet was distressed because he had no more visions, the revelations resumed and Muhammad began to preach to the polytheists of Mecca. Among the principal themes he emphasized during this early Meccan period was the idea that the many inexplicable wonders of the world, such as the fall of rain from the sky, the growth of plants from the ground, and the sequence of night and day, are "signs of God" that should induce the unbeliever to believe. The term *ayat Allah,* or "sign of God" (usually transliterated as *ayatollah*) is also the title of the highest ranking religious scholars in Shi'i Islam.[10]

Another leitmotif of the early Meccan verses of the Quran is the graphic depiction of the day of reckoning:

> On that day some faces will shine
> Laughing and rejoicing
> And on that day some faces will
> Be covered with dust
> Covered with darkness
> Thus will be those
> Who deny God
> And do evil.[11]

THE PROPHET AS LIBERATOR OF THE OPPRESSED OF MECCA

Fundamentalists often portray the early Meccan converts to Islam as "the oppressed" (al-mustad'afun), with Muhammad (like the earlier prophets before him) depicted as a man of God leading a social as well as a religious revolution. This is, as one might expect, especially true of the more radical literature. Thus Dr. 'Ali Shari'ati (1933–77), the principal theorist of the left wing of Iran's Islamic movement in the 1970s, has written:

> Muhammad, a young orphan, who used to take the sheep of the Meccans to graze on the outskirts, suddenly, from his sequestered life in the cave of Mount Hira comes down and declares war against the capitalists, the slave dealers of Mecca, and the farm owners of Taif. . . . Without delay, the enfeebled of his society, the strangers, [the] slaves, the deprived come round him and thus we hear of torture, flight, homelessness and the continuous war in the way of God.[12]

This interpretation of Muhammad is reminiscent of how Jesus has been interpreted by some liberation theologians in Latin America and demonstrates to what extent the most radical advocates of a strictly Islamic state and society have been influenced by Marxist thought.[13]

Just as the portrait of Jesus as liberator of the oppressed is in sharp contrast with the prevailing Christian view, Shari'ati's revolutionary conception of Muhammad differs fundamentally from the way the prophet is ordinarily perceived by Muslims. That does not mean, however, that such a view cannot have popular appeal, especially since the traditional biographies do stress the persecution of Muhammad and his early followers by the wealthy and powerful leaders of Mecca.[14]

MUHAMMAD'S STATE IN MADINA AS PRIMORDIAL UTOPIA

In 622, Muhammad fled from Mecca to Madina (then known as Yathrib). This "flight," or *hijra,* marks the beginning of the Islamic calendar (622 being the year 1) as well as the emergence of the Islamic polity which the prophet ruled until his death in 632. This period of the prophet's rule is portrayed as a golden age of justice, equality, and virtue in the fundamentalist literature. For example, Sayyid Qutb, the famous ideologist of Egypt's Muslim Brotherhood, writes:

> Society was purified of all social inequity and there arose "the Islamic system" in which the justice meted out was the justice of God measured by the scales of God. . . . And souls and morals were purified, as were hearts and spirits, with virtually no recourse to the punishments decreed by God. For supervision occurred in the conscience, and the yearning for the approval and reward of God, the fear of His wrath, and shame took the place of supervision and punishment.[15]

One of the principal themes of all the fundamentalist literature is that there was no distinction between religion and politics in Muhammad's Madinan polity and there should therefore be none in any truly Islamic state.[16]

VICTORY AND DEFEAT AS SIGNS OF THE FAVOR AND WRATH OF GOD

The "holy war," or *jihad,* between the Muslims and the unbelievers of Mecca escalated to a new level after the prophet's flight to Madina. And the Quranic depiction of this conflict, coupled with the depiction of the punishments inflicted by God upon those who rejected the prophets before Muhammad, established a conception of history that remains very much alive today.

In 624, two years after the hijra, the prophet and a band of about three hundred Muslims defeated a force of about a thousand Meccan unbelievers at the wells of Badr west of Madina. This victory convinced many polytheists to convert to Islam as it appeared to be a sign that God was indeed on the side of Muhammad. But then in the following year (625) some seven hundred Muslims barely avoided being routed by an army of three thousand Meccan unbelievers at the hill of Uhud on the outskirts of Madina. If Badr had been a sign of God's favor, Uhud was widely seen as a sign of God's wrath. In fact, the Quran explicitly explains the outcomes of the two battles in these terms. Thus the lack of victory at Uhud provoked a serious religious as well as political crisis that was not resolved until two years later, in 627, when the Muslims defeated a vast Meccan army that had besieged Madina for two weeks.[17]

From then on, the Muslims grew in strength until they occupied Mecca in 630, the eighth year of the Islamic calendar. By the time of the prophet's death in 632, they controlled almost all of western Arabia. And during the next century, they conquered most of the land from what is now Pakistan in the east to the Atlantic coast of Morocco in the west, as well as most of Spain. This extraordinarily successful expansion of the Islamic domain is explained in both the fundamentalist literature and traditional Islamic historiography as a sign that the early Muslims conformed to God's laws in every way. Conversely, the subsequent decline of the Islamic world, and especially the subjugation of the Islamic world by Europe in the nineteenth and twentieth centuries, is often interpreted (by fundamentalists as well as nonfundamentalists) as a sign that Muslims have disobeyed God's laws.[18]

Sayyid Qutb once said of the plight of the modern Muslims: "They have reached this wretched state because they have abandoned Islam, not because they are Muslims."[19] And in a letter sent to Iranian students in the United States and Canada in 1972, the Ayatollah Khomeini declared:

> If the Muslim governments and countries had relied on Islam and its inherent capabilities and powers instead of depending on the East (the Soviet Union) and the West, and if they had placed the enlightened and liberating precepts of the Quran before their eyes and put them into practice, then they would not today be captive slaves of the Zionist aggressors, terrified victims of the American Phantoms, and toys in the hands of the accommodating policies of the satanic Soviet Union. It is the disregard of the noble Quran by the Islamic countries that has brought the Islamic community to this difficult situation full of mis-

fortunes and reversals and placed its fate in the hands of the imperialism of the left and of the right.[20]

Khomeini's explanation of the subjugation of the Islamic world by the infidel conforms perfectly to the Quranic explanation of the near defeat at the hill of Uhud and—unlike some aspects of fundamentalist Islamic ideology—is deeply rooted in the popular Islamic imagination, as we can see from the following statement by a marginally literate peddler from Morocco:

> Why did God allow the Christians to rule over the house of Islam? Why did God allow the Jews to take Palestine and holy Jerusalem? Why does God allow the Christians to live like sultans in our land while we are like slaves in their land? This is God's punishment. And this is God's test. Muslims have left the path (*kharju min at-triq*) of Islam. Young people do not pray. The rich do not pray. Muslim girls bare their bodies like Christian women. And they walk hand in hand with their lovers. . . . The rich Muslim does not fast during Ramadan. And he drinks wine and whiskey. And he asks why it is that the house of Islam is like a toy in the hands of the Christian. The Christian domination is the wrath of God.[21]

In the Quran, as well as in the minds of many traditional Muslims today, there is but one explanation for the subjugation of the believer by the unbeliever: God is using the latter to punish the former for his sins. And only a return to a strictly Islamic way of life will induce God to free the faithful from the faithless. More generally, all kinds of affliction, including social injustice and poverty, are perceived as signs of God's wrath that only a return to God's law can efface. The power of this logic, in terms of the traditional Islamic worldview, is such that movements demanding a return to the pristine Islam of the prophet have repeatedly occurred at times of social crisis throughout Islamic history (primarily among Sunnis).[22]

This same logic has, of course, also played a central role in both Judaism and Christianity. The Zealots who revolted against the Romans in ancient Palestine were convinced that only strict conformity to the Torah would induce God to lead them to victory.[23] And more recently, the Reverend Jerry Falwell of the United States has written that "if Americans will face the truth, our nation can be turned around and can be saved from the evils and the destruction that have fallen upon every other nation that has turned its back on God."[24] This is precisely what most advocates of a "return to Islam" are saying.

In popular Islam, however, as in Judaism and Christianity, affliction is also perceived as a divinely ordained trial that one must patiently endure in the hope of happiness in the hereafter.[25] And this theme is often stressed in the Quran, as in the following passage:

> Be sure that We shall test you
> By fear, hunger, and loss of
> Goods, lives and fruits
> And bring glad tidings to
> Those who patiently endure
> Those who say, when affliction
> Afflicts them, "To God we belong
> And to Him we shall return."
> They are those upon whom descend
> The blessings and the mercy of God
> And they are the rightly guided.[26]

The fundamentalist Islamic ideologist attempts to substitute a more activist response to adversity than the notion of passive endurance (*as-sabr*) that is especially common among the poorest and least educated strata of Islamic societies. Thus one of the Quranic verses commonly cited in the fundamentalist literature is "God does not change the condition of a people until people change themselves."[27] This contrast between fundamentalist activism and popular fatalism is one of the most striking differences between fundamentalist Islamic ideology and popular Islam.

HOLY WAR (JIHAD)

Like most sacred texts, the Quran contains many contradictory and ambiguous statements that were originally spoken or written in very different situations. It is therefore usually possible to find scriptural justification for just about anything: capitalism as well as socialism, submission to authority as well as revolution, and peaceful coexistence with other religions as well as unrelenting hostility toward them. Those who seek to portray Islam as a tolerant and humane religion often cite Quranic verses such as "Let there be no compulsion in religion" (2:256) and "You have your religion and I have mine" (109:6). On the other hand, those who seek to portray Islam as an intolerant and inhumane religion often cite verses such as "O you who believe, fight the unbelievers around you; let them find harshness in you, and know that God is with those who fear Him" (9:123). All such verses are invariably taken out of their original contexts, as verses of any sacred scripture usually are. But the fact remains that both kinds of verses exist, as do both kinds of corresponding attitudes toward unbelievers.

Much of the Quran, like much of the Torah-cum-Old Testament, depicts a state of holy war between those who follow the one true religion and those who do not. In the early centuries of Islam, this meant fighting unbelievers so as to expand the Islamic domain throughout the world. The "people of the Book" (primarily Jews and Christians) were not usually forced to convert, but had to pay a special tax and submit to a number of restrictions that effectively subordinated them to Muslims in all aspects of social and political life. Their position in Islamic society was degrading, but far less difficult or vulnerable than that of the infidel in Christian Europe during the Middle Ages. During the past century the traditional restrictions on non-Muslims have been largely eliminated. But the fundamentalists would like to see them restored.[28]

The fundamentalists stress the need to revive the idea of fighting to create a single Islamic state to govern the entire world. They also reject modernist attempts to interpret jihad as a purely defensive form of warfare. Nor do they usually place primary emphasis on the idea of "the greater jihad" of the individual against his or her "bad inclinations." From their perspective, they are the slaves of God engaged in holy war against the slaves of Satan, the latter including all those Muslims who do not interpret Islam as they do.[29]

3

Islamic Sacred History in Popular Religion and Fundamentalist Ideology: The Shi'i Offshoot

In speaking of Shi'i Islam, we shall be referring specifically to the "Twelver" (or "Imami") sect to which all but a small minority of Shi'is belong. The adherents of Twelver Shi'ism believe in a line of twelve pure and sinless *imams,* or "spiritual leaders," the first of whom was the prophet Muhammad's patrilateral cousin and son-in-law, 'Ali, and the last of whom has been hidden from human view since the ninth century. This hidden twelfth imam is expected to return as a messiah near the end of time.

The Sunni-Shi'i dichotomy is of special interest insofar as this study is concerned because Iran is the only important country in which Shi'i Muslims constitute an overwhelming majority. It is also the only country to have experienced an Islamic revolution. About 85 percent of all Iranians are Twelver Shi'is, whereas roughly the same percentage of the world's total Muslim population is Sunni.[1]

Two other countries have less preponderant Twelver Shi'i majorities: Iraq and Bahrain. Iraq's population is roughly 55 percent Shi'i. And in the miniature state of Bahrain about 70 percent of the citizens (who numbered about a quarter of a million people in 1983) are estimated to be Shi'is. Although there were fundamentalist Shi'i movements in both Iraq and Bahrain in the late seventies and early eighties, they were ineffectual.[2]

There are also important Twelver Shi'i minorities in other countries east of the Suez Canal, notably Lebanon, where Twelver Shi'is constitute roughly a third of the population, and Saudi Arabia, where they included about 6 percent of an estimated 6 million Saudi citizens in the early eighties.[3]

ORIGINS: THE DISPUTE OVER THE SUCCESSION TO MUHAMMAD

In order to get some sense of what Shi'ism is and how it differs from the dominant Sunni sect of Islam, we need to return to the early sacred history of Islam following the death of Muhammad in 632. Once again, our primary goal is to convey a sense of how this sacred history is perceived by the believer rather than by the secular historian—with particular emphasis on the contrast between politicized fundamentalist interpretations and those of a more traditional religious character.

The prophet's death ten years after the hijra from Mecca to Madina caused both a religious and a political crisis since, as fundamentalist Islamic ideologists correctly emphasize, Muhammad was the religious as well as the political leader of the Islamic community, or *umma*. He was also the final prophet (*nabi*) and emissary (*rasul*) of God, a role that no one else could fill. His death thus raised the question of whether the Islamic polity could survive the loss of its charismatic creator. It did, of course, but not without generating a conflict that eventually led to the division of the Islamic world into the Sunni and Shi'i sects.

After the prophet died, some Muslims, known as the *shi'a,* or "faction," of 'Ali, felt that 'Ali should become the imam of the Islamic community. The beliefs of this group eventually coalesced into what came to be known as Shi'i Islam. But others felt that the successors of Muhammad should be chosen from among the men of the prophet's tribe of Quraysh by the elders of the Islamic community. Those in favor of this view came to be known as "the People of the Sunna and the Community" and their beliefs became those of Sunni Islam. (As noted in the last chapter, the *Sunna* is the exemplary practice of Muhammad as recorded in the *hadiths,* or "reports," concerning his words and acts.)

The majority of the elders of the Islamic community in Madina chose three other men as caliphs, or successors of the prophet, before finally selecting 'Ali in 656. All four of these men—Abu Bakr, 'Umar, 'Uthman, and 'Ali—are revered as "the rightly guided caliphs" (*al-khulafa' al-rashidun*) in Sunni Islam. And the period of their rule, from 632 through 661, is regarded by the fundamentalist ideologists of the Sunni world as an extension of the golden age of the prophet's rule in Madina from 622 through 632. But for Shiʻi fundamentalists, the golden age of Islam consists primarily of the ten years of the prophet's rule and the four and a half years (656–61) of the rule of ʻAli.[4]

Sunni Muslims often also point to both the Umayyad (661–750) and ʻAbbasid (750–1258) eras as a golden age when the Muslim empires were the most advanced superpowers of the world and Europe was among the underdeveloped regions. But both Sunni and Shiʻi fundamentalists view all history since the death of ʻAli in 661 as a long process of decay from the pristine Islam of the prophet Muhammad and his closest companions, with the Shiʻis generally also viewing the rule of the first three caliphs from 632 to 656 as a period of corruption.[5]

ON THE MEANINGS OF THE TERM *IMAM*

The Shiʻis regard the Sunni caliphs as usurpers except, of course, for the fourth one, ʻAli, who was from the Shiʻi perspective the first legitimate imam after the prophet's death. Shiʻis believe that the imams of Islam had to be pure and sinless as Muhammad had been. Only ʻAli and the patrilineal descendants of ʻAli had inherited Muhammad's purity and sinlessness, and therefore only they were capable of leading the Muslim community (the umma). The idea that the Islamic community should elect its leaders is thus emphatically rejected in traditional Shiʻi doctrine. And one sometimes hears Sunnis describe Shiʻi Islam as "authoritarian" as opposed to the more "democratic" character of the early and ideal Sunni caliphate.[6]

Related to the Shiʻi idea of the purity and sinlessness of the imams is the belief that only they had inherited the prophet's understanding of the inner esoteric meaning of Islam and that therefore only they had the authority to interpret the Quran and the hadiths of Islam.[7] (While the Shiʻis share many Sunni hadiths concerning the prophet, they also have many specifically Shiʻi hadiths concerning the imams.)

Dr. ʻAli Shariʻati condemns the popular Shiʻi conception of the imams as twelve "pure, sacred and preternatural souls, superhuman beings who are the only means of approaching and having recourse to God."[8] In keeping with the general fundamentalist emphasis upon political activism rather than religious quietism, Shariʻati says that the "true" meaning of the institution of the imamate is "pure, revolutionary leadership for guiding the people and the true construction of society."[9] Shariʻati translates the Shiʻi conception of the imams' *ʻisma,* traditionally understood to mean "purity and sinlessness," into the less ethereal concepts of "piety, purity of ideas and social leadership."[10]

Shari'ati's interpretation of the word *imam*, which is radically innovative in the Shi'i context, is at least partially similar to Sunni usage, which refers to Islamic religious leaders in general as *imams*—by analogy to *imam* in its basic sense of "one who stands in front" of a congregation of worshipers and leads them in congregational prayer. (In both Sunni and Shi'i Islam, any pious Muslim man in a state of ritual purity can serve as imam in this sense of "leader of congregational prayer.") Sunnis often refer to their caliphs as imams, and the founders of the four principal schools of law in Sunni Islam—Abu Hanifa, Malik Ibn Anas, al-Shafi'i, and Ibn Hanbal—are also all known as imams. The Sa'udi leaders of the Wahhabi movement in Arabia used to be called imams. And the "Epistles" of Hasan al-Banna, the founder of the Egyptian Muslim Brotherhood, were published under the title *The Collection of the Epistles of the Martyred Imam Hasan al-Banna (Majmu'at Rasa'il al-Imam al-Shahid Hasan al-Banna)*.[11]

So whereas both Sunnis and Shi'is refer to a leader of congregational prayers as an imam, Iranian Shi'is also use this term to refer to the twelve pure and sinless imams beginning with 'Ali, and Sunnis use it to refer to any venerated Islamic leader. Shi'i usage in Arabic-speaking countries (notably Iraq and Lebanon) tends to incorporate both Iranian and Sunni meanings of the term. Shi'is sometimes also use the term *imam* to refer specifically to the twelfth imam who will return near the end of time as a messiah, as in the name of the Shi'i religious tax called *sahm-i imam*, "the share of the imam." Thus only the context enables one to know what meaning of the word *imam* is intended. In this work, it will be used primarily to refer to the twelve pure and sinless imams of Twelver Shi'ism.[12]

Iranian students influenced by the radical ideas of Dr. 'Ali Shari'ati stress that the attribution of the title *imam* to the Ayatollah Khomeini during the Iranian Revolution simply meant that he was "the symbolic leader of the revolution and the charismatic leader who expresses the popular will of the people."[13] Khomeini himself never claimed to be the messianic hidden imam and would certainly regard such a claim as blasphemous, as would other Iranian *ulama*, or "religious scholars." But many less educated Iranians did associate Khomeini with the messianic imam for whom the Shi'is have been waiting for over a millennium.[14] And his absence from Iran from 1964 to 1979 was sometimes likened to the absence of the twelfth imam from 874 to the present. After Khomeini's return from exile on a plane chartered from Air France, Iran's Ayatollah Shari'atmadari, a prominent critic of Khomeini's Islamic Republic, once joked that nobody had ever expected the twelfth imam to return on a jumbo jet.[15] As this joke illustrates, not all Iranians, not even all devoutly religious Iranians, approved of the messianic aura surrounding Khomeini.

PURITY AND PATRILINEAL DESCENT FROM THE PROPHET

The Shi'i view of the imamate reflects, among other things, the role of patrilineal descent in seventh-century Arabia, since 'Ali was the prophet's patrilateral cousin (the son of his father's brother) and Muhammad's only two sons had died in infancy. But since the prophet had another patrilateral cousin ('Abd Allah, son of 'Abbas) whose right to lead the umma was never accepted by most Shi'is, the role of 'Ali in Shi'i sacred history cannot be explained solely in terms of patrilineal descent. Another factor is that 'Ali was married to the prophet's daughter Fatima and had two sons by her, Hasan and Husayn. The fact that Muhammad's own sons had died in infancy gave descent from the prophet through this daughter Fatima and his patrilateral cousin 'Ali a significance it would not have otherwise had in patrilineal Arabia. And in addition to the issue of descent per se, there was the close bond that existed between 'Ali and the prophet by virtue of the fact that 'Ali's father, Abu Talib, had raised the prophet as a boy, and the prophet had in turn raised 'Ali as a boy.[16]

THE REVOLT AGAINST 'ALI

When 'Ali was elected caliph in 656, some Muslims challenged his right to the caliphate, ostensibly on the grounds that he had been involved in the assassination of the third caliph, 'Uthman. And after suppressing an initial revolt, 'Ali was forced to fight a protracted battle in 657 against a rebel army at Siffin in Syria. The rebel army was led by Mu'awiya, the governor of Syria and a member of the Umayyad clan of the murdered caliph 'Uthman. Mu'awiya's father had been the principal leader of the Meccan opponents of Muhammad before he eventually converted to Islam. And Mu'awiya himself was to become the first caliph of the Umayyad dynasty that ruled the Islamic world from 661 to 750.[17]

After a series of indecisive skirmishes and negotiations at the battle of Siffin, Mu'awiya's men put pages of the Quran on the ends of their lances and requested that the dispute between Mu'awiya and 'Ali concerning the death of 'Uthman be arbitrated according to the word of God. 'Ali accepted this idea of arbitration, although he eventually rejected the actual decision of the arbitrators since they ruled against him.[18]

'Ali's acceptance of arbitration infuriated some of his supporters who later became known as the *Kharijites* (*Khawarij*), or "those who go out." This name probably originally referred to the departure of many men from 'Ali's camp because of the arbitration issue, but it came to be interpreted as referring to those who leave the Islamic community. Both Sunnis and Shi'is regard Kharijism as heretical.[19]

The Kharijites condemned both 'Ali and Mu'awiya and began to disseminate a doctrine of radical egalitarianism and strict conformity to the Quran. Whereas the Shi'is said that only 'Ali and his patrilineal descendants could be the imams of the Islamic state, and the Sunnis said that only members of the prophet's tribe of Quraysh could be caliphs, the Kharijites argued that any virtuous Muslim could be chosen as caliph even if he were a slave. The Kharijites also viewed all Muslims who did not accept their doctrines or who had committed a major sin as apostates.[20]

'Ali was able to defeat a Kharijite army at the Nahrawan Canal in Iraq in 658, but the Kharijite insurrection continued. And 'Ali was assassinated in 661 by a Kharijite who, according to Shi'i tradition, stabbed him while he was praying the dawn prayer at the main mosque of the southern Iraqi town of Kufa. 'Ali is believed to be buried six miles west of Kufa in the town of Najaf, which has therefore become one of the holy places of Shi'i Islam. (The Ayatollah Khomeini lived and taught in this city for thirteen years—from October 1965 to October 1978.)[21]

Kharijite revolts continued sporadically during the Umayyad dynasty (661–750) as well as in the early centuries of 'Abbasid rule (750–1258). But eventually the more radical forms of Kharijism were suppressed, and the less political wing became the Ibadi sect of Islam. Less than 1 percent of the world's Muslims are now Ibadis. And, except in the sultanate of Oman where they constitute slightly more than half the population (which was less than a million in the early 1980s), the Ibadis are of no political significance in the modern world.[22]

Some ulama in Egypt have referred to the Islamic fundamentalists of the twentieth century as Kharijites in part because they often stress radical egalitarianism and refer to Muslims who do not accept their ideas as apostates. But while praising some aspects of Kharijite thought, modern Islamic fundamentalists do not usually call themselves Kharijites—presumably because this label tends to imply doctrinal deviance and fanaticism.[23]

THE MARTYRDOM OF IMAM HUSAYN IN SHI'I SACRED HISTORY

After 'Ali's assassination by a Kharijite in 661, most of the Islamic world recognized Mu'awiya, the governor of Syria, as caliph. Mu'awiya is condemned by Sunni fundamentalists for transforming the elective caliphate of the four rightly guided caliphs into a hereditary monarchy. But whereas he is a relatively marginal figure in Sunni sacred history, he is central to the mythic structure of Shi'ism because of his opposition to 'Ali and his persecution of 'Ali's son Hasan (the first and second Shi'i imams, respectively), and because of his son Yazid's persecution of the third and most venerated Shi'i imam, Imam Husayn, "Lord of the Martyrs" (*Sayyid al-Shuhada'*). Shi'is believe that Mu'awiya promised 'Ali's first son, Hasan, the caliphate after his own death in exchange for Hasan's submission to his rule during his lifetime. Then instead of adhering to this agreement, Mu'awiya had Hasan poisoned and arranged to have his own son Yazid become caliph in 680.[24]

Although Shi'is revile Mu'awiya for all the reasons listed above, his son Yazid has become the archetypal symbol of evil in Shi'i Islam because he ordered the death of Imam Husayn, the archetypal Shi'i symbol of good. Husayn had been the third imam ever since his brother Hasan's death in about 671. When Yazid became caliph in 680, he demanded that Husayn pledge allegiance (*bay'a*) to him, and Husayn, unwilling to do so, sought refuge in the Sacred Mosque of Mecca, which was and remains (in principle) an inviolable sanctuary. Husayn remained here for almost four months. He received many letters from the southern Iraqi city of Kufa (where 'Ali had ruled and died) asking him to lead the people of that city in a revolt against the oppressive regime of Yazid. Husayn, his family, and closest supporters therefore left the sanctuary of Mecca to go to Kufa. Before leaving Mecca, Husayn told the pilgrims gathered there that he knew he was going to be martyred, but he had to fight Yazid's "government of injustice and tyranny."[25]

The caliph Yazid heard of the letters to Husayn and had the Shi'i leaders of Kufa killed and then had an army surround the imam and his followers at Karbala near the Euphrates River in southern Iraq. For the first nine days of the month of Muharram in the sixty-first year of the Islamic calendar (A.D. 680), Yazid's army encircled Imam Husayn and his companions in the desert and refused to let them drink the water of the Euphrates. On the tenth day, after having spent the night in prayer, Imam Husayn and most of his family and followers were slaughtered by Yazid's army of thirty thousand men. The heads of almost all of the men were severed from their bodies while the women, including Husayn's famous sister, Zaynab, were taken prisoner. Husayn's head was carried to Damascus, "where the caliph Yazid is said to have beaten it with a stick in a vain attempt to keep it from reciting the Qur'an."[26]

These events are narrated and reenacted every year on 'Ashura, "the tenth day" of the month of Muharram and the holiest day of the Shi'i year. Karbala, where Imam Husayn's decapitated body is buried, is the most venerated *haram,* or "sacred space," of Shi'i Islam and is visited by hundreds of thousands of Shi'i pilgrims every year. One of the most common slogans of the Iranian Revolution was the following hadith attributed to the twelfth imam: "Every day is 'Ashura and every place is Karbala."[27] This illustrates how sacred myths about specific times and places—for example, deliverance from bondage in Egypt and the crucifixion of Christ—can serve as paradigms in terms of which all times and all places are understood. But the different ways in which the myth of 'Ashura is understood illustrate to what extent the interpretation of such mythic models is determined by the social situation of those who interpret them.

HUSAYN THE ETHEREAL INTERCESSOR
AND HUSAYN THE RIGHTEOUS REVOLUTIONARY

We have already seen that many fundamentalist Islamic ideologists (Shi'i as well as Sunni) portray the prophet Muhammad as a righteous revolutionary struggling on behalf of "the oppressed," whereas in popular Islam the prophet is more typically viewed as an ethereal being who intercedes on behalf of the Muslim at the paradigmatic moment of crisis, the day of reckoning, as well as at ordinary moments of crisis in everyday life. In Shi'i Islam (and as usual, we are speaking primarily of Twelver Shi'ism), we find a similar dichotomy in fundamentalist and popular interpretations of Imam Husayn.

In popular Shi'ism, Imam Husayn is believed to be capable of forgiving sins and granting admission to heaven by virtue of his role as intercessor before God. Mourning for Husayn's martyrdom at Karbala is believed to be an especially effective means of obtaining his intercession. Thus weeping during the customary melodramatic narratives describing the suffering of Husayn is more than a mere emotional response to tragedy; it is also a ritual act intended to produce some benefit to the weeper in this world or the next. This is also true of the self-flagellation performed by black-shirted young men on 'Ashura. These men flail their backs with chains or beat their chests with open palms while chanting verses about Karbala. They are symbolically atoning for the sin of the Kufans who failed to support Husayn while at the same time mourning his death and participating in his pain.[28]

In addition to mourning for Husayn, Shi'is give him gifts in return for his assistance. (Such gifts are also offered to the other imams.) Mary Hegland cites the case of a man in an Iranian village who had been jailed for smuggling opium. The smuggler implored Imam Husayn to have him released and promised that if the imam did so, he would give three public meals in his honor during Muharram—the month of the massacre at Karbala. Hegland notes that the conception of the believer's relationship to Husayn inherent in the opium smuggler's request is analogous to the typical villager's conception of his or her relationship to the wealthy and powerful in this world. In both cases, the individual feels dependent upon a powerful patron to whom gifts and homage are due. In both cases, the villagers attempt to curry the favor of a powerful patron in order to obtain some advantage for themselves.[29]

But in the sixties and seventies, the Ayatollah Khomeini and 'Ali Shari'ati stressed that Imam Husayn, Lord of the Martyrs, was a revolutionary leading the oppressed against their oppressors. And rather than passively beg for his intercession, good Muslims should actively emulate his revolution. For example, on November 23, 1978, a week before the month of Muharram (the first ten days of which are devoted to the mourning of the martyrdom of Husayn) and less than three months before the establishment of the Islamic Republic, the Ayatollah Khomeini issued a statement to the Iranian people that began as follows:

> With the approach of Muharram, we are about to begin the month of epic heroism and self-sacrifice—the month in which blood triumphed over the sword, the month in which truth condemned falsehood for all eternity and branded the mark of disgrace upon the forehead of all oppressors and satanic governments; the month that has taught successive generations throughout history the path of victory over the bayonet; the month that proves the superpowers may be defeated by the word of truth; the month in which the leader of the Muslims [Imam Husayn] taught us how to struggle against all the tyrants of history.[30]

Thus Khomeini likened his own struggle against the shah to that of Imam Husayn against Yazid, as did many other Iranians. And he made people see Husayn's martyrdom as an event to be actively emulated rather than passively mourned. In this respect, his interpretation of the martyrdom of Imam Husayn corresponds to Shari'ati's interpretation of the Shi'i imams in general as revolutionary leaders—although Shari'ati's ideas are generally more radical and iconoclastic than are Khomeini's.[31]

The activist revolutionary interpretation of the martyrdom of Husayn was not completely new. As we have already seen in the case of the term *imam,* religious symbols have a wide range of meanings that emerge in different contexts. Khomeini was simply stressing a meaning of the Karbala myth that had been latent rather than manifest in the popular imagination. And he was not the first to do so. During Iran's constitutional revolution of 1905–11, a prominent ayatollah compared the Qajar dynasty that then ruled Iran to the Umayyads who had slaughtered Imam Husayn and his family.[32] In the 1960s, an Iranian textbook used by fifth and sixth graders stated: "Imam Husain did not accept oppression (*satamgaran*) and injustice (*zolm.* . . . His martyrdom at Karbala served as an example of resistance against tyranny."[33] And during Muharram of 1963, shortly before a wave of antigovernment demonstrations and riots, many of the customary *rawza* sermons describing the suffering of Husayn and his family emphasized the need to revolt against the "tyranny and oppression" of the shah just as Husayn had revolted against the "tyranny and oppression" of Yazid.[34]

But the mere existence of the story of Husayn's martyrdom has never, in and of itself, induced Shi'is to revolt against oppressive government. During the more than thirteen hundred years since the slaughter at Karbala, Shiʻis (and Twelver Shiʻis in particular) have usually passively accepted whatever government was in power at the time. Only when social and political conditions are conducive to revolt does the revolutionary interpretation of the myth of Karbala become paramount and politically effective.[35]

THE MESSIANIC THEME

Twelver Shiʻis generally believe that all but the last of their twelve imams died as martyrs—the notion of martyrdom for the cause of God being more important in Shiʻism than in Sunnism. The twelfth imam is believed to have been in a state of "lesser occultation" (*al-ghayba as-sughra*) from about 874 through 940, during which period his wishes were transmitted to his followers by four deputies who were the only people who could see him. As of 940, he entered the state of the "greater occultation" (*al-ghayba al-kubra*) which will last until he returns shortly before the end of time to fill the earth "with justice and equity, just as it was filled with injustice and oppression." This last imam is variously known as "the imam of the age," "the hidden imam," and *al-mahdi,* "the rightly guided one."[36]

The idea of a mahdi, or messiah, who will usher in an age of justice and happiness inspired many Shiʻi revolts in the early centuries of the Islamic era. This was especially true among the Ismaʻili Shiʻis, whose sect emerged out of a dispute as to who should be the seventh imam. Although the messianic theme never became as central to Sunni Islam as it is to Shiʻism, it did become part of the popular Sunni worldview. And messianic Sunni revolts have occurred periodically throughout Islamic history. The most famous of these revolts in the past century have been the Sudanese mahdist rebellion of the 1880s and the mahdist takeover of the Sacred Mosque of Mecca in November 1979. Thus in Islam, as in Judaism and Christianity, the idea of a messiah ushering in a utopian world has inspired many radical millenarian movements. But in all three of these religions, the messianic theme has usually been an eschatological vision inducing acceptance of the status quo. Religious symbols that legitimate revolt in certain social contexts can inhibit it in others.[37]

SACRED HISTORY AND POLITICAL THEORY IN SUNNI AND SHIʻI ISLAM

The Ayatollah Khomeini, among others, has argued that Shiʻi Islam has always been a more revolutionary doctrine than Sunni Islam, which has usually encouraged acceptance of the status quo:

According to Shi'i belief, only the Imams or those who act on their behalf are the legitimate holders of authority; all other governments are illegitimate. This belief has been expressed throughout history in Shi'i uprisings against different governments. . . .

Many Sunnis, however, may regard this rebellion against oppressive government as incompatible with Islam. . . . That is because of the belief that even an oppressive ruler must be obeyed, a belief that is based upon an incorrect interpretation of the Qur'anic verse concerning obedience. . . .

This is the root of the matter: Sunni-populated countries believe in obeying their rulers, whereas the Shi'is have always believed in rebellion—sometimes they were able to rebel, and at other times they were compelled to keep silent.[38]

If this view of the differing political implications of Shi'i and Sunni Islam were correct, then it would seemingly resolve the problem of why an Islamic revolution occurred only in Iran, the only Muslim country with an overwhelmingly Shi'i population. But Khomeini's view is not entirely accurate.

It is true that some medieval Sunni theologians insisted that rulers, even unjust rulers, should be obeyed so as to avoid disorder, but some of the most important of the twelve imams of Twelver Shi'ism (notably the fifth and sixth imams, Muhammad al-Baqir and Ja'far al-Sadiq) also commanded Shi'is not to rebel against their rulers under any circumstances.[39] Moreover, the doctrines propounded by medieval Sunni scholars did not prevent Sunnis from repeatedly revolting against their rulers throughout the course of history as can be seen by reading any history of the Islamic world.

As for the notion that Shi'is regard all governments other than those of the pure and sinless imams or of their representatives as illegitimate, it has been the subject of some debate among specialists in Iranian history.[40] But even if we assume that Shi'is *have* usually viewed governments as illegitimate, this idea has rarely induced them to revolt. Hamid Algar observes:

Both activist and quietist attitudes to prevailing authority could be deduced from the Imami belief, but it is clear that the latter came gradually to dominate the mainstream of Shi'ism. . . . Insofar as any attitude to the state and existing authority can be deduced from the teachings of the Imams, it is one that combines a denial of legitimacy with a quietistic patience and abstention from action. The Imam Ja'far as-Sadiq, sixth in the succession and from whom originates so much of Imami hadith (traditions concerning the sayings and deeds of the Prophet and the Imams), recommended to his followers total abstention from even so much as verbal dispute with their opponents.[41]

Like the idea that history reflects the will of God and the idea that the messianic hidden imam will usher in an age of perfect justice, the idea that all governments of men rather than imams are illegitimate can induce resignation as well as revolution. Social and political conditions dictate how such ideas are understood. This is not to say that they are insignificant, just that they are not immutable.

4

The Ulama, Popular Religion, and Fundamentalist Ideology in Sunni and Shi'i Islam

One of the most conspicuous differences between Sunni and Twelver Shi'i Islam is the greater religious (and thus political) authority of the ulama in the latter. This authority was a crucial factor in Iran's Islamic revolution of 1978–79.

Strictly speaking, there are no clerics in Islam. That is to say, there are no men with an essential mediating role between the believer and God (although we shall see that this is truer in Sunni Islam than it is in Shi'ism). The Friday congregational prayers as well as holy day prayers are supposed to be led by a man who stands in front of the worshipers and gives a sermon. This imam does not have to be a professional man of religion. He can be any pious Muslim male.[1] Often, however, he is a religious scholar or at least a man who has memorized the Quran and teaches it to young children (primarily boys).

The word *ulama* (*'ulama'*) means "those who have knowledge." Ulama are men who have studied Islamic doctrine and law for many years and make a living out of the knowledge gained through such study. They often serve as judges, teachers, and professors. Given the expansion of secular law and education in the twentieth century, they are generally less influential than they used to be—with the notable exception of the Iranian ulama since 1979. And to understand this exception, we need to examine the evolution of the role of the Twelver Shi'i ulama of Iran since the sixteenth century.[2]

29

TWELVER SHI'ISM BECOMES THE RELIGION OF IRAN

In the early sixteenth century, the Safavid dynasty transformed Twelver Shi'ism from a persecuted sect into the official religion of Iran. The Safavids had originally been a Sunni Sufi order that emerged in northwestern Iran in the fourteenth century. (Sufism is the mystical tradition of Islam.) In the fifteenth century, the Safavid order assimilated many of the ideas of the more extremist Shi'i sects, with the leaders of the brotherhood claiming to be incarnations of the pure and sinless imams and even of God. The head of the order at the end of the fifteenth century sometimes portrayed himself as the hidden messianic imam, or mahdi. And in 1501, this same leader of the Safavid order was crowned shah (king) of Iran and declared that the official religion of Iran would henceforth be Twelver Shi'ism.[3]

The Safavids imported Twelver Shi'i ulama from Lebanon, Bahrain, and Iraq to teach Twelver doctrines to the people of Iran, who were still mostly Sunnis in the early sixteenth century. And the Safavids diluted some of their earlier claims to divinity. Thus instead of portraying themselves as incarnations of the hidden imam, the later Safavid shahs claimed to be his deputies and thus the legitimate successors of the four deputies who had communicated the hidden imam's wishes to all believers during the lesser occultation (874–940). The Safavids also claimed legitimacy by virtue of their alleged descent from the seventh imam and, at least in the early Safavid era, by virtue of their continued role as leaders of the Safavid Sufi order. Like the Sunni caliphs, the Safavid shahs assumed the title of "Shadow of God on Earth" in the manner of the ancient Persian kings.[4]

During the period of Safavid rule from 1501 to 1722, the Twelver Shi'i ulama of Iran rarely questioned the legitimacy of the Safavid shahs—despite the highly questionable orthodoxy of even their more moderate claims. This was perhaps partially due to the fact that the ulama were largely dependent on government subsidies at this time. And perhaps they did not want to challenge the first government actively to propagate Twelver Shi'ism. At any rate, for whatever reasons, the Twelver Shi'i ulama generally worked for and supported the Safavid shahs throughout the sixteenth and seventeenth centuries. In the late seventeenth and early eighteenth centuries, however, the ulama became increasingly influential as the Safavid shahs became increasingly weak. And their situation was transformed in 1722 when Afghan armies invaded Iran and effectively terminated Safavid rule.[5]

During the late 1720s and early 1730s, a soldier named Nadir Khan led Iranian armies to victory over the Sunni Afghans in the east as well as over the Sunni Ottoman Turks in the west. And in 1736, Nadir Khan had himself crowned shah. The new shah outraged the Shi'i ulama by trying to transform Shi'ism into a fifth legal school of Sunni Islam and by confiscating many of the *waqf* properties (religious endowments) upon which the ulama depended for their living. Nadir Shah's assassination in 1747 put an end to all of this. But his reign, coupled with the Afghan invasion of 1722, severed the close ties that had existed between the Shi'i ulama and the Iranian state under the Safavids.[6]

After the Afghan invasion, the leading Shi'i ulama of Iran had fled to Najaf, Karbala, and other Shi'i holy cities in Iraq—which was then part of the Ottoman Empire. (It will be recalled that the tomb of Imam 'Ali is in Najaf and that of Imam Husayn in Karbala.) The leading ulama of Twelver Shi'ism generally continued to live and teach in these cities until the early 1920s, when many of them went to the Iranian city of Qum because of their opposition to the imposition of British rule in Iraq. The presence of the leading Iranian ulama in Iraq for roughly two centuries enabled them to criticize the shahs of Iran with relative impunity. Khomeini demonstrated the significance of this factor during his Iraqi exile from 1965 through 1978.[7]

THE EVOLUTION OF THE *MUJTAHID* CONCEPT

In the wake of the threats to their social position posed by the Afghan invasion, the collapse of the Safavid dynasty, and the reign of Nadir Shah, a growing number of Shi'i ulama advocated the doctrine that all Shi'is should be guided by a leading religious scholar known as a *mujtahid*, whose interpretations of Islamic law (and of the will of the hidden imam) are absolutely binding on all his followers. The term *mujtahid* is derived from the notion of *ijtihad*, or "independent judgment." The mujtahids of Twelver Shi'ism have been able to exercise such judgment more freely and with much greater authority than have the ulama of the Sunni world. During the course of the twentieth century, the Shi'i mujtahids have come to be known as *ayatollahs*, or "signs of God."[8]

Underlying the idea that all Twelver Shi'is should obey the decrees of a particular mujtahid is the belief that the mujtahids are the deputies of the hidden imam until he returns at the end of time—precisely the role claimed by the Safavid shahs. At least one Western scholar has denied that the medieval texts of Shi'ism justify such a notion.[9] But this objection is irrelevant insofar as we are interested in what Twelver Shi'is actually believe—as opposed to what medieval texts say they ought to believe. And most Twelver Shi'is of the nineteenth and twentieth centuries have believed that their mujtahids are in some sense the deputies of the messianic hidden imam.[10]

In addition to the idea that all believers should be the followers of a particular mujtahid, most Twelver Shi'is came to accept another important idea by the early nineteenth century, that of a foremost mujtahid—a *marja'-i taqlid,* or "source of imitation"—to whom even other mujtahids should defer. A marja'-i taqlid is a religious scholar renowned for his writings as well as his piety. He emerges by virtue of a consensus among the high-ranking Shi'i ulama rather than by a formal process of selection. In principle, there is supposed to be one such marja'-i taqlid at any given time, and this has often been the case. In recent decades, however, there have usually been more than one. In 1975, for example, there were seven such men (the Ayatollahs Khu'i and Khomeini in Najaf, the Ayatollahs Gulpayagani, Shari'atmadari and Mar'ashi-Najafi in Qum, the Ayatollah Khunsari in Tehran, and the Ayatollah Milani in Mashhad.)[11] Every Twelver Shi'i anywhere at that time was supposed to be the "follower" (*muqallid*) of one of these men, each of whom was usually dominant in a particular region. (Thus the Ayatollah Shari'atmadari's followers were primarily in the Turkish-speaking region of Azarbayjan in northwestern Iran.) By the time of the revolution of 1978–79, the Ayatollah Khomeini had of course become far more important politically than all of his fellow "sources of imitation." But in principle at least, he did not have any more religious authority than they did.[12]

THE MUJTAHIDS AND THE SHI'I TITHE

Shi'is are supposed not only to obey their mujtahid's rulings, but also to pay him a tithe in the form of half of the *khums,* or "one-fifth," a religious tax on income and property. A Western scholar has noted that there are no medieval texts to legitimate this practice, and it was repudiated by the president of the Twelver Shi'i Supreme Court of Lebanon in the 1960s.[13] But again, we are concerned with what most believers actually believe rather than with what medieval texts or isolated jurists say they ought to believe. And the overwhelming majority of Twelver Shi'is in the nineteenth and twentieth centuries have be-lieved that they should pay the tithe known as "the share of the imam" (*sahm-i imam;* half of the khums tax) to their mujtahid in his capacity as deputy of the hidden imam.[14]

The mujtahid usually uses most of the "share of the imam" money for the maintenance of mosques and religious colleges (*madrasas*) and for the incomes of the ulama and religious students who teach and study in such colleges. The other half of the khums tax is supposed to be given to poor *sayyids* (patrilineal descendants of the prophet Mu-hammad through 'Ali and Fatima). Like the *zakat* alms tax, which is paid by Sunnis as well as Shi'is, the money for the sayyids can be given to one's mujtahid to distribute or it can be distributed directly.[15]

Michael Fischer describes how one woman paid her khums tax to a mujtahid of the holy city of Qum in 1975:

> Picture the marja'-i taqlid (leading mujtahid) as a grandfatherly man with a white beard and twinkling eyes seated on a mat in a small room amid piles of books, or seated on a wooden platform in a court-yard amid pomegranate trees. . . .
> A woman enters and is politely ignored until she arranges her pieces of paper and her veil. She lists all her possessions and income and asks that her khums be calculated and the receipts of previous payments be subtracted. The marja' does this quickly, giving a bank account number to which she may deposit further payments. The woman then asks what kind of monthly payments should be made and is told that she should see how her situation is; the work of God does not proceed on monthly payments; whenever she has it she should contribute. The woman then gives him an apple to say a prayer over for her heart condition. This he does and returns the apple.[16]

Many people pay their religious taxes to a local *mullah* who keeps a share for himself and the maintenance of his mosque before sending the bulk of it to his mujtahid.[17] (Strictly speaking, the term *mullah* refers only to low-ranking men of religion who teach the Quran to children, but it is often used more generally to refer to the ulama as a whole.)

Because of the khums tax, the mujtahids of Twelver Shi'ism, who have come to be known as ayatollahs in the twentieth century, have had greater financial resources as well as greater authority than their Sunni counterparts. Both Sunni and Shi'i ulama traditionally had other sources of income: notably revenue from waqf religious endowments and money earned as judges, notaries, teachers, and scribes. But whereas secular governments have been able to control and circumscribe these revenues, they could no more prevent Shi'is from paying their "share of the imam" tax than they could prevent them from praying the daily prayers.

ON THE CHARISMATIC AUTHORITY OF THE SHI'I MUJTAHIDS

Unlike the ulama of the Sunni world, the Shi'i mujtahids of recent centuries have been charismatic leaders venerated by ordinary Shi'is in a way that many Sunni ulama regard as idolatrous. They have charismatic authority in the specifically religious sense that they are revered, and obeyed, because of their role as the sacred deputies of a supernatural being—in this case the hidden imam.[18] This was already true in the late Safavid period (1501–1722):

> They were said to be the means of clinging to the infallible Imams as the "Ark of Salvation"; their pen was superior to the blood of the martyrs; they were doors to heaven, and insulting them would bring the wrath of God upon the offender. The pages of the *Qisas al-'Ulama'* are replete with the lengthy accounts of the *karamat* [minor miracles] attributed to the eminent Shi'i divines. In addition, the *'ulama'* arrogated to themselves the function of *Shafa'a* or intercession in the hereafter.[19]

In the nineteenth century, many Iranians believed that the water with which the mujtahid Aqa Sayyid Muhammad performed his ablutions before prayer "acquired miraculous properties from contact with his person."[20] And when this same mujtahid arrived at the reigning shah's summer residence at Sultaniyya in 1826, an English observer described his reception as follows: "Much enthusiasm was manifested by the populace. To the Sied's person they could get no access, but they kissed the litter, kissed the ladder by which he had ascended it, and collected the dust which had the impressions of the mule's feet which bore him."[21]

Comparable veneration of a mujtahid has been witnessed on television screens all over the world since the Ayatollah Khomeini's return to Iran in February 1979. But Khomeini's charisma has transcended that of any other Shi'i mujtahid—for reasons that will become clear in later chapters.

POPULAR RELIGION AND ORTHODOXY IN SUNNI AND SHI'I ISLAM

The fact that Shi'i ulama have greater authority than their Sunni counterparts relates to another important point—the greater gap between orthodox and popular religion among Sunnis than among Shi'is. Ernest Gellner has spoken of a "pendulum swing" between the puritanical, egalitarian orthodox Islam of the learned and the ritualistic, hierarchical popular religion of the illiterate.[22] This model, however, applies primarily to Sunni Islam rather than Shi'ism. Fundamentalist movements demanding a return to austere orthodoxy have periodically arisen in the Sunni world throughout most of Islamic history. But such movements have been rare among Shi'is, and when they have occurred, primarily in twentieth-century Iran, they have not been accompanied by the condemnation of popular religion that has almost always characterized Sunni fundamentalism.[23]

Gellner has likened the contrast between orthodox and popular Islam to that between Protestantism and Roman Catholicism.[24] Useful primarily in the Sunni context, this analogy also applies to the contrast between Sunni and Shi'i Islam. (In fact, the hostility of educated Sunnis toward Shi'ism is strikingly similar to that of fundamentalist Protestants toward Roman Catholicism.) Whereas orthodox Sunni doctrine emphasizes the unmediated relationship between man and God, both Shi'ism and popular Sunni Islam emphasize the role of mediators: the twelve imams and their patrilineal descendants in Shi'ism, saints and their patrilineal descendants in popular Sunni Islam. Just as Shi'is visit the shrines of their imams and beseech them to grant their requests, so too do Sunni Muslims visit the shrines of their saints. Whereas orthodox Sunni Islam stresses the equality of all believers, both Shi'ism and popular Sunni Islam emphasize the purity and sinlessness of venerated holy men—usually believed to be the patrilineal descendants of Muhammad in both cases. And whereas orthodox Sunni Islam emphasizes puritanical piety and sobriety, both Shi'ism and popular Sunni Islam incorporate spectacular rituals involving music, dancing, and states of trance. The Sunni ulama horrified by the emotionalism, pageantry, and self-flagellation in the Shi'i rite of 'Ashura are equally horrified by the emotionalism, pageantry, and self-flagellation in some rituals of popular Sunni Islam.[25]

Shi'i ulama too have often condemned the popular rituals associated with 'Ashura, but never with the same vehemence as their Sunni counterparts. And although the Ayatollah Khomeini has condemned some aspects of popular Shi'ism, for example, magic, he has defended others, notably praying at shrines.[26] Most Sunni ulama and all Sunni fundamentalists condemn such practices—which are as commonplace in popular Sunni Islam as they are in Shi'ism.

Whereas the ulama are to a large extent divorced from popular religion among the Sunnis, they are very much a part of it in Shi'i Islam, especially in the cities. When traditional Shi'i families in Iran travel, they visit their marja'-i taqlid, who whispers prayers in their ears so as to protect them on their trip.[27] And we have already seen the case of the Shi'i woman who, after arranging to pay her tithe, gave an apple to her marja' asking him to say a prayer over it so that her heart condition would improve. Sunni ulama would condemn this as a perversion of Islam (as would some Shi'i intellectuals).

There have, of course, been many charismatic holy men venerated by Sunnis during the course of history. But these men were not venerated because they were religious scholars whom every believer should obey. They were typically venerated because of their role in popular institutions of marginal orthodoxy, namely saintly lineages and Sufi brotherhoods. In the twentieth century, various reformist and fundamentalist movements have succeeded in discrediting these popular Sunni institutions—in the eyes of the educated anyway. But the principal twentieth-century Islamic movements of the Shi'is have not condemned the popular veneration of charismatic holy men. They have, in fact, been led by such men, whose role in popular Shi'ism is as pivotal as it is in orthodoxy. These Shi'i movements have thus been grounded in popular religious belief and practice to a far greater degree than their Sunni counterparts.[28]

The gap between popular and orthodox belief in Sunni Islam should not be exaggerated. The religious scholar as well as the peasant and the peddler pray the same daily prayers and share the same basic beliefs concerning the day of reckoning and heaven and hell. Conversely, the extent of the gap between popular religion and orthodoxy in Shi'i Islam should not be underestimated. As has already been noted, many Shi'i ulama do disapprove of the more spectacular popular rituals associated with 'Ashura. Nonetheless, the fact remains that the Shi'i ulama have generally not been as hostile to popular religion as their Sunni counterparts. And they are a part of popular religious practices in a way that Sunni ulama are not.

ISLAM AS IDEOLOGY

Those who seek to revive or defend tradition inevitably reconstruct it and infuse it with a political significance it did not formerly have. This is certainly true of most of the twentieth-century Islamic movements that seek to create strictly Islamic polities. Fundamentalist ideology differs from popular religion as well as conventional orthodox belief in both Sunni and Shi'i Islam—most obviously by virtue of the very fact that it is an *ideology,* that is, a blueprint for political action. The principal shibboleth of the fundamentalists in both sects is that Islam is an all-encompassing way of life in which there can be no distinction between religion and politics. But the very frequency with which the fundamentalist ideologists feel compelled to emphasize this point demonstrates that most Muslims do not understand their religion this way. This is especially true of the less educated masses—the workers, the urban poor, and the peasants.[29] The fundamentalists do not constantly stress that Muhammad was the prophet of God or that there is a heaven and a hell because they know that all Muslims take these things for granted. But they do constantly stress that "real" Muslims are committed to the creation of a strictly Islamic state because they know that this is not in fact how most Muslims interpret their religion.

Hasan al-Banna, the founder of the Egyptian Muslim Brotherhood, once told his followers: "Our mission is in reality but an assault on familiar habits and a transformation of customary practices."[30] Unlike many Western scholars and journalists who echo the fundamentalist claim that Islam does not distinguish between religion and politics, Hasan al-Banna knew that his politicized conception of Islam conflicted sharply with the more strictly religious conception of Islam that exists in the minds of the overwhelming majority of Muslims. It is all very well to say there was no distinction between religion and politics at the time of the prophet Muhammad, but there certainly has been such a distinction throughout most of the twentieth century—and for many centuries before that according to some scholars.[31]

We have seen repeated examples of the disparity between fundamentalist and popular interpretations of Islam in the previous chapters—for example, with respect to the role of Muhammad and Imam Husayn as righteous revolutionaries in the fundamentalist literature and their role as ethereal intercessors in the popular imagination. Another example involves the very notion of what it means to be a *Mus-*

lim, literally, "one who submits" to God (Allah). The fundamentalists often insist that only those Muslims who are totally committed to the goal of a strictly Islamic state are real Muslims. And the more radical fundamentalists even condemn devoutly religious rulers such as Sadat of Egypt, Hasan II of Morocco, and Fahd of Saudi Arabia as "infidels" and purveyors of what is sometimes referred to as "the Islam of the merchants of oil and the agents of the Americans."[32] But most Muslims, even those hostile to Sadat, Hasan, and Fahd, do not view such men as infidels. And they are inclined to view those who do as somewhat bizarre. In short, the politicized fundamentalist interpretation of Islam differs profoundly from the worldview and ethos in terms of which most Muslims live their everyday lives. This is especially true of the more radical forms of fundamentalism.[33]

This disparity between fundamentalist ideology and the religion of Islam as understood by most Muslims exists among Shi'is as well as Sunnis. Most obvious in the radical Islamic writings of 'Ali Shari'ati, it is also evident in Khomeini's conception of an Islamic government, which—like much of what fundamentalists have to say—is an innovation portrayed as a return to tradition. But despite his innovative ideas, Khomeini's public persona is nonetheless profoundly traditional. And this traditional persona has enabled him to radically transform traditional Shi'ism.[34]

PART II

Islam and Politics since the Late Nineteenth Century

5

Iran

During the course of the nineteenth century, Russia and England inflicted a series of humiliating military defeats and economic treaties upon Iran. By the end of the century, European businessmen were paying the Iranian shahs for concessions to various resources and products, the most controversial of these being the monopoly over the production, sale, and export of all Iranian tobacco granted to an Englishman in 1890.

The ulama and the *bazaaris* (merchants and artisans) led protests against the tobacco concession in all the principal cities of Iran. And late in 1891, a decree attributed to Mirza Hasan Shirazi, the sole marja'-i taqlid of the time, forbade the smoking of tobacco until the tobacco concession was canceled. All over Iran, people (including the shah's wives) stopped smoking, and the shah, Nasir al-Din, was forced to cancel the concession in 1892. This "tobacco protest" of 1891–92 was the first example of nationwide opposition to foreign domination led by the formerly apolitical ulama and the merchants and artisans of the bazaar.[1]

One individual involved in the tobacco protest was the Iranian intellectual Jamal al-Din al-Afghani (1839–97), who was expelled from Iran in 1891 because of pamphlets he wrote in which he condemned the shah for "selling Iran to the infidel."[2] Although some scholars have suggested that al-Afghani may have actually been a freethinker who exploited Islam as a means of mobilizing Muslims to fight European imperialism, he is revered by Islamic fundamentalists, both Sunni and

Shi'i, because he articulated many of the themes that remain basic to their ideological conception of Islam, notably the idea that Muslims could overcome European domination by uniting and returning to the pristine Islam of the Quran.[3]

THE CONSTITUTIONAL REVOLUTION OF 1905–11

Years of protest by ulama, merchants, and intellectuals disturbed by growing Russian influence in Iran in the early twentieth century culminated in the constitutional revolution of 1905–11. The revolution is usually said to have begun in December 1905, when the governor of Tehran had the soles of two prominent merchants beaten on the pretext that they were responsible for the high price of sugar. The bazaar of Tehran shut down to protest these beatings, and several thousand merchants, mullahs, and religious students, led by two mujtahids, Sayyid 'Abd Allah Bihbihani and Sayyid Muhammad Tabataba'i, took sanctuary in a shrine near Tehran. From this sanctuary, the protesters demanded the replacement of the governor of Tehran who had had the two merchants bastinadoed, enforcement of Islamic law, dismissal of the Belgian official in charge of customs, and the establishment of a House of Justice—the precise nature of which was not defined. After the shutdown of the Tehran bazaar had lasted a month, the shah finally agreed to implement the protesters' demands in January 1906. But his promises remained unfulfilled.[4]

The next phase of protest was triggered by the arrest of a local preacher of Tehran in the summer of 1906. The preacher had criticized the government in the following terms (as translated by an employee of the British Legation at the time):

> O Iranians! O brethren of my beloved country! . . . In bygone days we had everything, and now all is gone. In the past, others looked on us as a great nation. Now, we are reduced to such a condition that our neighbors of the north and south already believe us to be their property and divide our country between themselves when they choose. . . . The Monarchs, at the same time, despoil you with their power over your property, your freedom, and your rights. And with all this come the strangers who receive from you all your money, and instead furnish you with green, blue, and red cloth, gaudy glassware, and luxury furniture. These are the causes of your misery, and the great luxury of Monarchs, some clerics, and the foreigners.[5]

During the protest that followed the arrest of this preacher, the police shot a religious student who was also a sayyid (a patrilineal descendant of the prophet Muhammad). Then the shah's Cossack Brigade further outraged the ulama by firing upon the mourning procession of religious students, mullahs, and bazaaris who were carrying the "martyred" sayyid's body through the streets of Tehran.[6]

On July 15, 1906, over a thousand ulama and religious students led by the mujtahids Bihbihani and Tabataba'i went to the holy city of Qum (famous for its shrines and seminaries) ninety miles south of Tehran. They said they would not return to Tehran until the shah fulfilled the promises he had made during the past year. Four days later, about fifty merchants and mullahs opposed to the shah took refuge at the spacious summer quarters of the British legation a few miles north of Tehran. (Since the shah was supported by the Russians, his opponents sought the support of the British.) Within days, thousands of merchants, artisans, ulama, students, and various secular intellectuals were camped in the gardens of the summer legation. The secular intellectuals soon convinced the more traditional merchants, artisans, and ulama to demand a constitution that would transform Iran into a constitutional monarchy with a nationally elected legislature.[7]

The shah initially condemned the protesters as "a bunch of traitors hired by the British."[8] But because of a general strike of merchants and artisans in Tehran and widespread support for it elsewhere, the shah finally signed a decree on August 5, 1906, authorizing the writing of a constitution. The ulama, the merchants, the students, and the secular intellectuals returned from Qum and the British legation in triumph.

But it was in fact the secular intellectuals rather than the ulama who had triumphed. They were the ones who wanted a constitution along European lines. It is true that most of the ulama accepted this demand at the time (1906), but they did not really know what it entailed. Sayyid Muhammad Tabataba'i, one of the most important constitutionalist mujtahids, later observed, "We had not experienced constitutional government, but had been told by those who had visited constitutional countries that it gave them security and prosperity. We therefore wished to establish a constitutional system here."[9] The secular intellectuals exploited such naïveté in order to create a parliamentary democracy that the ulama would never have sought on their own.

After hurried elections, in which the poor and propertyless could not vote, the first National Assembly convened in October 1906. About 20 percent of the members were ulama, with 41 percent being merchants and artisans. The first part of the constitution this body wrote was called the "fundamental laws" and was signed by the reigning shah, Muzaffar al-Din, on December 30, 1906—five days before his death. The fundamental laws basically declared that the National Assembly would henceforth have final authority over most governmental policies. The next part of the constitution, known as the supplementary fundamental laws, was signed by the new shah, Muhammad 'Ali, in October of 1907 in the wake of proconstitutionalist demonstrations by bazaaris and others in almost all the cities of Iran. The supplementary fundamental laws extended the authority of the National Assembly and included a bill of rights. Both the fundamental laws of 1906 and the supplementary fundamental laws of 1907 were largely based on the Belgian constitution. Together they remained the constitution of Iran until 1979, although they had little impact on the actual political structure of Iran after the collapse of the constitutional movement in 1911.[10]

During the course of 1907, it became increasingly clear that not all the ulama were in favor of the new constitution. The leader of the anticonstitutionalist ulama was the mujtahid Shaykh Fadl Allah Nuri. Nuri had joined the antiroyalist protests of 1906, but by the following year he was condemning the constitutionalists as "heretics and apostates" for trying to import "the customs and practices of the realm of infidelity" into Islamic Iran.[11] Nuri felt that the constitutionalist movement had been taken over by secular intellectuals who sought to create a Western-style democracy rather than the strictly Islamic state that he and many other ulama wanted. He was right.

Nuri's open letters of 1907, which were disseminated throughout Iran by sympathetic mullahs, convinced many ulama and religious students who had previously been either constitutionalists or neutral that the constitution was a threat to Islam. Some ulama, however, continued to support and even lead the constitutional movement, notably two of the three mujtahids in Tehran and three of the five leading mujtahids of Karbala and Najaf. Thus while some of Shi'i Islam's most venerated men of religion were now supporting the shah, others were leading the constitutionalist forces against him.[12]

In June of 1908, the constitutionalist movement appeared to be doomed when the shah had his Cossack Brigade, commanded by a Russian colonel, bombard the National Assembly building and arrest or execute many of the constitutionalist leaders. Although the intelligentsia and many merchants and artisans remained staunch constitutionalists, most of the urban poor now joined the landed aristocracy in supporting the shah. Civil war between the royalists and constitutionalists continued until July of 1909, when two constitutionalist armies (including one composed of Bakhtiari tribesmen) occupied Tehran and took over the Iranian government. Nuri was hanged on July 31, 1909.[13]

Although the constitutionalists eliminated Nuri himself, they could not eliminate his ideas. The members of the resurrected National Assembly were now increasingly divided between the secular intellectuals, some of whom were socialists, and the ulama, who shared many of Nuri's basic values. Just as Nuri had once labeled all constitutionalists "heretics and apostates," so too did many of the constitutionalist ulama now view their former secular allies as enemies of Islam.[14]

In 1911, as the secular-religious constitutionalist alliance was unraveling, Russian and British troops occupied parts of northern and southern Iran. In November of that year, the Russians issued an ultimatum. In order to avoid the Russian occupation of Tehran, the Iranian government would have to dismiss an American financial administrator who had curbed Russian influence in the north, promise not to hire any more foreigners without British and Russian approval, and pay the Russians an indemnity—for the expenses the czar's army had incurred in invading northern Iran. Since the Iranian army could not have resisted a Russian advance on Tehran, the government accepted the ultimatum. The National Assembly, where secular intellectuals and ulama had united to reject the Russian demands, was dissolved. The constitutional revolution was over.[15]

KUCHIK KHAN AND THE JANGALI REVOLT, 1917-21

During the years following the demise of the constitutionalist movement, Russian troops remained in the north, as did British troops in the south. The Russians gradually began to leave after the Bolsheviks seized power in 1917, and the British then replaced them in many areas. But the central government was impotent and various regional revolts occurred, the most famous of these being the revolt of the Jangalis (Forest Men) near the Caspian Sea.

The Jangali revolt was initially led by a former religious student named Kuchik Khan, who has come to be revered as one of Iran's greatest Islamic revolutionaries by the nation's radical Islamic activists. Kuchik Khan was a devout Muslim known for his support for the constitutionalist movement and his opposition to Russian and British domination of Iran. By the end of 1917, when they no longer had to fight czarist troops, Kuchik Khan and the Jangalis controlled much of Gilan Province near the Caspian Sea. Referred to as the "Robin Hoods of the Caspian Marches" by an English observer, they financed their revolt by kidnapping wealthy landlords.[16] But, like the constitutionalist movement, the Jangalis were crippled by tension between their Islamic wing (led by Kuchik Khan) and their secular wing, led by Marxist intellectuals. The latter took over the movement with the assistance of Bolshevik forces that landed on the Iranian shores of the Caspian Sea in May of 1920. The Soviet Union's withdrawal of its troops in September of 1921, as well as the split between Kuchik Khan's Islamic loyalists and the secular communists, enabled the Iranian government to suppress the Jangali movement in the fall of 1921. Kuchik Khan himself escaped to the mountains of Gilan, where he froze to death in a snowstorm.[17]

REZA KHAN AND THE ULAMA, 1921–24

Reza Khan, the colonel whose troops crushed the Jangali revolt, overthrew the Iranian government in February 1921. His coup was supported by the commander of the British forces in Iran—who withdrew all his troops from the country during the following four months. From 1921 through 1924, Reza Khan won tremendous popularity by suppressing various regional revolts in addition to that of Kuchik Khan. Already in 1922, two hundred merchants sent him an open letter declaring: "Before our beloved commander saved us, the Islamic Empire of Iran was fast disintegrating. The army had collapsed, the tribes were looting, the country was the laughing stock of the world. Thanks to the army commander, we now travel without fear, admire our country, and enjoy the fruits of law and order."[18]

In the years following the coup of 1921, Reza Khan wanted to abolish the monarchy and establish a republic with himself at its head. But the ulama vehemently opposed this idea—in part because they associated republicanism with the secular reforms implemented by Mustafa Kemal in Turkey. (Kemal had established a republic in 1923 and had abolished the caliphate and Islamic legal and educational systems the following year.) After meeting in Qum with three leading mujtahids who all stressed the importance of preserving the monarchy, Reza Khan gave up the idea of creating a republic in Iran. Although no longer in the forefront of Iranian political life as they had been during the constitutional revolution, the ulama still had enough influence to determine the form of Iran's government.[19]

It is ironic that in the 1920s Iran's most influential ulama condemned republican rule, whereas in the 1970s they established Iran's first republic. In the twenties, the idea of a republic was seen as a heretical innovation because, in addition to the association with the secular reforms in Turkey, republics did not exist among Muslims at that time (except for the artificial ones foisted upon the Muslims of the Soviet Union). The idea of Muslims being governed by a republic was inevitably associated with the idea of Muslims being governed by the laws of unbelievers, specifically the unbelievers of Europe. Thus Sayyid Hasan Mudarris, a prominent mullah of the time, declared that an attack on the monarchy was an attack on Islamic law. And the elders of the guilds of Tehran organized a march in which the merchants and artisans chanted: "We want to keep the religion of our fathers, we don't want a republic. We are the people of the Koran, we don't want a republic."[20]

By the 1970s, on the other hand, republics were the rule rather than the exception in the Islamic world, most of which had experienced decades of European colonial rule. The idea that republics were contrary to Islam had largely disappeared. It was thus easy to accept Khomeini's contention that monarchical rule was contrary to Islam in the late 1970s, whereas virtually no one would have accepted such a claim in the 1920s. Once again we see that ostensibly immutable ideas and institutions have different meanings in different historical contexts.

REZA SHAH AND THE ULAMA, 1925–41

Convinced of the futility of trying to establish a republic in the face of the opposition of the ulama and their bazaari supporters, Reza Khan had himself declared Iran's shah in 1925. He was now Reza Shah, the founder of the Pahlavi dynasty. *Pahlavi* was the name of a language used in pre-Islamic Iran. Reza Shah took it as his family name to symbolize his intention to emphasize Iran's national rather than Islamic identity much as Mustafa Kemal took the name of *Ata-turk*, "Father of the Turks," to emphasize the same idea in Turkey.[21]

If the ulama thought that by preventing the establishment of a republic they could prevent the kinds of secularist reforms implemented by Mustafa Kemal in Turkey, they were mistaken. No other country besides Turkey experienced such rapid secularization as Iran in the 1920s under Reza Shah. A new secular educational system of European inspiration supplanted traditional Islamic schools. A new secular legal system of European inspiration supplanted Islamic law (except with respect to family law). And the government supplanted the ulama with respect to control over some waqf properties. These various reforms stripped the ulama of many of their most important sources of income (but not the religious tax) and violated many of their most basic values. And yet their protests were surprisingly mild and ineffective.[22]

Europe was rich and powerful, and like Mustafa Kemal, Reza Shah was determined to imitate it in every way, even with respect to clothes. He tried to force all Iranian men to wear European brimmed hats that made it impossible to place one's forehead on the ground during prayer. And he tried to force Iranian women to stop wearing the chador. The Iranian economist Homa Katouzian likens the 1936 law prohibiting the chador to a law compelling European women to wear topless dresses—it violated basic conceptions of how much of a "decent" woman's body could be exposed.[23] Men would carry their mothers, wives, and sisters to the public baths in sacks to circumvent the chador prohibition. The Iranian writer Reza Baraheni notes that on one such occasion a policeman stopped his father and asked him what he had in his sack. His father said it was full of pistachio nuts. The policeman then claimed he wanted some and started tickling the obviously human form within the sack. Baraheni's grandmother laughed at first and then wriggled out and ran away. Baraheni's father was arrested.[24]

Reza Shah's clothing laws affected all Iranians and violated the basic values of most. Yet there was no Islamic revolution in the twenties and thirties—although there certainly *were* protests. In 1928 the leading mujtahid of Qum sent Reza Shah a telegram protesting the initial law requiring men to wear Western clothes as well as the fact that policemen were forcibly tearing off the traditional clothes of religious students. But "the regime paid no attention to this protest."[25]

In 1935, a mullah preaching in the mosque of the shrine of the eighth imam in Mashhad, the holiest shrine in Iran, demanded the repeal of the clothing laws as well as lower taxes. Many of the men present removed their European hats in defiance of the government. Although shrines are in principle inviolable, troops surrounded the building and opened fire within it, killing dozens, perhaps over a hundred. But there was little subsequent protest, let alone an Islamic revolution.[26]

In terms of both self-interest and basic values, the Irᵣ ᵢian ulama of the twenties and thirties had every reason to lead a revolution against Reza Shah. And the overwhelming majority of all Iranians in the cities had every reason to follow. In addition to the outrage provoked by Reza Shah's forced Westernization, there was widespread discontent caused by high taxes, high prices, low wages, the prohibition of unions, the monopolization of foreign trade by the state and a few wealthy merchants, the forced sedentarization of Iran's nomadic tribes, and the brutal suppression of all opposition to the government. But there was no revolution during the reign of Reza Shah.[27]

KASHANI AND MUSADDIQ, 1951–53

After the German invasion of Russia in June of 1941, Great Britain and the Soviet Union demanded that Reza Shah expel his many German advisers so as to protect the supply lines from the Persian Gulf to the beleaguered Russians. The Iranian monarch, who never tired of emphasizing that most Iranians were of "the Aryan race," was on good terms with the Nazis and rejected the Allied demand. So in August 1941, British and Russian troops once again occupied southern and northern Iran. Reza Shah abdicated in favor of his twenty-two-year-old son Muhammad Reza (1919–80). He died three years later in Johannesburg.[28]

During the 1940s, Iran experienced parliamentary democracy for the first time since the constitutional revolution. But the free elections and the fiery speeches in the National Assembly had little impact on the real political situation in Iran during World War II—since British, Russian, and, as of 1942, American troops occupied the country. By 1943, American officials were running the Iranian economy as well as the army and the national police force. And in this same year, Churchill, Roosevelt, and Stalin met in Tehran without even pretending to consult the Iranian government.[29]

In late 1945, Soviet troops prevented the Iranian army from repressing Russian-backed rebellions in the northwestern provinces of Azarbayjan and Kurdistan, and the Soviet Union refused to comply with an earlier agreement to withdraw its forces by March 2, 1946, although American and British troops had left Iran early that same year. This provoked a major confrontation with the United States. The Russians finally left in May 1946, after Iran's prime minister promised them the oil concession they had been demanding for years. The departure of the Russian troops enabled the Iranian army to suppress the Azarbayjani and Kurdish "republics" much as the withdrawal of Russian troops in 1921 had made possible the suppression of the Jangali revolt. And in 1947, with strong encouragement from the United States, Iran's National Assembly overwhelmingly rejected the oil concession to the Soviet Union.[30]

Although the weakness of the Tehran government in the 1940s enabled the ulama to regain some of the political influence they had lost in the twenties and thirties, they remained less politically significant than they had been during the constitutional revolution. In 1948, fifteen mujtahids issued a legal decree (*fatva*) forbidding women to shop in the bazaar unless they wore the chador. Rather than endorse this decree, the prime minister at the time simply asked the leading mujtahid of Tehran to "prevent illegal demonstrations and to curb attacks on women in public places on the part of religious zealots."[31]

In 1950, the Ayatollah Burujirdi, who was the sole marja'-i taqlid of Twelver Shi'ism from 1947 until his death in 1961, convened a conference of some two thousand ulama in Qum. The participants agreed that ulama would henceforth be prohibited from involvement in Iranian politics. Burujirdi himself conformed to this rule most of his life. But many ulama did not, notably, the Ayatollah Kashani.[32]

Kashani (d. 1962) was for a while associated with a small militant Islamic group known as the *Fada'iyan-e Islam* (those who sacrifice themselves for the sake of Islam). But in the spring of 1951, Dr. Muhammad Musaddiq became prime minister and Kashani became one of his most influential supporters in the National Assembly. The Fada'iyan, who were best known for assassinating secular politicians and intellectuals in the late 1940s, wanted to be included in Musaddiq's government. Kashani rejected this demand, and by June of 1951, the Musaddiq government had imprisoned all the Fada'iyan leaders and shut down their newspaper.[33]

Musaddiq became prime minister by virtue of his position as head of the National Front—a coalition of parties that shared a common hostility toward British imperialism and toward British control of Iranian oil in particular. This coalition drew its support primarily from the traditional and modern middle classes—bazaaris and ulama on the one hand, and professionals and civil servants on the other. Once again, as in the constitutionalist revolution, bazaaris and ulama (many of them anyway) joined with secular nationalists to oppose foreign domination and a shah perceived as its instrument. And once again, many of the ulama eventually came to view their secular allies as a greater threat than the foreigners or the shah.[34]

Musaddiq nationalized the Anglo-Iranian Oil Company in 1951, thus becoming a symbol of Iran's defiance of Western imperialism, much like Nasser in Egypt after the nationalization of the Suez Canal in 1956. But although the ulama generally supported Musaddiq's efforts to rid Iran of British domination, they did not share his domestic goals. For example, when some of Musaddiq's advisers advocated giving women the right to vote in 1952, the ulama, including the normally apolitical Ayatollah Burujirdi, contended that this would be contrary to Islamic law. One person was killed and ten seriously wounded when religious students in Qum staged a demonstration to protest the idea of extending voting rights to women. And by the summer of 1952, Kashani openly opposed Musaddiq, in part because of the latter's request for an extension of emergency powers that Kashani called "dictatorial" and in part because of his fear of the influence of the communist *Tudeh* (masses) party, but more fundamentally because Kashani and Musaddiq had irreconcilable conceptions of the kind of society they wanted to see emerge in Iran.[25]

Like some of Iran's ulama, many people in England and the United States perceived Musaddiq as a communist sympathizer when in fact he was a mildly socialist nationalist. An elderly man from a wealthy landowning family, Musaddiq had often clashed with the Russian-controlled Tudeh party. He had been among the most vehement critics of the Soviet Union's demand for an oil concession in the 1940s, which the Tudeh party had dutifully endorsed. And in the early 1950s, he tried to obtain American help in resolving the conflict with Great Britain over the nationalized oil fields. Iran's communist newspapers regularly vilified him as a puppet of the United States at the very time that many American newspapers were vilifying him as a puppet of the Russians. On September 16, 1951, *Besu Ayandeh* declared that "Dr.

Mossadeq, by following the policy of obeying the instructions of the Americans, is wasting the fruits of victory this nation has obtained in its movement to free Iran from the clutches of the imperialistic oil magnates."[36] On October 1, 1951, *Razm* informed its readers that "Dr. Mossadeq and his friends in the so-called National Front are dancing to the tune of imperialistic America." And on January 22, 1952, *Moadda* accused Musaddiq of allowing the Americans to replace the British as the "masters" of Iran. Meanwhile the CIA was planning Musaddiq's overthrow.[37]

Despite the Tudeh party's hostility toward Musaddiq and the "bourgeois" nationalism of the National Front, it did organize strikes and demonstrations in all the major cities and oil fields of Iran in support of Musaddiq when the shah, who was widely perceived as a lackey of the British, tried to prevent his prime minister from also becoming minister of war in July 1952. Kashani and the ulama played an even more important role in mobilizing popular support for Musaddiq at this time. And in the wake of the resultant nationwide demonstrations of support, Musaddiq obtained the ministry of war and the shah was once again reduced to being an impotent figurehead, which was what he had been ever since the British and the Russians put him on his father's throne in 1941. During the rest of 1952 and the first half of 1953, the Tudeh party staged a number of large rallies that caused many Iranians and foreigners to fear that it was preparing to seize power. And the relations between Musaddiq and Kashani grew worse and worse.[38]

On August 16, 1953, Musaddiq's government thwarted an attempted coup directed by the CIA (on the basis of a plan conceived by the Anglo-Iranian Oil Company). The next day, the shah fled to Baghdad and then to Rome, and excited Tudeh supporters surged through the streets of Tehran and other cities destroying royal statues and in some cases occupying government buildings. On August 18, at the insistence of the American ambassador to Tehran, Musaddiq had the army and the police disperse the pro-Tudeh crowds. Thus on the following day, August 19, 1953, the communists did nothing to prevent the coup that overthrew Musaddiq.[39]

Kashani and Iran's most prominent ulama strongly endorsed the CIA coup. And the Ayatollah Muhammad Bihbihani (whose father had been a leader of the constitutional revolution) actually organized a lumpenproletarian demonstration of support for the pro-shah troops that surrounded Musaddiq's residence. Kermit Roosevelt, however, who directed the whole operation, claims that the CIA gave up trying to involve the ulama in Musaddiq's ouster because they were asking for too much money! And there are conflicting views of Kashani's own role in the events of August 1953. But despite these as yet unresolved problems concerning ulama participation in the coup, it is clear that Kashani and most mullahs were delighted by Musaddiq's downfall—which they could have easily prevented by mobilizing their followers as they had in 1952. These facts are not usually mentioned by the Ayatollah Khomeini when he condemns the CIA for overthrowing the government of Iran in 1953.[40]

The parallels between the Musaddiq period and the constitutional revolution of 1905–11 are striking. In both cases, a secular-religious coalition based on shared opposition to Western domination crumbled when the ulama realized how incompatible the goals of the secularists were with their own. In both cases, certain socialist tendencies of the secularists also disturbed the ulama and their merchant supporters. And in both cases, the ulama were sharply divided. Despite the Ayatollah Burujirdi's position as the sole marja'-i taqlid in the early fifties, he was never able to force activist ulama such as Kashani to stay out of politics. And despite Kashani's break with Musaddiq, some ulama continued to revere the old man who had defied the British Empire long after August 1953.

The CIA coup was successful for a number of reasons. For one thing, after the nationalization of the Anglo-Iranian Oil Company in 1951, the British had organized an international boycott of Iranian oil, which was the Iranian government's primary source of revenue. This crippled the Iranian economy and caused widespread discontent. But the crucial factor appears to have been Musaddiq's alienation of two of the most powerful political forces in Iran in the early fifties—the communists and the ulama. Had the communists or the ulama come to Musaddiq's rescue, as they had in July 1952, he would not have been overthrown. A handful of CIA agents with suitcases full of dollars could not have toppled Iran's government if the politically conscious segments of Iranian society had not allowed them to do so. On the other hand, however, it seems unlikely that the shah could have ever overthrown Musaddiq's democratically elected government without the help of the CIA's men and dollars.[42]

THE ULAMA AND MUHAMMAD REZA SHAH, 1960–64

After the coup of 1953, Muhammad Reza Shah banned the political parties that had flourished since the British and the Russians had installed him on the throne in 1941. Many political activists were imprisoned or executed, and others escaped to Europe. With the assistance of the CIA, and the FBI, and Israel's Mossad, the shah established the secret police force SAVAK, the primary purpose of which was to suppress all domestic opposition. But the shah made every effort to please the ulama, with whom he maintained good relations at least until 1959, when a number of ayatollahs protested government proposals concerning women's enfranchisement and land reform.[43]

In the summer of 1960, serious domestic opposition to the shah's post-coup regime surfaced for the first time when secular intellectuals with ties to the National Front protested the patently rigged elections to the Majlis (National Assembly). The shah was anxious to avoid antagonizing the new Kennedy administration, which was known to favor the liberalization of authoritarian regimes. So he announced that "free" elections would be held in January 1961. But National Front as well as Tudeh candidates were generally excluded from these elections, which therefore further outraged the professional, student, and bazaari supporters of the Front. (The Tudeh party was moribund in Iran by this time, although it remained influential among some students and intellectuals abroad.) Then in the spring of 1961, the regime was shaken by a teachers' strike in Tehran, which was the most dramatic of a series of strikes triggered by prolonged inflation and the government's subsequent austerity measures.[44]

The shah responded to all of this, as he did in the late seventies, with a combination of carrot and stick. On the one hand, he instituted a series of reforms designed to please the National Front's largely middle-class supporters (as well as the Kennedy administration and Iran's peasants and workers). On the other hand, he had the National Front's leaders jailed and their rallies (usually at the University of Tehran) broken up by paratroopers. These tactics succeeded. By 1963, the shah's liberal democratic opposition had been muzzled. But then came Khomeini.[45]

Most ulama had not participated in the secular democratic demonstrations of 1960–62, although some of them *had* criticized the government's land reform bill as well as the idea of women's suffrage. (It will be recalled that the enfranchisement of women was one of the issues that had led to the conflict between Musaddiq and the ulama.) When the shah announced in February 1963 that women would be allowed to vote, the ulama organized demonstrations and bazaaris closed their shops in all of Iran's major cities. The government responded by an attack on the Fayziyya Madrasa (seminary) in Qum, which soon became the center of Islamic opposition to the shah.[46]

On June 3, 1963, which was 'Ashura, the hitherto obscure Ayatollah Khomeini (b. 1902) likened the attack on the Fayziyya Madrasa to the slaughter at Karbala and warned the shah that unless he stopped trying to eradicate Islam and the ulama from Iranian society, he would die in exile like his father. Before dawn the next morning, Khomeini was arrested at his home in Qum, as were many other prominent ulama and religious students. These arrests, especially Khomeini's, sparked demonstrations that soon turned into riots in Qum, Tehran, Isfahan, and Shiraz.[47]

Amir Taheri, the editor-in-chief of Iran's leading newspaper until 1979, contends that "the largest demonstrations took place in Tehran itself where crowds of women in black *chadors* and men in white burial shrouds started to move towards the city center from the poor districts of the south."[48] In addition to the urban poor, Iran's ulama, religious students, and bazaaris were active in the uprising of June 1963. Some students from the Student Committee of the National Front at Tehran University also participated, although they had previously refused to cooperate with mullahs opposed to women's suffrage. But most university students and secular intellectuals sympathetic to the National Front still viewed the ulama as reactionaries and were not involved in the events of June 1963.[49]

The government used troops to suppress the demonstrations and riots, with orders to shoot to kill if necessary. As in the 1978–79 revolution, estimates of the number of people killed vary. Nikki Keddie speaks of "loss of life in the hundreds or more," although the figure of fifteen thousand dead is often given by Khomeini's supporters.[50] The American political scientist Marvin Zonis, who saw troops open fire in front of the Tehran bazaar on the first day of violence, says that the total number of people wounded or killed during June 1963 "certainly reached many thousands."[51] Whatever the actual number of casualties, the army's tactics worked. All protest was stamped out in less than a week.

In April 1964, Khomeini was allowed to return to Qum, where he was given a hero's welcome. The head of SAVAK at the time claimed that Khomeini had agreed not to participate in political activities any more, but the ayatollah was soon criticizing the shah as vehemently as ever. In October 1964, the Majlis passed a bill giving diplomatic immunity to American military and civilian personnel in Iran and another bill approving a $200 million loan from the United States. Khomeini saw the latter as a payment for the former and condemned both:

> Do you not know that this agreement reduces the Iranian people to a rank lower than that of an American dog?
> If someone runs over an American dog with his car, he is subject to investigation and prosecution even if he is "the shah" himself. But if an American cook runs over "the shah of Iran" himself, or any other important person, he will not be subject to prosecution.[52]

Khomeini also asserted that the authorities were trying to reduce the authority of the ulama because they had understood that so long as the men of religion had extensive influence on the people, the government "would not be able to enslave the people and sell them to the English one day and to the Americans another."[53]

The shah then decided to exile Khomeini, presumably for fear of the consequences of killing him. The ayatollah was flown to Turkey on November 4, 1964. In sharp contrast to the demonstrations and riots following his arrest (and that of other mullahs) in 1963, Khomeini's exile provoked virtually no protest. And in October 1965, the shah allowed Khomeini to move from Sunni Turkey to the Shi'i shrine city of Najaf in Iraq. It seemed as though that the aging deputy of the hidden imam (he was sixty-three at the time) would spend his remaining years quietly praying and teaching.[54]

THE ISLAMIC OPPOSITION, 1965-77

From 1964 until late 1977, the Islamic opposition was relatively mute, but far from dead. Khomeini continued to condemn the shah from Najaf, where he taught thousands of Arab and Iranian religious students during the course of his exile. And his sermons, lectures, and speeches were clandestinely distributed in Iran. There were also periodic protests against government policies by other ulama and religious students in Iran.[55]

Another facet of the Islamic opposition in Iran during the sixties and seventies was represented by Mahdi Bazargan (b. 1906) and the Liberation Movement of Iran, which he helped establish in 1961. Bazargan, the son of a wealthy bazaari from Azarbayjan, was an engineer who had been active in the National Front and had served in the Musaddiq government. He was in a sense Iran's Muhammad 'Abduh. That is to say that, like 'Abduh in Egypt, Bazargan stressed the compatibility of Islam with both democracy and science. His reformist and rationalist conception of Islam appealed to some middle-class Iranians. But most Iranians never read his books and pamphlets and he lacked the popular appeal of a Musaddiq or a Khomeini.[56]

Far more politically significant than Bazargan was Dr. 'Ali Shari'ati. Shari'ati, whose father was a mullah, urged Iranians to return to Islam as a means of regaining their authentic cultural identity and freeing their country from foreign domination. Influenced by Marx and Frantz Fanon while a graduate student in Paris, Shari'ati interpreted Shi'i Islam as a kind of Islamic liberation theology. His iconoclastic writings antagonized many ulama but were extremely popular among university students and the Westernized intelligentsia. And because of Shari'ati's ideas, many students previously attracted to Marxism began to speak of the need for an Islamic revolution.[57]

During the late sixties and early seventies, several guerrilla groups emerged to oppose the shah's regime, notably the Marxist Fada'iyan (not to be confused with the Islamic Fada'iyan of the forties) and the radical Islamic Mujahidin, or "Holy Warriors." The Mujahidin were founded by a few young graduates of Tehran University shortly after the uprising of June 1963. They endorsed Shari'ati's view that the struggle for a truly Islamic society entailed revolt against "class inequality, cartels, multinational corporations, racism, cultural imperialism, and the blind worship of the West."[58] They began a series of bombings, assassinations, and bank robberies in 1971, but like the Marxist Fada'iyan, they were never able to attract mass support outside of Iran's universities.[59]

As late as 1977, Iran's Islamic movement, which was in fact a congeries of different groups with different goals, appeared to be incapable of seriously threatening the shah's regime. The radical quasi-Marxist Islamic opposition, embodied by Shari'ati who died in London in 1977, was strong on university campuses but weak elsewhere. The reformist Islamic opposition, embodied by Bazargan who was living quietly in Tehran, seemed to exist only in a handful of books, pamphlets, and articles that virtually nobody read. And the militant and relatively traditionalist Islamic opposition, embodied by Khomeini who was still in Iraq, appeared to have been crippled by the exile and imprisonment of its principal leaders. Despite the serious inflation and consequent austerity measures of the mid-seventies, the shah seemed invincible. And yet by February 1979 Khomeini ruled Iran.[60]

THE PROTESTS OF 1977: HARBINGERS OF REVOLUTION

During the spring and summer of 1977, secular intellectuals in Iran openly criticized the shah's regime for the first time since 1960–62. The shah had initiated a few "liberalizing" measures as early as 1975–76 in response to growing criticism of SAVAK's methods by liberal politicians and journalists in the United States. Further liberalization followed the election of Jimmy Carter in November of 1976. Carter was a liberal Democrat critical of the human rights abuses in many of the third world dictatorships with close ties to the United States. His election thus dismayed the shah and delighted his moderate opposition. Bazargan, who was to become the first prime minister of the Islamic Republic in 1979, has said, "we did not believe the Shah when he started the liberalization policy, but when Carter's human rights drive lifted the hope of the people, all the built-up pressure exploded."[61] On the other hand, the more radical opposition, both religious and secular, tended to dismiss Carter's human rights policy as a public relations gimmick without substance.[62]

The various protests of the spring and summer of 1977 were in no sense a mass movement. They were simply a series of open letters and manifestos by secular upper-middle-class intellectuals who demanded a democratic form of government. The best known of the open letters was issued by three members of the National Front (Dr. Karim Sanjabi, Dr. Shahpur Bakhtiar, and Dariush Furuhar) on June 12, 1977. It concluded as follows:

> The only way, therefore, to restore individual freedoms, re-establish national co-operation and solve the problems that threaten Iran's future is to desist from authoritarian rule, to submit absolutely to the principle of constitutionality, revive the people's rights, respect the Constitution and the Universal Declaration of Human Rights, abandon the single-party system, permit freedom of the press and freedom of association, free all political prisoners, allow exiles to return, and es-

tablish a government based on a majority that has been popularly elected and which considers itself answerable to the Constitution.[63]

Such statements, which were all of a reformist rather than revolutionary character, never appeared in the strictly censored mass media. And the overwhelming majority of Iranians never read them. But the fact that most of the people who wrote them were neither imprisoned nor tortured encouraged many of the shah's more radical opponents to emerge publicly.

By the fall of 1977, the genteel letters and leaflets of the National Front intellectuals had given way to more strident protests. Squatters on the outskirts of Tehran fought government demolition crews sent to raze their illegal settlements. University students of both Marxist and radical Islamic orientations organized large demonstrations—both in Iran and in the United States. And by early December most Iranian universities had been shut down by student strikes. University and high school students, especially those influenced by Shari'ati, would continue to provide many of the revolution's organizers and martyrs until the final collapse of the shah's regime on February 11, 1979.[64]

When Khomeini's son Mustafa died in Najaf at the end of October, the ulama added mourning rites to the variety of protests that would eventually coalesce into the Islamic revolution. Although it is not clear exactly how Khomeini's son died, many Iranians hostile to the shah attributed his death, like Shari'ati's five months earlier, to SAVAK. A memorial service for Mustafa was held in Tehran. At the service, which was reportedly attended by over 3,000 people, the Ayatollah Tahiri Isfahani urged all those present to pray for the good health and "speedy return" of "our one and only leader, the defender of the faith and the great combatant of Islam, Grand Ayatollah Khomeini." The congregation responded to the mention of Khomeini's name by chanting *Allahu akbar,* "God is greater."[65] Similar memorial services were held in many other cities. After thirteen years of exile and apparent oblivion, Khomeini's name was now on many lips.[66]

All these activities by secular intellectuals, students, the ulama, and the urban poor in 1977 constituted the most serious opposition the shah had faced in decades. But no one realized that they were the first tremors of an upheaval that would transform Iran into an Islamic republic. On December 31, 1977, President Carter visited Tehran and toasted the shah, declaring that "Iran, because of the great leadership of the Shah, is an island of stability in one of the more troubled areas of the world."[67] These words did not seem ridiculous at the time they were spoken.

THE REVOLUTION OF 1978-79

On January 7, 1978, a week after Carter's famous toast, a leading Iranian newspaper published an article at the "request" of the minister of information. The article condemned mullahs opposed to the shah as "black reactionaries" and charged that the Ayatollah Komeini had been employed as a British spy and had lived a licentious life. Outraged by this attack on a deputy of the hidden imam, thousands of mullahs, religious students (*talabehs*), and bazaaris demonstrated in the streets of Qum. According to the Iranian journalist Amir Taheri, the demonstrators attacked and burned banks, girls' schools, secular book stores, the homes of government officials, and the only two restaurants in Qum where men and women could eat together.[68]

> By early afternoon [on January 9, 1978] the crowd, which had now grown to some 20,000 and was led by overexcited *talabehs,* felt confident enough to head for the central police station with cries of "Muslims, take up arms, Islam is in danger." Seeing the angry crowd approach, the nervous police began firing from the rooftop of the central police station. . . . It was the arrival of army troops on the scene shortly before sunset that finally restored peace.[69]

According to the government, only two people died in this clash at Qum, but opposition sources claimed that seventy were killed and over five hundred injured. Such discrepancies persisted throughout the revolution, with government figures always too low and opposition figures always too high. But no matter how many people died in Qum in January 1978, their deaths marked a turning point in the Iranian Revolution of 1978-79. From this moment on, the revolution was clearly Islamic—although it was not yet clearly a revolution. This is not to say that everyone who participated in anti-shah protests after January 9, 1978, wanted an Islamic state. But from that day on, the dominant symbols of the opposition (notably that of "Imam" Khomeini himself) were Islamic ones.[70]

In Shi'i Islam, mourning services are held on the third, seventh, and fortieth day after death. The fortieth-day mourning ceremonies for the martyrs of the January 9 riot in Qum took place on February 18, 1978. In all the main cities, memorial services were held in mosques while bazaars and universities were closed. (Mosques, bazaars, and universities were to remain the centers of protest throughout the revolution.) As would often be the case during the following months, the fortieth-day mourning rites of February 18 were demonstrations of rage as well as of sorrow.[71]

In the northwestern city of Tabriz, rite became riot after a policeman killed a student protester. The enraged but unarmed protesters attacked symbols of despotism (for example, police stations and offices of the shah's Resurgence party), symbols of wealth (luxury hotels and large banks), and symbols of Western immorality (liquor stores and movie theaters with sexy billboards). These were among the principal targets of rioters throughout the revolution. The Tabriz riot lasted two days, February 18 and 19, until the army regained control of the city by means of tanks and helicopter gunships. European eyewitnesses estimated that almost a hundred people died during the rioting, thus creating many new martyrs to be mourned.[72]

The cycle of martyrdom and mourning begun in Qum and Tabriz continued to some extent throughout the revolution, but especially during the first five months of 1978. Those who died in the February 18 and 19 riots in Tabriz were mourned forty days later in March. These mourning processions again became riots and those killed by the police were mourned forty days later in May. These rites too erupted into riots, with more deaths. The cycle was broken in June, on the fortieth day of mourning for the martyrs of May, when the Ayatollah Shari'atmadari and other ulama called for a peaceful general strike.[73]

Although dozens of Iranians were martyred and mourned during the summer of 1978, Iran seemed relatively calm until August 19 (the twenty-fifth anniversary of the CIA coup of 1953), when hundreds of people in a movie theater burned to death in a fire. The government blamed the fire on the mullahs. But the widespread belief that SAVAK had deliberately caused hundreds of Iranians to burn to death so as to discredit the ulama heightened hostility toward the shah.[74]

Shaken by the protests following the fire, the shah appointed a new prime minister and offered the opposition a number of concessions, notably the closure of casinos, the restoration of the Islamic calendar, and the promise of free elections. Although some of the secular nationalists and the moderate mullahs (such as the Ayatollah Shari'atmadari) welcomed these changes, Khomeini and his supporters dismissed them as purely cosmetic.[75]

Huge protest marches at the end of Ramadan (the month of fasting) in early September induced the shah to impose martial law during the night of September 7, 1978. The next morning troops opened fire on thousands of people gathered in Jaleh Square to mourn and protest the deaths of several martyrs a week earlier. As usual, the exact number of people killed on this "Black Friday" is disputed. The government said fewer than a hundred. The opposition said thousands. Whatever the actual figure, the massacre of September 8, 1978, horrified and outraged many Iranians who had not previously openly opposed the shah.[76]

The main participants in the mourning rites, demonstrations, and riots of the winter, spring, and summer of 1978 appear to have been merchants and artisans of the bazaar, university and high school students, religious students, and mullahs. As for the secular intellectuals whose open letters had engendered more radical opposition in 1977, they continued to march in all the main marches and even helped organize them on occasion. And they still had a great deal of support from the Westernized middle class. But they could not compete with Khomeini and the ulama. The secular nationalists would continue to hope that they could use Khomeini much as secular nationalists had used the ulama during the constitutionalist revolution and the Musaddiq era. But this time it was the ulama who would use the secular nationalists.[77]

In the fall of 1978, professionals and white- and blue-collar workers joined the bazaaris, ulama, students, intellectuals, and the urban poor in challenging the shah on a large scale. By the third week of October, strikes had shut down most bazaars, universities, high schools, government offices, factories, oil fields, and refineries. Meanwhile the wealthy elite was escaping to the West, taking over $2.5 billion out of Iran in the last three months of 1978. The revolution was now clearly a revolution.[78]

The shah had asked the government of Iraq to expel Khomeini early in October in the hope that this would decrease contact between the ayatollah and the opposition in Iran. But Khomeini went to France, from where he was able to speak to his supporters in Iran far more freely than ever before. His sermons and speeches were recorded in a French studio and the tapes were distributed in Iran by the thousands. Moreover, BBC news broadcasts to Iran enabled every Iranian with a radio to know exactly what Khomeini was saying day after day (at least what he was saying to Western reporters). The technology and political freedom of the West brought Khomeini closer to Iran in France than he had been in Iraq.[79]

The largest demonstrations of 1978 occurred during Muharram, the month of mourning, which began on December 2. After hundreds of demonstrators had been killed during the first few days of the month, the government agreed not to interfere with the religious processions on the two holiest days (the ninth and tenth of Muharram) if the marchers would keep to a certain prescribed route and avoid direct criticism of the shah.[80]

Somewhere between 300,000 and 3 million people participated in the march of the ninth of Muharram (December 10, 1978). Old National Front nationalists in suits and ties marched, as did ulama in cloaks and turbans. University and high school students in jeans marched, as did seminarians in robes. Elegantly dressed women with bare faces, arms, and legs marched, as did women covered by chadors. Bazaaris, laborers, and peddlers marched, as did doctors, lawyers, and engineers. It seemed as though everyone in Tehran was marching, except for the shah, his soldiers, and the very rich—who were either busy packing or already in Beverly Hills or Paris.[81]

The following day was 'Ashura. The crowds were even larger than the previous day (estimates range from 2 million to 4 million people). Despite efforts by mullahs to avoid chants that would provoke the army, the marchers could not be restrained from chanting some of the principal slogans of the revolution:

> Khomeini, you are the light of God, the cry of our hearts!
> Khomeini is our leader, Shari'ati our inspirer!
> Death to the shah!
> Shah, we shall kill you because you killed our fathers!
> Death to the American dog!
> Shah held on a leash by the Americans!
> We will destroy Yankee power in Iran!
> Hang this American king![82]

By now, the United States was desperately trying to arrange a compromise between the shah and his secular nationalist opposition in order to prevent Khomeini from taking power. On December 30, the shah appointed Shahpur Bakhtiar of the National Front as prime minister. On January 16, 1979, "His Imperial Majesty, Muhammad Reza Pahlavi, Shah of Shahs, Light of the Aryans," fled his country, leaving behind him ecstatic crowds rejoicing in the streets of every city. Bakhtiar was expelled from the National Front, and it was obvious from the moment that he took office that his government could not govern. On February 1, Khomeini returned on a jumbo jet chartered from Air France, and millions of jubilant Iranians turned out to welcome "the imam" after his long absence.[83]

A few days after his return, Khomeini asked Mahdi Bazargan to form a provisional Islamic government and had his Revolutionary Council negotiate with the chiefs of staff of the Iranian armed forces. Then on February 9, the shah's Imperial Guard attacked a large military base in Tehran to punish hundreds of air force technicians for having publicly expressed support for Khomeini. Guerrillas of the Marxist Fada'iyan and the radical Islamic Mujahidin, who had not played an important role in the revolution until now, rushed to assist the rebels. Along with men from a nearby popular quarter, the guerrillas and technicians forced the Imperial Guards to withdraw. And during the next two days, with the help of many soldiers and some Tudeh party members who joined them, the guerrillas attacked police stations, prisons, army garrisons, and armories all over Tehran. At 2 P.M. on February 11, 1979, the Supreme Council of the Armed Forces declared its neutrality. Bakhtiar fled to Paris, and the last vestiges of the Pahlavi regime collapsed.[84]

THE UNRAVELING OF THE REVOLUTIONARY COALITION OF 1978–79

As in most revolutions, once the raison d'être of the coalition that overthrew the old regime was gone—namely the old regime itself—previously submerged differences came to the surface. The secular nationalists, the Westernized middle class, and many students and bazaaris wanted democracy as well as less foreign domination. Instead they got an autocrat even less sympathetic to democracy than the shah. This should not have surprised them. But many well-educated Iranians never bothered to read Khomeini's writings or simply assumed that they could manipulate him as an earlier generation of secular intellectuals had manipulated the ulama during the constitutionalist revolution of 1905–11. Khomeini himself, perhaps on the advice of his secularly educated advisers, encouraged such wishful thinking while in exile. But as the Islamic Republic took shape in 1979, all illusions were soon dispelled.[85]

The ulama had played an important role in all the major events of modern Iranian history, notably the tobacco protest of 1891–92, the constitutionalist revolution of 1905–11, Musaddiq's nationalization of oil in 1951–53, and the riots of 1963. But the revolution of 1978–79 gave the ulama greater power than they would have imagined possible—or legitimate—in earlier decades. Khomeini's notion of a government led by a leading religious scholar was an innovation that many ulama, not to mention other Iranians, regarded as heretical. But such people have been suppressed along with the various liberals and leftists whose leaders are now in the cemeteries of Iran or the cities of the West.[86]

The seizure of the American embassy by Islamic militants in November 1979, the consequent hostage crisis, and above all the Iran-Iraq War begun in September 1980 strengthened the Islamic Republic because of the rally-around-the-flag syndrome in times of external threat. Moreover, Khomeini's own charisma was such that any attempt to overthrow him was widely perceived as "Satanic"—as the radical Islamic Mujahidin learned in 1982. After he dies, however, the imam will take much of his charisma to his grave.[87]

6

Saudi Arabia

In 1745, the religious scholar Muhammad Ibn 'Abd al-Wahhab and Muhammad Ibn Saud, the ruler of a small territory in the Najd plateau of central Arabia, agreed to join forces to spread the doctrine that has come to be known as Wahhabi Islam. The basic themes of this doctrine were common to most of the fundamentalist movements that periodically emerged in Sunni Islam: the need to return to the pristine Islam of the Quran and the Sunna, that is, the "customary practice" of the prophet Muhammad, and the condemnation of all innovations that deviated from the worship of God alone, especially the veneration of saints' tombs that had spread throughout the Islamic world.[1]

During the course of the late eighteenth and early nineteenth centuries, the Saudi-led Wahhabis succeeded in conquering most of the Arabian peninsula and much of what is now Jordan and Syria. Disturbed by this spreading revolt within his empire, the Ottoman sultan sent an army from Egypt to crush the Wahhabi movement, which it eventually did in 1818. A new and less powerful Saudi state was soon reborn, however, and survived in the Najd plateau until 1891, when the Saud family fled to Kuwait after having been defeated by the Rashid clan of the tribe of Shammar.[2]

Then in 1902, 'Abd al-'Aziz Ibn 'Abd al-Rahman Al Saud, best known in the West as Ibn Saud, regained control of the Najdi town of Riyadh. And by the outbreak of World War I, he governed the entire Najd plateau and most of eastern Arabia. Like most of the other local rulers of the Arabian peninsula, Ibn Saud became a client of the

British Empire. In 1916, he agreed to maintain a force of four thousand men to fight the pro-Ottoman Rashid clan in return for a monthly stipend of five thousand pounds, four machine guns, and three thousand rifles "with an ample supply of ammunition."[3]

IBN SAUD AND THE IKHWAN, 1912–30

Seeking to create an army that would transcend tribal ties and tensions, Ibn Saud organized the *Ikhwan,* or "Brethren," in about 1912. He established settlements for the Ikhwan and provided them with land, seeds, and tools, as well as instruction in growing crops, hoping to transform them into sedentary agriculturalists as well as holy warriors. Ibn Saud also provided the Ikhwan with arms, ammunition, and teachers who instructed them in the basic tenets of the Wahhabi doctrine.[4]

The Ikhwan enabled Ibn Saud to conquer most of the Arabian peninsula, including the holy cities of Mecca and Madina, which were occupied in 1924 and 1925, respectively. But Ibn Saud was frequently forced to restrain the religious fervor of the Ikhwan so as to avoid antagonizing the British and the majority of the world's Muslims who tended to view the Ikhwan as bizarre fanatics. For example, in 1926, Egyptian pilgrims brought their annual gift of a black and gold cloth cover for the Ka'ba, the sacred cube at the center of the Sacred Mosque (*al-Masjid al-Haram*) in Mecca. The Egyptians carried the cloth on an ornate litter (*mahmal*) and were accompanied by buglers and armed soldiers. The puritanical Ikhwan, for whom music of any kind was anathema, regarded the gaudy procession as a perversion of Islam and stoned the Egyptians, killing some, until Ibn Saud intervened to restore order.[5]

The conflict between the Ikhwan and Ibn Saud festered for years until the Ikhwan returned to the Najd after the conquest of the Hijaz. Then at a conference in 1926, leaders of the Ikhwan openly criticized Ibn Saud for (1) sending his son Saud to Egypt, which was occupied by the Christian English and inhabited by "infidel Muslims," that is, non-Wahhabi Muslims; (2) sending his son Faisal to infidel England; (3) using automobiles, telephones, radios, and telegraphs, all of which were "Christian innovations and inventions of the devil"; (4) taxing the tribes in the Hijaz and the Najd; (5) allowing the infidel (the non-Wahhabi) tribes of the newly created states of Iraq and Transjordan to graze their flocks in the lands of the Muslims (the Wahhabis);

(6) prohibiting trade with Kuwait and the Kuwaitis; and (7) failing to force the Shi'is of eastern Arabia to become Wahhabi Muslims.[6]

These demands were an interesting mixture. Most of them articulated outrage provoked by the violation of religious belief. But some of them also reflected the self-interest of Najdi bedouin whose traditional livelihoods were threatened by the new Saudi kingdom they had helped create. (The transformation of the Najdi bedouin into sedentary agriculturalists was far from complete.)

Ibn Saud responded to the Ikhwan challenge by convening a conference of leading Ikhwan and ulama in January 1927 at which he stressed that he was a "faithful servant of Islamic law."[7] A month later, the ulama of the Najd issued a fatwa, or "legal decree," in which they supported some of the Ikhwan demands while rejecting others. They demanded the implementation of Islamic law throughout the Saudi domain, the demolition of idolatrous shrines, the conversion of the Shi'is of eastern Arabia to Wahhabi Islam, the prohibition of grazing by the flocks of Shi'i tribes from Iraq within the Saudi domain, and the abolition of taxes not authorized by Islamic law. On the other hand, the ulama rejected the Ikhwan view that the jihad, or "holy war," against non-Wahhabis should be continued, saying that this was to be decided by Ibn Saud. The ulama also decreed that the Ikhwan did not have the right to revolt against Ibn Saud even if he did not abolish the non-Islamic taxes. And they refused to condemn technological innovations such as the telegraph on the ground that there are no references to such things in Islamic law. Ibn Saud agreed to conform to this fatwa, which ultimately served to strengthen him vis-à-vis the disgruntled Ikhwan.[8]

Despite the decree of the ulama, Ikhwan resentment of British restrictions on their right to raid Shi'i tribes on the Iraqi side of the recently demarcated Najdi-Iraqi border soon triggered open defiance of Ibn Saud. In 1927, the British-controlled Iraqi government sent twelve workmen and seven policemen to build the first of a series of police posts near the Najdi-Iraqi border. Ibn Saud protested that the building of this post violated the terms of the 1922 'Uqayr protocols that had established the border between the Najd and Iraq. And in September 1927, a band of Ikhwan (who had been raiding the tribes of southern Iraq for years) attacked the workmen and policemen, killing all but one of them. Further Ikhwan forays into Iraq followed, with the British Royal Air Force responding by air attacks on the Najdi bedouin. Ibn Saud condemned the raids of both the British and the Ikhwan while trying to avoid armed conflict with either. He attempted to negotiate with the British, and in October 1928, he held another congress of the Ikhwan in Riyadh in a vain attempt to placate their rebellious leaders.[9]

For much of 1928, it seemed as though Ibn Saud would be unable to suppress Ikhwan opposition to his rule. But then in February 1929, one of the rebel leaders, Ibn Bijad of the 'Utayba tribe, made the mistake of murdering some Najdi camel merchants as well as some men of the Najdi tribe of Shammar. These massacres outraged most Najdi townsmen as well as many Najdi bedouin and enabled Ibn Saud to recruit an army of thousands with which he defeated the Ikhwan at the battle of al-Sabila in March 1929. Despite this defeat, the revolt continued until January 1930, when the principal rebel leaders surrendered to the British in Kuwait. The Ikhwan were incorporated into the new National Guard and never again challenged Saudi rule.[10]

OPPOSITION TO THE SAUDI REGIME IN THE FIFTIES AND SIXTIES

In the decades following the suppression of the Ikhwan revolt of 1928–30, the Saudi regime, presiding over what officially became the Kingdom of Saudi Arabia in 1932, was secure politically but hard-pressed financially. It was the need for cash that induced Ibn Saud to allow Standard Oil of California to explore for oil, which was first discovered in marketable quantities in 1938. During World War II, when revenue from oil and the pilgrimage to Mecca fell drastically, Saudi Arabia received aid from both Great Britain and the United States. It was not until the 1950s that the Saudis began to earn great wealth from their oil. It was also in the 1950s that the Saudi regime began to face new forms of domestic opposition.[11]

In 1953, Arab workers in the ARAMCO (Arab American Oil Company) oil fields went on strike to demand higher salaries, better working conditions, and the elimination of the segregation of Americans and Arabs. The government jailed the strike leaders but did grant salary increases and better working conditions. The oil workers struck again in 1956 after the harsh suppression of a demonstration protesting American "imperialism." Once again, the Saudi government punished the strike leaders but granted a few concessions. High salaries, improved working conditions, and a severe law prohibiting strikes combined to inhibit the growth of a strong labor movement in following years.[12]

In the fifties and sixties, the government also faced opposition from educated young men of the new middle class and a handful of liberal princes from the royal family. These young people, who were attracted to Nasser's Arab nationalism, advocated democracy and a diminution of American influence. They tended to view the Saudi regime's ties to the United States as treasonous in the light of American support for Israel. But Egypt's humiliating defeat in the Six-Day War of 1967 tarnished Nasser's image as the anti-imperialist hero of the Arab world and many of the Nasserist Saudi rebels of the sixties became pillars of the establishment in the seventies.[13]

In addition to these various strands of secular opposition, the Saudi regime also faced some less organized religious opposition in the 1960s. Early in the decade, the opening of a girls' school provoked riots. In 1963, a delegation of ulama protested to King Faisal when a woman's voice was broadcast for the first time on Radio Mecca. And when television was introduced in 1965 despite the protests of some ulama, a grandson of Ibn Saud led a small band of zealots in an unsuccessful attack on the television station in Riyadh. But these various protests were of minor significance when compared with the seizure of Mecca's Sacred Mosque in November 1979.[14]

THE SEIZURE OF MECCA'S SACRED MOSQUE IN 1979

During the 1970s, a bearded young man named Juhayman al-'Utaybi traveled throughout Saudi Arabia condemning the Saudi regime for its decadence. Al-'Utaybi's name was derived from that of the tribe of 'Utayba, some segments of which had participated in the Ikhwan revolt of 1928–30. Juhayman and the followers he collected during the late seventies called themselves Ikhwan and, like many of their fathers and grandfathers in earlier years, wore long beards and short robes. Juhayman had served eighteen years in Saudi Arabia's National Guard before becoming an itinerant preacher. Most of his followers, some of whom were foreigners, were students of Islamic law and theology at the Islamic University of Madina, where Juhayman himself may have attended the courses of the religious scholar Shaykh 'Abd al-'Aziz Ibn Baz. This university was founded in the 1960s by Egyptian fundamentalists who had fled to Saudi Arabia after Nasser's crackdown on the Muslim Brotherhood.[15]

During the 1970s, Juhayman wrote a series of pamphlets in which he condemned rulers who did not govern according to the Quran and the Sunna. He specifically condemned the Saudi royal family for its corruption, its close ties to infidel governments, and its persecution of all domestic opposition. Although he praised some ulama for warning the government about corruption, he condemned most of them, and Shaykh 'Abd al-'Aziz Ibn Baz in particular, for serving as lackeys of the Saudi regime. Ironically, Ibn Baz (who once claimed that the sun revolved around the immovable earth) had induced the government to free Juhayman and ninety-eight of his followers after their arrest for subversion in 1978.[16]

Juhayman and several hundred of his followers seized Mecca's Sacred Mosque at dawn on November 20, 1979, as the fifteenth century of the Islamic calendar was about to begin. Juhayman declared that his brother-in-law Muhammad Ibn 'Abn Allah al-Qahtani was the messianic mahdi who had come to rid the world of injustice and corruption. But even among Saudi Arabs hostile to the government, there was little support for Juhayman's revolt. The prevailing view was that the rebels had desecrated the holiest place in Islam, where violence is not supposed to occur. King Khalid had no trouble convincing the leading ulama of Saudi Arabia, including Ibn Baz, to issue a legal decree condemning the seizure of the mosque and permitting the government to use force to subdue the rebels if they did not surrender peacefully.[17]

Within two weeks, troops had retaken the mosque. Whereas his allegedly messianic brother-in-law was killed in the first few days of fighting, Juhayman himself was taken alive on December 5, 1979, exactly two weeks after the revolt began. Handcuffed and defeated, he stared defiantly at the television cameras, "thrusting forward his matted beard, his eyes fierce and piercing like a cornered beast of prey."[18] On January 9, 1980, Juhayman and sixty-two of his followers were beheaded. In addition to forty-one Saudi Arabs (most of them in their early and mid-thirties), the executed included ten Egyptians, six South Yemenis, three Kuwaitis, one North Yemeni, one Sudanese, and one Iraqi.[19]

Despite the presence of so many foreigners, there is no evidence that Juhayman's anachronistic millenarian revolt was organized outside of Saudi Arabia. But the Ayatollah Khomeini suggested on Tehran Radio that "it is not beyond guessing that this is the work of criminal

American imperialism and international Zionism."[20] Rumors to this effect sparked the burning of the American embassy in Pakistan, an attack on the U.S. mission in Libya, and demonstrations in many other Islamic countries.[21]

THE SHI'IS OF SAUDI ARABIA

While the Saudi government was trying to suppress Juhayman's Meccan revolt during the last week of November 1979, thousands of Shi'is rioted in the oil-rich eastern region—where almost all of Saudi Arabia's Shi'is are concentrated. Already in the summer of 1979, emboldened by the Iranian Revolution, Shi'i ulama of the predominantly Shi'i town of al-Qatif had announced that Shi'is would commemorate the martyrdom of Imam Husayn publicly that year, despite the Saudi ban on such activities. And the Shi'is did so on 'Ashura, which fell on November 28, 1979.[22]

The mourning rites became demonstrations in which the Shi'is demanded an end to discrimination against them. The demonstrations led to the burning of cars, the looting of shops, and violent clashes with police. Seventeen people were killed and dozens wounded before Saudi troops succeeded in restoring order. Four more Shi'is died in a later riot on February 1, 1980, the first anniversary of Khomeini's return to Iran. On this occasion, a sermon in the main mosque of the predominantly Shi'i town of al-Qatif led a crowd to demonstrate against the government and attack the town's largest bank and currency exchange. The demonstrators carried photographs of the Ayatollah Khomeini.[23]

Although exact figures are lacking, Shi'is constitute only about 6 percent of Saudi Arabia's population, which was around 6 million in 1980. But their economic and political significance is far greater than these numbers would suggest because of their concentration in the oil fields near the Persian Gulf. At least 35 percent of ARAMCO's employees are Shi'is—most of them manual laborers.[24]

Given their condemnation of the veneration of anyone but God, the Wahhabis have always been outraged by the virtual apotheosis of 'Ali and Husayn in Shi'i Islam. And nothing could be more offensive to the sober and puritanical Wahhabi ethos than the frenzied weeping and self-flagellation of 'Ashura. The Wahhabis thus traditionally reviled the Shi'is as the worst of all "infidels." In 1802, Wahhabis had raided the Shi'i holy city of Karbala. "The inhabitants were killed without mercy in the streets and houses; the great dome of the tomb of Husain was demolished, and the bejeweled covering of his grave carried off as spoil."[25] In the following year, a Shi'i assassinated the Saudi ruler who had led the raid on Karbala. Over a century later, when Ibn Saud reimposed Wahhabi rule on the Shi'is of the eastern province, the Ikhwan demanded that he force the Shi'is of Arabia and Iraq to convert to the "true" Islam of the Wahhabis. Although endorsed by the ulama of the Najd, this demand was never implemented. However, like other Saudi rulers before and since, Ibn Saud did not allow the Shi'is to practice their distinctive rituals in public, this being particularly true with respect to the mourning rites of 'Ashura.[26]

The discovery of oil in the 1930s improved the Shi'is' economic status, but did not alter the traditional Wahhabi view of them as despicable heretics. Although not found among all Saudis, this view remains widespread, and it has prevented Shi'is from taking advantage of all the opportunities available to their Sunni compatriots. The Iranian Revolution encouraged the Shi'is to protest this situation.[27]

Although the Saudi government imprisoned hundreds of Shi'is after the riots of 1979, it also acknowledged that they had some legitimate grievances, which it attempted to redress by means of well-publicized plans to improve government services in the largely Shi'i eastern region near Bahrain. This new interest in the Shi'is' well-being seems to have eased tensions since the eastern province has remained relatively quiet since 1980—despite regular Iranian radio broadcasts in Arabic exhorting the Shi'is to revolt against the Saudi government.[28]

But Shi'i opposition to Saudi rule persists. The clandestine Shi'i group known as the Organization of the Islamic Revolution in the Arab Peninsula advocates the overthrow of the Saudi regime and the establishment of a revolutionary Islamic republic similar to that of Iran. The following passage from a tract distributed during the 1981 pilgrimage in Mecca exemplifies the rhetoric of this movement:

> At the time when the Muslim ummah is turning to real Islam as the only hope for progress, freedom and complete independence, the ummah faces a dangerous enemy represented by ruling regimes of the so-called Islamic states. The Saudi family is one of these regimes. . . . Their regime is the most dangerous enemy of Islam because they use the cover of religion to legitimate their otherwise unIslamic [*sic*] rule. . . . Ask yourselves: does Islam allow a royal family to have luxurious palaces and share in commercial firms?[29]

The Organization of the Islamic Revolution in the Arab Peninsula espouses Sunni-Shi'i unity in its tracts, but it is in fact an exclusively Shi'i movement with close ties to the Islamic Republic of Iran. It is therefore incapable of leading an Islamic revolution in Saudi Arabia. But a few well-trained terrorists could wreak havoc in the oil fields and refineries from which Saudi wealth flows. This possibility terrifies the Saudi government as well as the tens of thousands of American managers and technicians in the eastern region where both oil and Shi'is are found.[30]

CONCLUSION

Saudi Arabia is often viewed in the West as the epitome of "fundamentalist" Islam, and in many ways it is. The government is explicitly based on Islamic law, and infractions of this law are, in principle, severely punished. Liquor is prohibited, although easily obtainable for those who can afford it. Women are not allowed to drive cars or travel alone. And there has been a general tendency toward stricter enforcement of Islamic law because of the fears engendered by the fall of the shah, the seizure of the Sacred Mosque, and the entire Islamic revival of the late seventies.[31]

But coupled with this puritanism is the well-known profligacy of the Saudi elite, which is condemned by a wide range of Saudis far less marginal than Juhayman or the Organization for Islamic Revolution in the Arab Peninsula. Resentment of this profligacy is compounded by middle-class resentment of the concentration of wealth and power in the hands of the royal family (which includes several thousand people at least) and the Saudi regime's role as a client of the United States. These various discontents could eventually threaten the Saudi government. But there do not appear to be any Islamic movements (or secular ones for that matter) capable of translating them into a revolution in the immediate future.[32]

7

Egypt

Egypt in the nineteenth century, like most of the rest of the Arabic-speaking world, was a province of the Istanbul-based Ottoman Empire. But during the second half of the century, Turkish rule was gradually replaced by that of Great Britain. British troops occupied Egypt in 1882 to suppress a nationalist revolt led by Colonel Ahmad 'Urabi. And Britain effectively controlled the country for the next seventy years until forced to leave in the 1950s by another nationalist revolt led by another colonel—Gamal Abdel Nasser. Although never officially a colony, Egypt experienced British rule far more directly than either Iran or Saudi Arabia.

THE REFORMIST ISLAM OF AL-AFGHANI, 'ABDUH, AND RIDA

During the decade preceding the British occupation, Jamal al-Din al-Afghani (1838–97) had taught at Cairo's famous Islamic university of al-Azhar. As already noted in the context of his involvement in the Iranian tobacco protest of 1891–92, al-Afghani stressed the need for Muslims to unite and return to what he portrayed as primordial Islam in order to resist European imperialism. His ideas influenced a number of young Egyptian intellectuals, notably Muhammad 'Abduh (1849–1905). But whereas al-Afghani had refused to cooperate with British imperialism in any way, 'Abduh served the British government in Egypt in various important legal positions. As the most influential member of a government committee appointed to reform al-Azhar, he proposed a series of innovations aimed at integrating Western science and thought into the curriculum. These proposals outraged the more traditional ulama.[1]

'Abduh's reformist ideas were given a more fundamentalist twist by his disciple Muhammad Rashid Rida (1865–1935). Rida, a Syrian religious scholar who spent much of his life in Egypt editing the journal *al-Manar*, advocated the militant anti-imperialism of al-Afghani, with particular emphasis on the need to resist Western domination by returning to a purely Islamic state and society. But like 'Abduh, Rida was more a polemicist than a political leader.[2]

FROM THE UPRISING OF 1919 TO THE DISSOLUTION OF THE BROTHERHOOD IN 1948

By the end of World War I, many Egyptians hoped that Great Britain would grant Egypt its independence. In November 1918 a group of prominent secular nationalists led by Sa'd Zaghlul formed a "delegation" (*wafd*) to present the case for Egyptian independence at the Paris Peace Conference. In 1919, the British arrested Zaghlul and two other leading nationalists and exiled them to Malta in the hope that this would put an end to the widespread demonstrations in support of their delegation. But the exile of Zaghlul, who was coming to embody Egyptian nationalism much as Nasser would in the fifties and sixties, triggered a series of demonstrations, strikes, and riots, in which virtually all segments of Egyptian society participated, Christian Copts as well as Muslims. (The Copts constitute about 10 percent of Egypt's population.) This national upheaval finally induced Great Britain to grant Egypt nominal independence in 1922, but real power remained in British hands.[3]

Among the many students who participated in the uprising of 1919 was Hasan al-Banna (1906–49), the founder of the Muslim Brotherhood. Al-Banna's father was a minor religious scholar and watch repairer who served as imam, muezzin, and Quranic teacher in a little town of the Nile Delta. Al-Banna himself became a schoolteacher. He started teaching in the Suez Canal town of Isma'iliyya in 1927 and founded the Muslim Brotherhood in 1928. (This organization, called *al-Ikhwan al-Muslimun* in Arabic, should not be confused with the Ikhwan of Arabia, although the two groups had similar views on many issues.) Al-Banna contended that the Muslim Brotherhood had two basic goals: "That the Islamic nation [*watan*] be liberated from all foreign powers" and "that there arise in this free nation a free Islamic state that will function according to the rules of Islam."[4]

By the late forties, the Brotherhood had become the most powerful Islamic movement in the world, with perhaps as many as half a million members and a complex network of businesses, schools, and clinics in Egypt alone—plus an important branch in Syria. Its activist members were primarily students, professionals, and civil servants of the new middle class. Disturbed by the movement's growing strength and the terrorist activities of its "secret apparatus," Prime Minister Nuqrashi dissolved it on December 8, 1948. Twenty days later, Nuqrashi was assassinated by a Muslim Brother. And two months later, al-Banna was in turn assassinated—probably by a government agent. By July of 1949, there were about four thousand Brothers in Egyptian prison camps.[5]

THE MUSLIM BROTHERHOOD UNDER NASSER, 1952–70

When Nasser and the "Free Officers" overthrew the Egyptian monarchy on July 23, 1952, the Muslim Brothers were initially delighted since they believed their troubles were now over. The officers shared the Brotherhood's goal of freeing Egypt from British domination and were, by and large, devout Muslims. But personal piety is one thing and ideological commitment to the goal of a strictly Islamic state is another. Nasser and most of the Free Officers definitely lacked the latter, so that conflict was inevitable. And it occurred in 1954, when Nasser outlawed the Brotherhood after one of its members tried to assassinate him. By the end of 1954, over one thousand Brothers had been arrested, and six of them had been hanged. Nasser's repression at this time, coming so soon after the repression of 1948–49, permanently crippled the movement, which never regained the power it had enjoyed in the late forties.[6]

After nationalizing the Suez Canal and surviving the English, French, and Israeli invasions of 1956, Nasser became a larger-than-life symbol of Arab nationalism. The Muslim Brothers could not have threatened him even if most of their leaders had not been in prison or exile. This probably remained true in 1964, when Nasser freed a few prominent Brothers, including Sayyid Qutb, who was of a more militant orientation than the current leadership of the Brotherhood. But in 1965, Qutb and many other Brothers were once again imprisoned— on charges of participating in a conspiracy to overthrow the government. And in 1966, Qutb was hanged, despite pleas for clemency from all over the Muslim world.[7]

Until Egypt's humiliating defeat in the 1967 war with Israel, Nasser remained, in the eyes of most Egyptians, the hero of Suez, the third world David who had defied the Goliaths of the West. Despite his protracted and unsuccessful war in North Yemen, despite the failure of his quasi-socialist economy, and despite his ruthless suppression of all opposition, Nasser continued to embody the aspirations of most Egyptians, indeed of most Arabs. The Six-Day War forced Egyptians and Arabs generally to recognize that Nasser the man could not fulfill the goals of Nasser the myth. The shock of that realization, and the anxiety it entailed, led many Egyptians to turn to religion—especially since many devout Muslims interpreted Israel's victory as a sign that the Arabs had deviated from the laws of God. But the wave of religious fervor that swept Egypt after 1967 did not result in the immediate rebirth of the Muslim Brothers, thousands of whom remained in prison or in exile until Anwar Sadat had them released in 1971 and 1975.[8]

THE MUSLIM BROTHERHOOD UNDER SADAT, 1970–81

Sadat, who became president after Nasser's death in September 1970, decided to free the Brothers as part of a plan to utilize Islam to legitimate his campaign of "de-Nasserization." This campaign involved a shift away from socialism and dependence on the Soviet Union toward free enterprise and dependence on the United States. Sadat's position was strengthened by the October War of 1973, which was depicted as a great Egyptian victory in Egypt's government-controlled media. (The initial crossing of the Suez Canal was called "Operation Badr" after the first great victory of the prophet Muhammad, and it was widely believed that angels had aided the Egyptians just as they had aided the prophet over thirteen centuries earlier.) But Nasserists and Marxists continued to oppose Sadat's policies. And he thought that encouraging the Brotherhood as well as Islamic groups on university campuses (where Nasserists and Marxists were strong) would be an effective way to offset his leftist opposition.[9]

The resurrected Brotherhood's tacit alliance with Sadat was soon strained by the latter's trip to Jerusalem in 1977, the Camp David accords of 1978, and the signing of the Egyptian-Israeli peace treaty in 1979. The Brothers agreed with the leftists and others who felt that Sadat had betrayed the Palestinians—especially after it became clear that the "autonomy" talks were going nowhere. But unlike the leftists, the Brothers expressed their hostility toward Israel in virulent diatribes that parroted the shibboleths of twentieth-century European anti-Semitism.[10]

The Brotherhood's criticism of Egypt's new relations with Israel led Sadat to arrest hundreds of Muslim Brothers (among other people) in September 1981. Another source of conflict had been the Brotherhood's opposition to the personal status law which gave women greater rights with respect to divorce, alimony, and custody of children. Sadat had to enact this law by presidential decree in 1979 because of fierce opposition in the People's Assembly during the previous five years.[11]

But despite its eventual conflict with Sadat, the Brotherhood of the seventies and eighties was never a revolutionary movement. Many of its most prominent supporters were wealthy businessmen and professionals who definitely did not want an Islamic revolution along the lines of Iran's. Before their interdiction in 1981, the Brotherhood magazines tended to stress the need for a strictly Islamic legal system and for the elimination of immorality in the mass media. They did not advocate the radical transformation of the social and political structures of Egypt or the use of violence to achieve their goals. But other Islamic groups did.[12]

THE MORE MILITANT ISLAMIC GROUPS UNDER SADAT, 1970–81

During the late sixties and early seventies some young advocates of a strictly Islamic society decided that the Muslim Brotherhood had lost whatever revolutionary fervor it may have had in the days of Sayyid Qutb. And they started more militant Islamic groups of their own, notably *Munadhdhamat al-Tahrir al-Islami* (Islamic Liberation Organization), *Jama'at al-Muslimin* (Society of Muslims), and *al-Jihad* (Holy War).

The Islamic Liberation Organization (ILO) was founded in 1971 by Dr. Salih Siriyya, a Palestinian with a Ph.D. in science education. Siriyya, who was in his mid-thirties when he started the group, had been a member of the Jordanian branch of the Muslim Brotherhood known as the Islamic Liberation Party. Most of the members of the ILO were students or recent university graduates. In 1974, Egyptian police suppressed an attempted coup by Siriyya and his followers, and the ILO effectively ceased to exist after this.[13]

The Society of Muslims was also founded by an educated former Muslim Brother in his mid-thirties, namely Shukri Mustafa, who had a B.S. in agricultural science. Arrested for distributing Brotherhood pamphlets at the University of Asyut in 1965, Mustafa started his movement while in prison and recruited hundreds of students and recent university graduates after his release in 1971. His group was usually referred to in the Egyptian media as *al-Takfir wa al-Hijra,* or "Excommunication and Emigration," because of its belief that all Muslims who did not share its views were infidels and that real Muslims should withdraw from the unbelieving society around them. The group first attracted attention in 1977, the year of the January food riots and Sadat's November trip to Jerusalem. In July of this year, members of the Society of Muslims kidnapped a prominent religious scholar, Muhammad al-Dhahabi, who was a former minister of waqf properties (mortmain properties used for the maintenance of mosques and other Islamic institutions). The kidnappers demanded a ransom of about half a million dollars and the release of their "brothers" in prison. When the government rejected their demands, they killed their hostage. This led to the arrest of all the group's leaders and over six hundred of its members. Shukri Mustafa was hanged and his movement appears to have disintegrated since.[14]

The third prominent militant Islamic group to have emerged during the seventies was al-Jihad, the group that assassinated Sadat in 1981. Like the ILO and the Society of Muslims, al-Jihad appealed primarily to students and other young people who had recently graduated from or dropped out of high schools, universities, or technical institutes. But the group also had some adherents in the armed forces, notably Khalid al-Islambuli, the lieutenant who boasted "I have killed the Pharaoh" after Sadat's death.[15]

Two days after Sadat's assassination on October 6, 1981, members and sympathizers of al-Jihad seized control of the upper Egyptian town of Asyut. But Egyptian paratroopers crushed the revolt within days. The rebels had hoped that the assassination of "the pharaoh" would spark an Islamic revolution. It did not. The zealots of al-Jihad had far less popular support than they believed. Like the ILO after its seizure of the Technical Military Academy in 1974 and like the Society of Muslims after the kidnapping of al-Dhahabi in 1977, al-Jihad appears to have been destroyed, or at least permanently crippled, by the executions of its leaders and the arrests of hundreds of its members.[16]

The militants never had mass support. Even many students sympathetic to the protean notion of "a truly Islamic society" condemned the fanaticism and violence of groups such as al-Jihad. And all such groups were condemned by the Muslim Brotherhood as well as by Egypt's prominent ulama, who were in turn excoriated by the militants as lackeys of the "heathen" (*jahili*) government. However, one blind professor of Islamic studies at a college in Asyut, Shaykh 'Umar 'Abd al-Rahman, did serve as a legal counselor to al-Jihad. And some other ulama who opposed the methods of the militants echoed many of their demands, for example, the demand for a strictly Islamic legal code.[17]

EGYPT'S ISLAMIC MOVEMENT UNDER MUBARAK

After succeeding Sadat as president in 1981, Husni Mubarak attempted to improve his government's relations with its domestic opposition. He freed the Muslim Brotherhood's leaders and other moderate Muslim fundamentalists. And although he continued to prohibit the formation of any party based on a particular religion, he did allow the Brotherhood to participate in the 1984 parliamentary elections as part of the conservative Wafd party's slate of candidates. Only eight Brotherhood candidates were elected, however, and in the following years, the alliance with the secular Wafd fell apart.[18]

In the April 1987 parliamentary elections, the Brotherhood formed a new coalition with two small parties. This time, Brotherhood candidates and sympathizers from the two allied parties won about 10 percent of the parliamentary seats. But Mubarak's National Democratic party won over 76 percent of the seats. Even if we take into consideration the ruling party's ability to influence the electoral process, the election results reflect the fact that the Brotherhood's goals are not shared by most Egyptians. The most visible sign of this lack of widespread support was perhaps the absence of public protest when, on May 4, 1985, the Egyptian parliament rejected a proposal for the immediate implementation of a strictly Islamic legal code.[19]

One man who did protest the parliament's action was Shaykh Hafiz Salama, a religious scholar who had been active in Egypt's fundamentalist movement since the 1940s. As a young man, he had belonged to a group known as the Youth of Our Lord Muhammad, which had split off from the Brotherhood in 1939 because of al-Banna's compromises with the government. When Nasser banned this group in the fifties, Salama founded the Society for Islamic Guidance, which established a number of mosques, notably the Mosque of the Martyrs in Suez and the Mosque of the Light (*al-Nur*) in Cairo. The latter mosque in the popular quarter of 'Abbasiyya became a center of fundamentalist activity in the 1970s.[20]

During the war of 1973, Salama organized resistance to the Israeli army besieging Suez, thus preventing the occupation of that city. He was given a medal for his role at Suez by President Sadat. But in 1979, Salama condemned the treaty with Israel as a treaty of "surrender" (*istislam*) rather than "peace" (*salam*). Sadat, in turn, referred to Salama as "the mad imam."[21] The shaykh continued to badger the government after Mubarak became president. When parliament refused to implement Islamic law in May 1985, Salama said he would lead a huge march on the presidential mansion in Cairo if Islamic law were not implemented by June 14, which was the holiest day of Ramadan, the month of fasting. But the government forbade the march on June 13 and Salama canceled it.[22]

In July 1985, the government tried to undermine the Islamic movement by decreeing that all private mosques had to be controlled by the Ministry of Waqfs, which also had to approve all Friday sermons. Salama planned a large demonstration to protest the government's actions, but once again canceled it at the last minute. He did so, he said, to avoid a violent confrontation with the government's security forces. He was arrested and the Mosque of the Light was closed. But he was released a month later and allowed to make the pilgrimage to Mecca. Since returning to Egypt, he has continued to demand the implementation of Islamic law. But he has also stressed his opposition to the use of force to obtain this goal, and he has specifically denied allegations that he seeks to overthrow the government. He has said he simply wants it to implement Islamic law.[23]

As for the more militant Islamic groups, they remain powerful on university campuses and nowhere else. In the student elections of November 1985 at Cairo University, candidates from "Islamic societies" (*al-jama'at al-islamiyya*) won over 80 percent of the contested seats in the Law School, 70 percent of the seats in the School of Information Sciences, and 70 percent in the School of Arts and Letters. But such numbers do not necessarily translate into overwhelming support for a strictly Islamic state. One of the electoral strategies used by the fundamentalist students was to stand by the entrance to the voting rooms and ask entering students "Are you for the Quran and the Sunna or for unbelief and error?" For most devout Muslims, that is not much of a choice.[24]

Militant Islamic students continued to stage periodic demonstrations in the mid and late eighties—especially at the universities of upper Egypt where they are strongest. And they will undoubtedly continue to do so. But the lack of popular support for the abortive uprising at the University of Asyut in 1981 demonstrated their impotence. And the anthropological field work of Patrick Gaffney in Minya (in upper Egypt) suggests that they have even antagonized most of their fellow students. The fact is that most Egyptians, students as well as nonstudents, regard the militants as bizarre fanatics.[25]

The more moderate fundamentalists, as represented by Hafiz Salama and the Muslim Brotherhood, have considerably broader appeal than do the militants. But the elections of 1984 and 1987 as well as the dearth of protest after the parliament refused to implement Islamic law in 1985 suggest that not even Salama or the Brotherhood has the support of most Egyptians. And although Salama would appear to be the ideal person to play the role of a charismatic Khomeini-like leader (minus the latter's specifically Shi'i dimensions), he has yet to demonstrate the ability or the willingness to do so. Given Egypt's very serious economic difficulties, as well as widespread resentment of the Mubarak regime's dependence upon the United States, the government is certainly vulnerable. But Egypt's fragmented Islamic movement has been incapable of exploiting this vulnerability. And that will probably remain true for years to come.[26]

8

Syria

Until 1920, the name Syria (*al-Sham* in Arabic) referred to the entire region stretching from the Mediterranean to the Euphrates, and from the Sinai desert to the southern hills of Turkey. From the early sixteenth century through World War I, this area was part of the Ottoman Empire. After defeating the Ottomans in World War I, the French and the British divided Syria into mandates to be governed by France and Britain under the auspices of the League of Nations. Thus the mandated states of Lebanon, Palestine, and Transjordan were created, leaving a truncated Syria under French control. The French further divided their Syrian mandate into smaller autonomous regions predominantly inhabited by particular religious sects—'Alawis in the northwest, Druzes in the south, and Sunnis and a large Christian minority in the central heartland. (Both the 'Alawi and Druze sects are offshoots of mainstream Shi'ism.) These regions were reunited in 1942. And after decades of nationalist struggle, Syria gained its independence in 1946.[1]

A number of vaguely fundamentalist Sunni groups emerged in Syria during the 1930s. In the mid-forties, the religious scholar Mustafa Siba'i united most of these groups to form the Syrian branch of the Muslim Brotherhood, which was politically insignificant during the early years of its existence. Its candidates won less than 3 percent of the contested parliamentary seats in 1949, less than 4 percent in 1954, and less than 6 percent in 1961. The movement had virtually no support whatsoever in rural areas, although it was quite strong in the cities. In Damascus, for example, it won 23 percent of the parliamentary seats in 1949, 19 percent in 1954, and 18 percent in 1961.[2] During Syria's union with Egypt from 1958 to 1961, the Brotherhood was dissolved at Nasser's request. It regained influence after the Ba'thist coup of 1963.[3]

THE BA'TH VERSUS THE BROTHERHOOD IN THE 1960S

The *Ba'th,* or "Revival," party was founded in the 1940s by two schoolteachers, the Christian Michel 'Aflaq and the Sunni Muslim Salah al-Din al-Bitar. The Ba'thists emphasized opposition to Western domination, the need for Arab unity, and socialistic notions concerning the redistribution of wealth, all of which were also basic themes of Nasserism. Conflict between the Ba'thists and the Muslim Brothers was inevitable for several reasons.[4]

To begin with, the Ba'th's secular nationalism could not be reconciled with the Brotherhood's demand for an Islamic state. Moreover, a disproportionate number of Ba'thist leaders were from religious minorities, notably Christians (who constitute 14 percent of the Syrian population), 'Alawis (12 percent), Druzes (3 percent), and Isma'ilis (2 percent). For these minorities, the secular nationalist Ba'th was a means of overcoming their traditional subordination to the Sunni Arab majority (57 percent of the population). The Muslim Brotherhood on the other hand, despite its rhetoric about unifying all Muslims, has always been a Sunni Arab movement. Thus, just as it has never appealed to 'Alawis, Druzes, and Isma'ilis, it has never had much success among Syria's Kurds (9 percent of the population) and Turcomans (3 percent), who are Sunnis but not Arabs.[5]

Sunnis did hold many important positions in the Ba'thist government from 1963 through 1966, and even afterward, but 'Alawis gradually gained control of the higher echelons of power in the army and government by the late sixties. The conflict between the Ba'th and the Brotherhood thus became increasingly sectarian in character. This sectarian factor meshed with social tensions. Many of the 'Alawi officers who came to dominate the Ba'th were from peasant families traditionally exploited by Sunni landlords. And many Muslim Brothers were urban Sunni merchants and artisans hurt by the socialist policies of the Ba'thist government.[6]

During the year following their coup of March 1963, the Ba'thists nationalized Syria's banks and reduced civil service salaries by from

25 to 40 percent. These actions, coupled with widespread unemployment and inflation, led to the upheaval of April 1964, which was precipitated by the arrest of a high school boy in the city of Hama. (The boy had erased a Ba'thist slogan written by his teacher on a blackboard.) High school students protested the arrest, as did Sunni imams in their Friday sermons. When a student demonstrator was killed by police on April 11, 1964, Hama's merchants shut their stores the next day. At night, loudspeakers blared the cry "Islam or the Ba'th" from minarets throughout the city. And on April 14, troops shelled the Sunni Mosque of al-Sultan, killing dozens of people within it. The government claimed that the troops had been fired upon from the mosque's minaret.[7]

The shelling of al-Sultan Mosque outraged Sunnis in all Syrian towns and appeared to confirm the Muslim Brotherhood's depiction of the Ba'thist regime as "godless." It also acted as a catalyst that transformed the conflict in Hama into a nationwide series of strikes and demonstrations by merchants, artisans, ulama, engineers, doctors, lawyers, teachers, students, and some workers. Although some of these people belonged to, or sympathized with, the Muslim Brotherhood, others simply took advantage of the crisis to demand a democratic form of government. By early May of 1964 the uprising was over. Many of its ostensible leaders were arrested, and merchants were forced to open their stores. At the same time, free elections and credit for small merchants were promised. But further conflict soon followed.[8]

In January 1965, merchants shut their businesses while the Brotherhood and some ulama condemned the Ba'thist regime's nationalization of most Syrian industry and all foreign trade. As in the previous year, the Chamber of Commerce and some professional associations protested. But this time, the Brotherhood and the disgruntled merchants were not joined by the Nasserists and other leftist critics of the government. Many Sunni ulama also refused to participate. And the 1965 protests were quickly suppressed.[9]

Then in April 1967, after the radical wing of the Ba'th had seized power in 1966, an article in the Syrian army magazine provoked more merchants' strikes and protests led by ulama and Muslim Brothers. The article suggested that religion was a vestige of the past that Arabs should discard in order to progress:

Until now the Arab nation has turned toward God. It has sought ancient values in Islam and Christianity. It has based itself on feudalism, capitalism or other systems of bygone eras. But in vain, for all these values have made the Arab a miserable, resigned, fatalistic, dependent man who submits to his fate repeating the ritual phrase "There is no power and no strength except from God." . . . God, religion, feudalism, capitalism, imperialism and all the values that controlled ancient society are no more than mummies for the museum of history. In reality, there is only one value: the new man in whom we must henceforth believe, the man who counts only on himself, on his work and his contribution to humanity, and who knows that death is his inevitable end, nothing but death, without heaven or hell.[10]

Such an article in an official army magazine would probably cause a furor in most countries outside the iron curtain. It certainly did so in Syria. In order to calm the storm of protest (which involved Christians as well as Muslims), the article's author and the magazine's editor were condemned to hard labor for life—although they were later quietly released. On May 7, 1967, Radio Damascus declared that the "sinful" article had in fact been the product of a conspiracy hatched by the CIA, Israel, and reactionary Arabs.[11]

MILITANTS VERSUS MODERATES

Less than two months after the publication of the infamous article consigning religion to "the museum of history," Israel handed the Syrian government a more serious problem—the occupation of the Golan Heights about forty miles southwest of Damascus. The Muslim Brothers condemned the Ba'thist regime for its failure to mount a vigorous resistance to the Israeli occupation, even going so far as to suggest Ba'thist collusion with Israel.[12]

But the Brotherhood was unable to challenge the government during the late sixties—in part perhaps because of an internal conflict between a militant northern faction that favored an armed jihad against the Ba'thists and a moderate Damascene faction that favored nonviolent methods. Eventually the militants won secret elections held in 1971 and replaced 'Isam al-'Attar, the moderate inspector-general of the Brotherhood, by their own man 'Adnan Sa'd al-Din. Al-'Attar, a schoolteacher who had led the Brotherhood from exile in West Germany since 1964, refused to cooperate with the new militant leadership, as did many of his followers in Damascus. This division persisted throughout the seventies.[13]

The militant Muslim Brothers from the northern cities of Aleppo and Hama were led by a young agronomist named Marwan Hadid, who came from a family of relatively wealthy cotton growers near Hama. In the late fifties and early sixties, Hadid studied in Egypt, where he was influenced by Sayyid Qutb. The Nasser regime tried to arrest him in 1965, but he escaped to Hama where he founded a group called the Battalions of Muhammad (*Kata'ib Muhammad*). Like similar militants in Egypt, Hadid never led a large organization but was extremely popular with students and other young people. One member of Syria's Muslim Brotherhood describes Hadid's group as "a fringe movement on the periphery of the Brotherhood."[14] Hadid was eventually captured and died in prison in 1976. His death following a prolonged hunger strike provoked demonstrations in Hama and other cities and is sometimes said to have sparked the wave of terrorist attacks by Syria's Islamic militants in the late seventies.[15]

AL-ASAD AND THE ISLAMIC OPPOSITION, 1970–82

Like the Brotherhood, the Ba'th was seriously divided in the late sixties. In 1966, the party's left wing, which was led by 'Alawi officers, had overthrown its more conservative wing, which was led by a Sunni general. Then the left wing itself was torn by conflict between a radical faction led by the former general Salah Jadid and a more pragmatic faction led by the general Hafiz al-Asad. Both Jadid and al-Asad were 'Alawis, as were most of the powerful officials in the Ba'th party by the end of the sixties. In November 1970, al-Asad settled the dispute by seizing power and removing the radicals from their government positions.[16]

Al-Asad immediately set about improving his government's relations with Syria's largely Sunni business community by easing restrictions on the private sector while continuing to pay lip service to Ba'thist socialism. He also renewed relations with Arab governments condemned by the previous regime as "feudal" and "reactionary" as well as with Western governments previously condemned as "imperialist." These policies were similar to Sadat's de-Nasserization program in Egypt, although al-Asad never severed his ties to the Soviet Union nor did he sign a peace treaty with Israel.[17]

The al-Asad regime had its first serious confrontation with the Brotherhood early in 1973—ostensibly because the draft of a new constitution released in January made no mention of Islam except to say that Islamic law was *a* main source of legislation. The Muslim

Brothers and some ulama demanded that the constitution declare Islam the official religion of Syria—despite the country's 14 percent Christian minority and despite the fact that Islam had never been so designated before. The religious scholar Sa'id Hawwa, a prominent Muslim Brother, got many Sunni ulama to sign a petition condemning the draft constitution. Demonstrations began in Hama (as was often the case) and spread to Aleppo, Hums, and Damascus. The protests often turned into riots, as in Hama, where the offices of the Ba'th party and of Ba'thist youth and women's organizations were attacked. The Brotherhood was especially active in the northern protests while those in Damascus were led by Shaykh Habbanaka, a religious scholar also involved in the disturbances of 1964 and 1967. As in these earlier protests, Sunni merchants shut their shops. The government attempted to placate its Sunni critics by including a provision in the constitution restricting the office of president to Muslims. This did not satisfy many Muslim Brothers and the government was not able to repress the continuing protests until mid-April of 1973.[18]

In the years following the constitutional crisis of 1973, al-Asad went to great lengths to counter the Brotherhood's depiction of the 'Alawis as "infidels" by cultivating the image of a devout Muslim. He attended Friday congregational prayers, which 'Alawis do not usually do. He induced eighty 'Alawi religious leaders to declare, in 1973, that they shared the basic beliefs of Twelver Shi'ism and that the heretical ideas often attributed to them were the inventions of the enemies of Islam. And he maintained cordial and well-publicized relations with prominent Sunni ulama who often praised him in the sycophantic manner for which the Azhari ulama of Egypt are notorious. Thus the official magazine of the Syrian (Sunni) ulama lauded al-Asad as "combatant of the Holy War [and] defender of our sacrosanct religion," thanks to whom "the spirit of Islam reigns in Syria."[19] There were, of course, many Sunni ulama who spoke of al-Asad in quite different terms.[20]

Al-Asad's attempts to portray himself as a devout Muslim were dismissed as a farce by most Muslim Brothers. But he did not face any serious opposition from the Brotherhood and its sympathizers during the mid-seventies, in part perhaps because Sunni merchants were prospering. Saudi Arabia and other "feudal" and "reactionary" oil-rich states were giving "socialist" Syria $500 million to $600 million a year. And Syria's comparatively modest earnings from its own oil wells jumped from $67 million in 1973 to $412 million in 1974 because of the OPEC price increases. In addition to this oil wealth, Syria benefited from high prices for its own other main exports, phosphates and cotton. Thanks to al-Asad's support for the private sector, Sunni merchants shared in this general prosperity. So the economic discontent that had fueled the protests of the sixties largely disappeared.[21]

As of 1976, however, the Islamic opposition, led by the militants who now controlled the Muslim Brotherhood, began assassinating prominent 'Alawis. While Marwan Hadid's death in prison is sometimes said to have triggered this wave of terror, a more important factor was al-Asad's dispatch of Syrian troops to Lebanon. In June 1976, al-Asad sent Syrian troops to support the tottering Lebanese government against the forces of the Palestine Liberation Organization and the leftist Lebanese National Movement. The Lebanese government was controlled and supported by Maronite Christians. And although Christians such as George Habash and Nayif Hawatmeh led some of the best known Palestinian guerrilla groups, most Palestinians and Lebanese leftists were Muslims. Thus many Sunnis felt that al-Asad was helping Christians defeat Muslims, and the traditional Sunni view that the 'Alawis were not really Muslims at all was reinforced. Moreover, the Palestinian cause had always been strongly supported by most Syrian Sunnis, who were thus sickened by the spectacle of "their" army fighting the PLO. The Muslim Brothers, among others, accused al-Asad of helping Israel destroy the Palestinian guerrilla movement. And the Brothers reminded Syrians that al-Asad had refused to help the Palestinians during their "Black September" conflict with King Husayn of Jordan in 1970.[22]

By the late seventies, the outrage provoked by the Lebanese intervention coupled with a deteriorating economic situation and the enthusiasm generated by Iran's Islamic revolution encouraged the Muslim Brotherhood and various splinter groups to accelerate their holy war against the regime of al-Asad. Muslim Brothers and members of smaller Islamic groups assassinated prominent 'Alawis and attacked government and Ba'th party offices, police stations, and army units. The grisliest incident occurred in June 1979, when a Sunni officer and several accomplices gunned down eighty-three 'Alawi cadets at the Artillery Academy at Aleppo.[23]

The government had prominent Sunni ulama condemn the slaughter at the Aleppo academy as well as the Muslim Brotherhood in general. And fifteen political prisoners allegedly linked to the Brotherhood were executed. The Ba'thist leaders also attempted to curb (or at least give the appearance of curbing) the widespread corruption in the government. None of these measures had much impact. Sunnis continued to murder 'Alawis throughout 1979. In late August, the murder of an 'Alawi religious leader sparked a prolonged shootout between Sunnis and the predominantly 'Alawi security forces in the Mediterranean port of Latakia.[24]

By early 1980, assassinations or other acts of violence were almost a daily occurrence in the northern cities of Syria, especially Aleppo, where Muslim Brothers openly distributed their leaflets in the traditional markets. Russians were sometimes the targets of the Brotherhood's terrorist attacks (just as Americans were sometimes the targets of comparable attacks in Iran during the 1970s). In January 1980 a Soviet colonel and a military engineer were killed in Hama, and another Soviet adviser died during a machine-gun attack in Aleppo. But the strikes, demonstrations, and riots of March 1980 soon overshadowed such incidents.[25]

A strike of merchants in Aleppo in early March soon spread to the other major cities of the north, although not to Damascus. And, in a manner reminiscent of the protests of 1964, many secular groups joined in "the March uprising." Schools shut down. The associations of lawyers, engineers, doctors, academics, and other professionals supported the strikes (but not necessarily the Muslim Brotherhood) and issued manifestos demanding democracy, the release of political prisoners, and an end to the 'Alawi monopolization of power. Similar demands were voiced by various leftist groups as well as by some (but not all) ulama. Unlike the leftists, however, such ulama also demanded the implementation of Islamic law. By the end of March, in all of Syria's cities except Damascus, schools, universities, stores, and private offices were closed in an extraordinary display of opposition to the Ba'thist regime. It seemed that Syria was on the verge of an Iranian-style revolution. But that did not turn out to be the case.[26]

Al-Asad's response to the protests of March 1980 was harsh. On March 9, the day after the seventeenth anniversary of the Ba'thist "revolution" of 1963, troops killed some two hundred people in the town of Jasr al-Shughur southwest of Aleppo. In Aleppo itself, the army's special units, equipped with tanks, antiaircraft guns and helicopters, cordoned off several quarters and conducted house-to-house searches for Muslim Brothers and weapons caches. A similar operation took place in Hama. Thousands were arrested while an unknown number were killed. The various professional associations that were active in the March protests were dissolved. By mid-April, the opposition had been silenced.[27]

But terrorist attacks continued as before. On June 26, 1980, an Islamic militant tried to assassinate al-Asad. The next day, a unit of the government's Defense Brigades killed hundreds of political prisoners (mostly Muslim Brothers) at Palmyra Prison in the Syrian desert. The cycle of Brotherhood terrorism and government repression continued throughout 1980 with hundreds of innocent people killed by both sides.[28]

In July 1980, the government made membership in the Brotherhood a capital offense. But at the request of some ulama, it gave members of the outlawed organization a fifty-day grace period during which they could surrender before the new law would take effect. Over a thousand Brothers gave themselves up, most of them students, teachers, professors, or engineers in their twenties. Aware that they were losing ground in their struggle with the regime, the leaders of the Brotherhood created a new Islamic Front in the fall of 1980. This coalition consisted of the Brotherhood itself, several of its smaller offshoots, and many ulama and politicians. Meanwhile, the violence continued, with car bombs planted by Muslim Brothers killing hundreds in the fall of 1981.[29]

In January 1982, the government decided to eradicate the Brotherhood in its northern stronghold of Hama. In early February, the army began house-to-house raids. The Brothers revolted. On the evening of February 2, 1982, loudspeakers on minarets throughout Hama proclaimed a jihad against the Ba'thist regime. Islamic militants soon seized all government buildings in the city, and arms taken from armories and police stations were distributed among sympathetic Sunnis. An "Islamic Tribunal" was set up to try government and Ba'th party officials, over fifty of whom were executed. Ulama leaders of the Islamic Front urged all Syrians (actually they meant all Sunnis) to join the revolt.[30]

The insurrection was centered in the old quarters of Hama, which the Syrian army bombarded from tanks, heavy artillery, and helicopter gunships. Then bulldozers were sent in to raze some of these old neighborhoods to the ground. The exact number of people killed is not known, but was probably somewhere between five and ten thousand. By the end of February, all resistance (and much of the city) had been crushed. Some Sunni ulama with close ties to the government endorsed the army's attempt to put an end to "the filthy criminal acts" of the Brotherhood.[31] Except for minor incidents in Latakia and Aleppo, the Hama insurrection never spread to the rest of Syria.[32]

THE IRANIAN CONNECTION

It is worth noting that al-Asad's secular regime maintained good relations with Iran's Islamic Republic throughout the three weeks of the Hama uprising, even though the Syrian army was in the process of killing thousands of (Sunni) Muslims fighting for a strictly Islamic state. But in 1987, when Syrian troops killed about twenty Twelver Shi'i members of the Lebanese fundamentalist group *Hizb Allah* (the Party of God), Khomeini's officially designated successor, the Ayatollah Muntazari, referred to the incident as a "twentieth century Karbala."[33] As might be expected, the Brotherhood's initial enthusiasm for Khomeini's revolution has cooled considerably.[34]

The Khomeini regime, which has repeatedly stressed that Sunnis and Shi'is should unite to fight Western and Russian imperialism, denies that Iran's support for al-Asad has anything to do with the fact that the 'Alawis are Shi'is and the Muslim Brothers are Sunnis. Some officials of the Islamic Republic have echoed the Syrian regime's charge that the Brotherhood is supported by Israel, Egypt, and the United States because of al-Asad's role as leader of the "anti-imperialist" forces in the Middle East. Some Iranians also criticize the Brotherhood for receiving money from the Saudis although al-Asad's government has received billions of dollars from Saudi Arabia—which is reviled as an "American surrogate" by many Syrian Muslim Brothers.[35]

The truth would appear to be that the good relations between the Islamic Republic of Iran and the secular regime in Syria have been based largely on the fact that they have some common enemies and thus some common interests. Although both Syria and Iraq are governed by Ba'thist governments, their relationship since about 1973 has been envenomed by disputes over oil, water, ideology, and competition for regional influence. Thus Syria, like Libya, has supported Iran in its war against Iraq. Given Syria's military strength, it is definitely in Iran's interest to cultivate al-Asad's friendship and thereby avoid giving Iraq yet another powerful Arab ally. But the Syrian-Iranian connection has been severely strained by Syrian attempts to curb the pro-Iranian Twelver Shi'i fundamentalists in Lebanon. And if there are further clashes between Syrian troops and Iran's Lebanese protégés, they could mean the end of the curious alliance of the Islamic Republic with the secular Ba'thist regime of Syria.[36]

IMPOTENCE AFTER HAMA

The ruthless suppression of the Hama revolt had a devastating impact on Syria's Muslim Brotherhood. An obvious sign of the Islamic movement's weakness was the formation in March 1982 of a National Alliance for the Liberation of Syria composed of the Islamic Front (including the Brotherhood) and a wide variety of secular socialists, Nasserists, and disgruntled Ba'thists. Only impotence could induce the advocates of a strictly Islamic state to keep such company. And the most militant Muslim Brothers led by 'Adnan al-'Uqla refused to join this alliance.[37]

Al-'Uqla also condemned the leader of the Brotherhood, 'Adnan Sa'd al-Din, for his "complacent attitude toward the imperialism of the two superpowers" and his "ambiguous declarations on capitalism."[38] In a statement published in Paris on September 11, 1982, the Sa'd al-Din faction of the Brotherhood responded to these criticisms by claiming that al-'Uqla had been expelled from the Islamic Front by "the High Command of the Islamic Revolution in Syria." In January 1985, al-'Uqla and his followers accepted the government's offer of amnesty.[39]

The remnants of the Brotherhood still active in France, Germany, Jordan, and Iraq in the late eighties appear incapable of mobilizing much support within Syria itself. But the Brotherhood came back to life in the seventies after the repression of the mid-sixties. And it will no doubt come to life again after the repression of the early eighties. However despite all the protests, strikes, riots, and even insurrections led by the Brotherhood in recent decades, the fact remains that it has been, and remains, incapable of mounting a full-fledged Islamic revolution.

9

Social Bases

Religious and political movements, and politicized religious ones, appeal to specific social strata. They are rooted in the beliefs and discontents of particular kinds of people. And we need to know something about these people if we are to explain why one movement is able to topple a government while seemingly similar ones are not.[1]

STUDENTS AND THE EDUCATED YOUNG

One of the best documented generalizations that can be made about the Islamic movements of the seventies and early eighties is that students and recent university graduates were their most active supporters. In Iran, high school and university students played a crucial role in the revolution of 1978–79. In Saudi Arabia, many of Juhayman's followers were students at the Islamic University of Madina. In Egypt, a study of thirty-four members of radical Islamic groups imprisoned in the 1970s found that twenty-nine (or 85 percent) were either university students or recent graduates when arrested. In Syria, one of the leaders of that country's branch of the Muslim Brotherhood has stated that students and recent graduates were his movement's most militant activists. And scholars have noted the importance of students in Islamic movements elsewhere. Most of these students were educated in secular institutions, and many were students of engineering and other applied scientific fields (such as medicine and agronomy). Students of relatively traditional Islamic studies were also active in Iran and in Saudi Arabia.[2]

Although students usually constituted a majority of the activists in the Islamic movements of the seventies and eighties, however, such activists did not usually constitute a majority of students. In Egypt, the bullying tactics used by the Islamic militants (attacking couples holding hands, for example) often alienated other students. And many students who espoused a return to Islam in terms of personal values (and apparel) were not committed to revolution, or to any specific political agenda for that matter.[3]

Moreover, Marxist and socialist-cum-nationalist movements remained influential on university campuses in most of the Muslim world. Islamic groups were often involved in conflicts, verbal as well as physical, with such secular leftist groups—whose activists were also primarily students and other educated young people. And there were many students who did not participate in any political groups at all. In other words, although militant Islamic students tended to monopolize public attention in the late seventies and early eighties, they had no monopoly over the loyalties of their fellow students.[4]

ON THE SOCIAL ORIGINS OF FUNDAMENTALIST STUDENTS

It is difficult to determine the social origins of fundamentalist Islamic students. Michael Fischer has suggested that they are typically the children of the traditional petite bourgeoisie, namely shopkeepers (both merchants and artisans). And Ervand Abrahamian contends that many members of Iran's radical Islamic Mujahidin were the sons of ulama as well as of merchants. But although he has published some extremely valuable data concerning the occupations of arrested Mujahidin guerrillas, Abrahamian has not published much with respect to the occupations of their fathers. And the contention that Iran's educated young Islamic militants are typically the children of the traditional middle class has yet to be substantiated—or refuted for that matter. The available evidence is simply too meager.[5]

With respect to the social origins of Egypt's young Islamic activists, Saad Eddin Ibrahim notes that of the fathers of the thirty-four militants he and his associates studied, twenty-one, or 62 percent, were civil servants; four, or 12 percent, were high-level professionals; another four were small merchants; three were small farmers (owning between six and eleven acres); and two had working-class occupations. Clearly these findings, limited as they are, do not support Fischer's hypothesis that most educated Islamic militants of the late seventies and early eighties were the sons of shopkeepers. Rather they suggest that such militants were often the children of fathers of the "new middle class."[6]

Although evidence concerning this issue is scarce, it would seem logical to assume that most militant Islamic students are from either traditional or modern middle-class families. Children from very poor families have much less chance of attending a university than do those from the middle and upper classes.[7] In the words of a 1979 survey of students at Cairo University's Faculty of Arts, "belonging to political parties was more for the sons of the rich and middle classes and less for the sons of the poor and the very poor classes."[8]

THE NEW MIDDLE CLASS

In addition to the educated young, older members of the new middle classes of the Islamic world have also often been involved in Islamic movements—as one might expect given that most such people were once university students themselves. In Egypt for example, professionals, businessmen, and government bureaucrats were important supporters of the Muslim Brotherhood from the 1940s through the 1980s. During the course of attending meetings of the Brotherhood in Cairo for a year and a half from 1953 to 1955, Richard P. Mitchell found that the overwhelming majority of those in attendance were students, civil servants, teachers, clerks, office workers, and professionals in Western suits.[9] Mitchell observes, "That this membership largely represented an emergent and self-conscious Muslim middle class is obvious."[10]

In the late seventies, by which time the Brotherhood was ridiculed as an impotent relic of the past by Egypt's younger and more militant fundamentalists, it continued to appeal to many businessmen, civil servants, and professionals who were horrified by the more radical Islamic groups. Middle-aged professionals and civil servants were also among the most ardent supporters of reformist rather than revolutionary Islamic movements in other countries, including Iran. Thus, to some extent, the division between reformist and radical advocates of a strictly Islamic polity represents a generation gap, with older middle-class Muslims drawn to moderate groups and their children drawn to more militant groups. This relationship, however, is by no means universal. Egypt's Muslim Brotherhood has continued to win support among many students alienated by the more militant groups of the late seventies and early eighties.[11]

THE TRADITIONAL MIDDLE CLASS OF MERCHANTS AND ARTISANS

It has been argued that the Islamic movements of the late twentieth century have generally appealed to merchants and artisans. And it is certainly true that merchants and artisans (or bazaaris) have been active in the Islamic movements of modern Iran. In Syria, too, shopkeepers have supported the Muslim Brotherhood—much as the shopkeepers of Pakistan have supported the Jama'at-i Islam. But this pattern is by no means universal.[12]

None of the Egyptian Islamic militants studied by Ibrahim and his associates was a merchant or an artisan. Nor were merchants or artisans involved in al-Jihad's assassination of Sadat. Moreover, neither the assassination of Sadat nor the abortive uprising of Asyut two days later induced the shopkeepers of Egypt to shut their stores or take to the streets in the manner of their Iranian counterparts. And if the merchants and artisans of Egypt had been financing al-Jihad, that organization would presumably not have had to depend on robbing Coptic jewelry stores for funds.[13]

It is true that Gilles Kepel contends that 20 percent of the 302 people charged with belonging to al-Jihad in 1982 were merchants and artisans. But most of the people he calls artisans were carpenters, electricians, mechanics, and similar people who could be considered blue-collar workers. (This is a graphic illustration of how the taxonomic assumptions underlying statistics on occupational distribution can affect the conclusions drawn from them.) Moreover, the overwhelming majority of the men Kepel calls merchants and artisans were in their twenties, which suggests that most of them had recently been students. And it should be stressed that these men constituted a small minority of the 302 men charged with belonging to al-Jihad— of whom only 107 were eventually sentenced to prison.[14]

The fact is that the militant wing of Egypt's Islamic movement has not been able to mobilize that country's merchants and artisans. And the same is true of the more moderate wing represented by the Muslim Brotherhood. Egypt's shopkeepers do not have the tradition of Islamic activism for which their Iranian counterparts are renowned. Even at the height of the Muslim Brotherhood's strength in the fifties and sixties, relatively few merchants and artisans were ever arrested for involvement in that group's activities. And this pattern persisted in the seventies and eighties. Many Egyptian shopkeepers do undoubtedly sympathize with the reformist fundamentalist goal of a more strictly Islamic society, but they have not been active in efforts to implement that goal, nor have the shopkeepers of Morocco, Saudi Arabia, or Tunisia.[15]

THE ULAMA

With respect to the ulama, they have led the most important Shiʻi fundamentalist movements of the twentieth century, whereas they have not usually even participated in comparable Sunni movements. As has already been suggested, the greater political role of the Shiʻi ulama is largely due to their greater religious authority. It should be remembered, however, that the great majority of Iran's ulama did not openly oppose the shah's regime from 1964 until 1978, as the Ayatollah Khomeini's own son and spokesman Ahmad has emphasized. Even among Shiʻi ulama, passive acceptance of the status quo has been the rule rather than the exception.[16]

But Sunni ulama *have* tended to be more submissive than their Shiʻi counterparts. Most of them have unctuously endorsed the policies of whatever government was currently in power. In May 1952, the Egyptian religious scholar Hasan al-Zayyat praised the then reigning King Farouq as "defender of Islam and Arabism, protector of al-Azhar." After Farouq was overthrown a few months later, al-Zayyat referred to him as "a satan who dared transgress the religion of Allah and break all taboos."[17] Such ulama have condemned the militant Islamic movements of the 1970s and 1980s and the militants have in turn condemned them.[18]

But despite the servility of the most prominent Sunni ulama, there were nonetheless, in the seventies and eighties, at least a few religious scholars who openly supported moderate fundamentalist movements in all Sunni countries, while many others had similar sympathies. The activist ulama could usually be called low ranking as opposed those in exalted official positions, although there is no rigid hierarchy among Sunni ulama. In Syria, even some ulama in important government positions have sometimes challenged the government. But al-Asad has always been able to rely on a number of prominent Sunni ulama to endorse everything he does (in public at least). As for the rebellious Sunni ulama, such as Egypt's Hafiz Salama or Syria's Shaykh Habbanaka, they have never had the charismatic authority of a Khomeini, but they have certainly had broader support than the student militants.[19]

THE WORKING CLASSES

The working classes of the Islamic world did not usually participate in the Islamic movements of the seventies and eighties, with the partial exception of Iran. Even in Iran, it was only in the decisive oil field and factory strikes of the fall of 1978 that workers played an important role in the revolution. And these strikes were in fact often initiated and led by middle-class employees in management.[20]

We do find some working-class Muslims expressing sympathy for the goal of a return to a virtuous and truly Islamic society. But such diffuse sympathies, which are widespread in many social strata, do not entail participation in Islamic movements. Those blue-collar workers who did participate in these movements were typically former students who became active in them while they were still in school. The Islamic movements of the 1970s and 1980s (like most other political movements in the Islamic world) were not working-class movements.[21]

THE RURAL-BORN URBAN POOR

It is sometimes suggested that "anomic" and "uprooted" rural-urban migrants have participated in Islamic movements as a means of regaining the sense of security allegedly lost because of migration. One finds this argument in some of the most insightful analyses of modern Islamic movements. There is, however, no evidence to support such a view. Recent research in the Middle East, as well as in the third world generally, suggests that the rural-born urban poor usually remain closely tied to relatives and friends from their natal villages, many of whom are their neighbors in the city. These migrants are usually immersed in a cultural environment similar to that of their villages and are far less prone to suffer from alienation or anomie than are highly educated members of the middle class or elite.[22]

Those who view rural-urban migration as a disruptive experience leading to participation in Islamic movements sometimes point to the fact that twenty-one, or 62 percent, of the Islamic militants studied by Ibrahim and his associates in Egypt were born in villages or small towns and had gone to cities to study at universities. But since small towns are nonetheless towns, we should perhaps speak of 62 percent of Ibrahim's militants as being of *provincial* rather than specifically *rural* origin. This seems particularly true given than 74 percent of these militants were the sons of civil servants or professionals, most of whom are usually found in towns and cities rather than villages.[23]

Gilles Kepel and Hamied Ansari have noted that many of the Egyptians charged with belonging to al-Jihad in 1982 lived in poor peripheral neighborhoods of Cairo with large concentrations of migrants, and they therefore argue that many Islamic militants were themselves migrants. But most of the accused members of al-Jihad were students or other educated young people who lived in poor neighborhoods because they could not afford to live elsewhere. Some of these students may have migrated to Cairo from rural areas, but they were certainly not part of the lumpenproletarian urban poor. Although militants such as Muhammad 'Abd al-Slam Farag have often preached to the rural-born urban poor, there is no evidence that such preaching has produced many converts. And the argument that Cairo's rural-born urban poor suffer from anomie or uprootedness is not substantiated by recent anthropological studies of the urban poor of Cairo or by the earlier work of Janet Abu-Lughod.[24]

Boys, young men, and eventually women from the slums and squatter settlements of Iran did participate in many of the marches that coalesced into the Islamic revolution of 1978–79. But Farhad Kazemi, who did fieldwork in South Tehran in 1974–75 and 1977, suggests that the poorer migrants in squatter settlements were less active in the revolution than those with more secure incomes and housing. The same point is made by Janet Bauer, who did fieldwork in South Tehran and four rural areas from July 1977 through December 1978. Some squatters did protest the government's efforts to raze their shacks in 1977 and 1978. But these people were simply trying to protect their homes. They were not trying to overthrow the shah, although the government's attempt to destroy their neighborhoods presumably made them more receptive to revolutionary rhetoric than they would otherwise have been.[25]

The urban poor certainly increased the size of, and thus the psychological and political impact of, the antiregime marches in Iran, especially in the fall of 1978, by which time the shah's regime had already been severely shaken. But they were never the initiators or the leaders of political action. Bauer observes that many of the young people from the poor neighborhoods of Tehran who participated in the revolution appeared to have "initially taken part out of a sense of excitement and curiosity rather than out of strong ideological conviction."[26] The urban poor, like many ulama and students, were not actively committed to the goal of an Islamic state before they were caught up in the quasi-messianic fervor of 1978—by which time the shah's downfall seemed inevitable. They were not an important component of the Islamic movement's social base until then. The Iranian lumpenproletariat thus does not appear to be an exception to the general rule that the urban poor do not make revolutions, although their support (or hostility) can be crucial for those who do.[27]

PEASANTS AND TRIBESMEN

The fact that the urban poor rarely participated in Islamic movements is not surprising, since most of them were recently peasants or tribesmen. And these groups have almost never participated in the fundamentalist Islamic movements of the latter half of the twentieth century, except where such movements have been linked to anticolonial or ethnic separatist movements.

As has often been noted, Iran's Islamic revolution was primarily an urban upheaval in which the rural population (52 percent of the total in 1978) did not play a major role. Certain elements of rural society did actively support the revolution—notably young men with at least some high school education who worked as teachers, factory workers, technicians, and clerks. Many of these young men commuted to work in cities and towns, which is where they participated in marches and demonstrations. They were thus among the most urban of rural Iranians. But peasants and tribesmen per se played virtually no role in Iran's revolution.[28]

THE MILITARY

The fact that peasants and tribesmen rarely participated in the Islamic movements of the 1970s and 1980s is directly relevant to the appeal of such movements to the military—since most soldiers in the Islamic world (and the third world generally) are simply peasants and tribesmen in uniform. It comes as no surprise, then, that enlisted men were generally not attracted to the fundamentalist movements of the 1970s and 1980s. More educated military men sometimes were, however.

In Egypt, young officers and a sergeant assassinated Sadat, and four young officers were accused of planning a fundamentalist coup in December 1986. In Syria, some Sunni officers are said to be sympathetic to the Muslim Brotherhood—although resentment of 'Alawi predominance in the armed forces is probably a major factor in this case. In Tunisia, the radical Party of Islamic Liberation attracted some cadets at the Air Force Academy in the early 1980s. And in Iran, air force technicians and young officers were among the first elements of the military to support the Islamic revolution. A slowly growing number of enlisted men, however, were also deserting, and in some cases joining opposition marches, during the fall of 1978 and the winter of 1979.[29]

CONCLUSION: THE CONTRAST BETWEEN IRAN AND ELSEWHERE

In the latter half of the twentieth century, Islamic movements striving to bring about a strictly Islamic polity have most often appealed to the educated young—both civilians and, to a lesser extent, military officers. These people were usually educated in secular schools and universities, and they had often been trained in engineering and other applied scientific fields. Whatever their social origins, most of these young people were members of their countries' middle classes, if only by virtue of their education and the jobs to which it gave access. Older educated middle-class Muslims were also active in Islamic movements, usually less radical ones.

Merchants and artisans with their own shops were active in the Islamic movements of Iran, Pakistan, and Syria—in part at least because of hardships resulting from governmental economic policies. But such activity was not typical of merchants and artisans in many other countries, for example, Egypt, Morocco, and Saudi Arabia.

Generally speaking, the least educated and most traditional social strata were not active in the fundamentalist Islamic movements of the late twentieth century. Peasants have been conspicuously absent from such movements, as have the urban poor and blue-collar workers with regular jobs—although the latter two groups did eventually participate in Iran's revolution. The religious beliefs and practices of these less educated strata are far removed from the ideologized Islam of the educated fundamentalists. In the Sunni world in particular, there are sharp differences between the fundamentalist emphasis upon the need to struggle for a puritanical Islamic state and the popular world of saints, spirits, and amulets. These differences have inhibited the spread of Sunni fundamentalist ideology.[30]

As noted in chapter 4, in addition to having greater authority than their Sunni counterparts, the high-ranking Shi'i ulama are less divorced from popular urban religion. This makes it easier for them to organize the less educated urban social strata. And this is one reason Khomeini and his followers were eventually able to mobilize significant numbers of the urban poor and the working class of Iran, although not the peasantry (where ulama influence has been traditionally weak). Khomeini's messianic aura, his association with the hidden imam, and his populist rhetoric also all helped him appeal to the more traditional and less educated people in Iran's cities. But it is important to keep in mind that many of these people did not actually participate in the revolution until they felt they could do so with impunity.[31]

In sharp contrast with the Iranian situation, most Sunni fundamentalist movements have been incapable of mobilizing support outside the ranks of university students and recent graduates or dropouts. This is especially true of the more radical and militant movements. And even more moderate movements such as the Muslim Brotherhood have not succeeded in winning much support except among the educated and politically conscious middle classes. (The same could be said of most secular political movements in the Islamic world.)

These facts have often been overlooked. And they are crucial insofar as they suggest that further Islamic revolutions are not imminent. It is, of course, true that a well-organized party can seize power even if it does not have mass support—so long as the regime it is overthrowing does not have such support either. But the fact remains that Sunni fundamentalist movements have been incapable of mobilizing "the oppressed masses" (al-jamahir al-kadiha) on whose behalf they usually claim to speak. And they have been far more successful in making headlines than they have in making revolutions.

PART III

Explanations

10

Modernization and Revolution

The "commonsense" view that prevails in the West is that Islamic fundamentalists are reactionaries opposed to modernization because they perceive it as being contrary to their religious beliefs. And it is certainly true that religious belief can impel people to take political action. In the United States, abortion and school prayer are among the most volatile political issues of the late twentieth century. And the millions of Americans passionately opposed to abortion and in favor of school prayer are not primarily motivated by material self-interest— at least not insofar as these particular issues are concerned. Rather, they are motivated by moral outrage, outrage provoked by the violation of some of their fundamental conceptions of good and evil. The same is true of the Orthodox Jews in Israel who object to the excavation of the dead and violations of the Sabbath. The outrage provoked by the violation of fundamental values (religious or secular) clearly can motivate political action. And this is no less true in the Islamic world than it is in the United States or Israel.

However, the view that activists in Islamic movements are motivated by their opposition to modernization is not entirely accurate, nor does it explain why an Islamic revolution occurred only in Iran. To begin with, many of the activists in the Islamic movements of the late twentieth century have been university students in the applied sciences, as well as engineers and doctors. It seems unlikely that such people would oppose the *technological* modernization of recent decades, without which they would have no jobs. Moreover, when we

look at the writings of the principal ideologists of the Islamic movements of the late twentieth century, we do not find condemnation of
technological or economic innovation.[1]

The Ayatollah Khomeini never condemned the shah for trying to
industrialize Iran. On the contrary, he argued that the shah's regime
was one of many "puppet governments" established by Western im-
perialists to *prevent* the industrialization of the Islamic world. In his
lectures on "Islamic Government," which he presented to religious
students in Iraq in 1970, Khomeini declared:

> If you pay no attention to the policies of the imperialists, and consider
> Islam to be simply the few topics you are always studying and never
> go beyond them, then the imperialists will leave you alone. Pray as
> much as you like; it is your oil they are after—why should they worry
> about your prayers? They are after our minerals, and want to turn our
> country into a market for their goods. That is the reason the puppet
> governments they have installed prevent us from industrializing, and
> instead establish only assembly plants and industry that is dependent
> on the outside world.[2]

This is not the rhetoric of a man opposed to technological and economic development. Nor would the policies implemented by the
Khomeini regime since 1979 suggest hostility to such development.[3]

It is true that traditional Muslims (those who interpret their religion
as did earlier generations) have at times opposed technological innovations as have their counterparts in other religions. In 1926, the leaders of the rebel Ikhwan in Arabia criticized Ibn Saud for using
automobiles, telegraph, wireless, and telephones, all of which were
"Christian innovations, and inventions of the devil."[4] And the ulama
of Arabia were initially wary of the telephone until they heard the
Quran read over it. But such attitudes toward modern technology are
not generally found in the Islamic movements of the 1970s and 1980s.
It is worth noting in this respect that one of the principal weapons of
the Islamic movements of the seventies and eighties has been the cas-
sette tape, itself a decidedly modern piece of technology.[5]

But although opposition to technological and economic modernization is rare in the fundamentalist Islamic literature of the late twentieth century, opposition to social modernization is not. Modernization
in this sense implies more than just the replacement of the old by the
new. It implies a shift from a society in which people's social and legal
status is largely determined by characteristics they are usually born

with, such as sex, religion, and family, to one in which social and legal status is largely determined by what people achieve by their own effort. It should be emphasized that this distinction is a relative one—there are *no* societies in which sex, religion, and family are completely unrelated to social status.[6]

Understood in this sense, social modernization entails the diminution of the role of religion in society and state—but not in the life of the individual. And fundamentalist Islamic ideologists definitely do oppose such secularization. We have seen that one of the principal shibboleths of the fundamentalist Islamic literature is that Islam encompasses all aspects of life and that the idea of a secular state and society is therefore contrary to the laws of God.[7]

Moral outrage provoked by the violations of traditional Islamic values is frequently articulated in the fundamentalist literature. Hasan al-Banna, the Egyptian founder of the Muslim Brotherhood, once wrote that among the "social and educational" goals of the Brotherhood were the following:

> Putting an end to prostitution, in both its secret and public forms, and considering fornication an abominable crime the perpetrators of which are to be whipped.
> Putting an end to gambling in all its forms. . . .
> Waging war on alcoholic beverages and drugs. . . .
> Struggling against the display of women's bodies and licentiousness, and guiding women toward the way things ought to be. . . .
> Prohibiting the mixing of male and female students. . . .
> Shutting down licentious night clubs and dance halls and prohibiting dancing and all that is related to it.[8]

We find such evils as liquor, "half-naked women," and the mingling of men and women condemned in the writings of most of the other major fundamentalist Islamic ideologists of the late twentieth century. And the Islamic Republic of Iran has attempted to extirpate all these "vices." Women have been publicly flogged for swimming in areas reserved for men. They have been forbidden to participate in international athletic competition so as to avoid exposing their bare legs and arms. And according to a law passed in 1981, men and women convicted of adultery are supposed to be stoned or flogged. One could almost believe that Khomeini was deliberately trying to perpetuate all the standard stereotypes of Islam in the West.[9]

It is also significant that in 1979, Khomeini's son Ahmad, himself a mullah, published an article in which he divided Iran's ulama into three groups. The first group consisted of those ulama who had never wavered in their support for the shah because of the subsidies they received from his government. Khomeini's son argued that these ulama constituted a small minority. The second group, also a small minority, had vigorously opposed the shah's domestic and foreign policies. The third group, which included the vast majority of Iran's men of religion, had neither supported nor openly opposed the shah until the late 1970s. Ahmad Khomeini chides the ulama in this last group for their indifference to the shah's subservience to Western imperialism, and he claims that when they did oppose the shah, they did so primarily because of the "moral decadence" and "social filth" that he tolerated in Iran.[10]

All of these facts suggest that many Muslim fundamentalists are indeed outraged by the violation of traditional Islamic values. But such outrage did not suddenly emerge in the late 1970s, nor did it emerge only in Iran. Muslims have been complaining about secularization, the mixing of men and women, gambling, liquor, and other Western evils throughout most of the twentieth century. Yet fundamentalist Islamic movements seeking to create "truly" Islamic states and societies have been only sporadically significant during this period, and a successful Islamic revolution has occurred only once. In other words, it is true that Muslims are often outraged by social and cultural innovations that violate their traditional values, but the existence of such outrage does not entail an Islamic revolution. If it did, there would be a string of Islamic republics stretching from Morocco to Indonesia.[11]

One could, of course, argue that the degree of social and cultural modernization undertaken by the shah of Iran in the 1970s was far greater than that undertaken anywhere else at any other time in the Islamic world. But this explanation is ultimately circular in that the only real evidence to support it is the very fact it is supposed to explain—the Islamic revolution itself. The social and cultural innovations effected by the shah's father Reza Shah in the 1920s and 1930s violated people's traditional religious values far more than any of the innovations implemented by the shah in the 1970s. We have seen that from 1925 through 1936, Reza Shah radically curtailed the legal and social role of Islam in Iran and tried to force Iranian men and women to wear Western clothes, going so far as to prohibit the wearing of the veil by Iranian women in 1936. These innovations directly affected and outraged most Iranians. Yet the protests they provoked were easily suppressed.[12]

Why was there no Islamic revolution at the time of Reza Shah's drastic social and cultural innovations of the twenties and thirties rather than in 1978–79, by which time the secularizing policies of the Pahlavi dynasty had been in effect for over half a century? Were the exposed legs of modern Iranian women more shocking in the late seventies than they had been in the late thirties? This hardly seems likely. Once again we stress that although rapid and extensive cultural innovation may entail widespread moral outrage, widespread moral outrage does not entail revolution.

ON THE "DISRUPTIVE" EFFECTS OF
MODERNIZATION: RAPID ECONOMIC GROWTH

The "moral outrage" explanation examined above concerns the religious values of those who join or support fundamentalist Islamic movements. But the Iranian Revolution and the Islamic resurgence in general have also been explained as unconscious responses to the allegedly disruptive consequences of rapid economic growth and social modernization. Such growth and modernization are disruptive, according to this view, in that they erode traditional social bonds and engender unrealizable aspirations in emergent social groups, notably the new middle class. This argument, as well as that of moral outrage, is often implicit in the common view that "the shah modernized too fast."[13]

It is true that from 1970 through 1977, Iran had one of the highest economic growth rates in the world, with an average annual increase in per capita GNP of 9.9 percent. But all the OPEC countries were affected by the radical increases in the price of oil during the 1970s. And all of them experienced phenomenal rates of economic growth (as opposed to self-sustained economic development). From 1970 through 1977, Iraq and Saudi Arabia both had higher rates of economic growth than did Iran. Yet although these countries had active Islamic movements in the late seventies, neither underwent a full-fledged Islamic revolution. In fact the Islamic movements in both these countries never attracted mass support and appear to have dwindled in political significance during the 1980s. Moreover, other OPEC countries (for example, Algeria and the United Arab Emirates) experienced very little turmoil during the oil boom of the seventies, whereas countries with little or no oil (such as Egypt and Pakistan) experienced a great deal. So the argument that the Iranian Revolution was the result of the disruptive impact of the rapid economic growth engendered by the sudden influx of oil wealth is less than convincing.[14]

ON THE "DISRUPTIVE" EFFECTS OF
MODERNIZATION: RURAL-URBAN MIGRATION

Rural-urban migration is often cited as one of the most disruptive aspects of modernization because it allegedly uproots people from their traditional way of life and thus renders them susceptible to revolutionary doctrines. But, as has already been noted, countless studies of rural-urban migration in the Middle East and the third world generally have demonstrated that migration does not entail severe social and cultural disruption. Moreover, as we saw in the last chapter, the rural-born urban poor (who constitute the bulk of the migrants in the cities of the Muslim world) have generally played little or no role in the Islamic movements of the seventies and eighties, with the partial exception of Iran late in the revolution.[15]

The argument that the Iranian Revolution was somehow caused by massive rural-urban migration also overlooks the fact that this process was occurring throughout the Islamic world—as well as the rest of the third world. From 1970 through 1981, Afghanistan, Algeria, Iraq, Libya, Saudi Arabia, and the Sudan all had higher rates of urban population growth—which was partly due to rural-urban migration—than did Iran. And the urban populations of Jordan, Morocco, and Syria grew almost as rapidly as that of Iran during this same period. But only Iran had a revolution.[16]

ON THE "DISRUPTIVE" EFFECTS
OF MODERNIZATION: EDUCATION

Although the rural-born urban poor have not usually participated in fundamentalist Islamic movements, students of rural origin sometimes have. But this is also true of many students and other educated young people of urban origin. Education rather than migration would appear to be the crucial factor in such cases, since university students and recent graduates tend to be among the most politicized people in all third world societies, whereas uneducated rural-urban migrants tend to be among the least. The exposure of Muslims from very traditional families to secular Western-style education would seem to be more likely to engender alienation than migration. Such students, whether born in a city or a village, are often caught between two cultures—that taught in school and that taught at home. The urban poor, on the other hand, remain immersed in a culture similar to that of the villages from which they and/or their parents emigrated.[17]

Rapid and massive expansion of modern education does often produce political instability—in the short run at any rate. Such education tends to encourage students to question previously unquestioned values and political structures. It exposes them to revolutionary political ideologies that peasants and the urban poor have usually never heard of. It often engenders aspirations that cannot be realized without radical change. And since educational expansion in the third world often outpaces the expansion of employment opportunities for the educated, it can engender frustration and resentment in those graduates unable to find jobs commensurate with their educations. For these reasons, among others, the rapid and massive expansion of education does tend to produce a politically volatile social stratum implacably opposed to the regime that educated it.[18]

So one might argue that a major cause of the Iranian Revolution was the rapid expansion of Iran's educational infrastructure under the shah. This line of reasoning is of particular interest because of the importance of university and secondary school students in the revolution. But, once again, although there is no denying that education expanded remarkably under the shah, this was true throughout much of the Middle East and the rest of the third world. In fact, from 1960 through 1980, the secondary school systems of Algeria, Libya, Morocco, Saudi Arabia, and the Sudan all expanded more rapidly than did that of Iran. Similarly, from 1960 through 1979, higher education expanded more dramatically in Jordan, Libya, and Saudi Arabia than in Iran. But only Iran had an Islamic revolution. So although the expansion of educational opportunity was unquestionably of major importance, it did not, in and of itself, cause Iran's Islamic revolution.[19]

ON THE "DISRUPTIVE" EFFECTS OF MODERNIZATION:
THE DEMAND FOR POLITICAL PARTICIPATION

It has been argued that urbanization, industrialization, and the expansion of education and the mass media all combine to increase the number of politically conscious people who want to participate in a country's political system. If such people are not allowed some participation, typically in the form of elections, they will revolt. Jerrold Green, among others, has attempted to explain the Iranian Revolution in this manner. And there is certainly some truth to his argument. If democracy (which is the kind of political participation people usually want) had existed in Iran under the shah, the intelligentsia would not have needed to engage in the protests that eventually sparked the revolution of 1978–79.[20]

The letters and manifestos of 1977 demanded free elections, free speech, fair trials, and the elimination of torture. If Iranians had already enjoyed these rights, the hostility of many educated middle-class Iranians toward the shah would have been diluted. And they would have been able to articulate their other grievances as well, thus reducing the likelihood of their supporting Khomeini, who clearly had a different set of priorities. Moreover, if people had been free to criticize the government in the past, the fact that a few did so with impunity in 1977 would not have been perceived as a sign of weakness encouraging more radical opposition. It is true that the intellectuals who were most committed to free elections and human rights did not control the revolution of 1978–79. But their protests in 1977 sparked it, and the strikes by middle-class employees with similar aspirations helped make it succeed in the fall of 1978 and the winter of 1979. So it is quite possible that democracy, or even a certain degree of democracy, could have averted the revolution that toppled the shah.

However, the argument that the absence of democracy *entailed* the Iranian Revolution runs into a familiar problem. Although educated Iranians definitely did want a greater voice in Iran's political system, this was true of the educated middle classes of the rest of the Islamic world as well. There were no democratic governments in the Islamic world in the seventies or eighties. Political participation was as restricted in virtually all other Islamic countries as it was in Iran. But only Iran had an Islamic revolution.[21]

THE SELF-INTEREST OF TRADITIONAL SOCIAL GROUPS:
THE ULAMA AND THE BAZAARIS

One could argue that modernization causes revolution insofar as certain traditional social strata will oppose it out of material self-interest. And this argument has been made with respect to the Iranian ulama. It is true that in 1977, as part an austerity program aimed at curbing government spending and inflation, Prime Minister Jamshid Amuzegar reduced the subsidies that some ulama had been paid annually for the maintenance of mosques, schools, and other religious institutions. It is not clear precisely how much money was involved. Michael Ledeen and William Lewis speak of a reduction from $80 million to $30 million in mid-1977, but they give no source for these figures. Fereydoun Hoveyda speaks of the elimination of an annual subsidy of $11 million, but he too gives no source for his information. But whatever the amount of money involved, there was a significant reduction in payments to some ulama as part of a broader effort to cut government spending.[22]

The reduction of subsidies to the ulama in mid-1977, however, does not explain the Iranian Revolution. Reza Shah curtailed the revenues and privileges of the ulama in the twenties and thirties far more drastically than his son ever did, and yet he encountered only minor protests. Moreover, the ulama were not very active in 1977, when the cutback in government subsidies occurred. It was only after the Qum riots of January 1978 that they really began to lead the opposition to the shah. And many of the ulama who were most active in the revolution were either in exile or in prison in 1977. Such men would not have been affected by the cutback.[23]

Moreover, in his 1979 article criticizing the majority of Iran's ulama for not actively opposing the shah until the late seventies, Khomeini's son Ahmad does not mention the reduction in government subsidies. Given that this article is critical of most Iranian ulama, if such a reduction had been of major significance in precipitating overt opposition to the government, Ahmad Khomeini would have mentioned it. So while a reduction in governmental subsidies to the ulama may well have prompted some previously docile ulama to support the revolution, it certainly did not motivate the ulama who ultimately led the revolution to its successful conclusion.[24]

More significant than the cutback in subsidies to the ulama was the shah's treatment of the merchants and artisans, or bazaaris. As part of its efforts to curb inflation, the Iranian government initiated an antiprofiteering campaign in 1975. All over Iran, thousands of bazaaris were fined, imprisoned, and banned from their hometowns. By early 1976, every bazaari family in the country had been hurt by the antiprofiteering campaign. All students of Iran agree that this was a very important cause of bazaari hostility toward the shah.[25]

In addition to the antiprofiteering campaign, the shah's government had also antagonized Iran's bazaaris in other ways. Government-supported factories, import-export trade companies, and banks had undermined their traditional livelihoods. The Ministry of Health was planning to extend social security laws to the bazaar, which would hurt the bazaaris financially. The main bazaar in the holy city of Mashhad had been razed, and there was a plan to raze much of Tehran's main bazaar as well in order to build an eight-lane freeway. So aside from traditional Islamic values and close ties to the ulama, the bazaaris' opposition to the shah was undoubtedly motivated to some extent by material self-interest.[26]

But bazaari resentment of the shah's policies did not entail the revolution of 1978–79. The antiprofiteering campaign occurred in 1975–76. The first major protests did not occur until 1977, and the bazaaris were not involved in the earliest of these. And although the bazaaris certainly played a crucial role in the protests of 1978–79, so did many other Iranians unaffected by the antiprofiteering campaign or the razing of the bazaar of Mashhad.

ECONOMIC GROWTH AND FRUSTRATED EXPECTATIONS

It has been argued that revolutions occur when a period of rapid economic growth is followed by a worsening economic situation that frustrates the expectations heightened by the previous boom. This idea derives in part from de Tocqueville's famous observation that "evils which are patiently endured when they seem inevitable become intolerable when once the idea of escape from them is suggested."[27] De Tocqueville's point is a fundamental one that relates to grievances of all kinds, not just economic ones.[28]

We cannot simply explain revolutions or lesser forms of social turmoil in terms of hardships and inequities as perceived by an external observer. We need to know how such alleged hardships and inequities are perceived by those who experience them. Many intellectuals, for example, tend to view the Muslim workers in Europe as an exploited and oppressed underclass. And there may well be some truth to this characterization. But Moroccan workers in Europe often regard themselves as fortunate, and they are envied by their relatives and friends who work in Morocco for much less money. Similarly, many traditional Muslim women do not regard themselves as exploited or oppressed although they tend to be so regarded by educated Muslim women as well as by Western observers. The point of these examples is not to suggest that we can *judge* social situations only in terms of the insider's point of view. It is rather that we must *understand* this point of view in order to understand and explain why people do what they do (in this case, revolt).[29]

Those scholars, however, who have argued that revolutions are engendered by the frustration of heightened expectations have often simply assumed that economic growth followed by decline entails such frustration without really trying to determine to what extent this is true—and it is not always true. What may appear as economic growth and decline in statistical tables is not always perceived as such by ordinary people trying to keep bread on the table and a roof over their heads—especially since economic growth does not necessarily entail any immediate benefits for the masses.[30]

But even if we assume that periods of prosperity followed by periods of decline (as measured by the standard statistical indices) do frustrate heightened expectations, the fact remains that good times have followed bad throughout the course of human history without necessarily causing revolutions. A brief comparison of recent economic growth in Iran and several other Islamic countries should make this clear.

The OPEC oil price increases spawned an economic boom in Iran from 1973 through 1976, which resulted in a high rate of inflation, averaging around 50 percent from 1975 through 1977, according to some sources. This inflation and other problems induced the Iranian government to initiate an austerity program in 1977 that curtailed construction and increased unemployment, thus presumably frustrating the expectations of at least those who lost their jobs. But a much sharper shift from boom to austerity occurred in all of the OPEC countries in the wake of the collapse of oil prices in the 1980s. Yet no revolutions occurred.[31]

In short, explaining the Iranian Revolution in terms of the frustration of heightened expectations that were due to the recession following the boom of the early seventies is as inadequate as the many other variations on the theme of disruptive modernization. This is not to suggest that there is no truth whatsoever to any of these approaches, just that *in and of themselves* they do not explain why an Islamic revolution occurred only in Iran and only in 1978–79.

11

Resentment of Foreign Domination and the Quest for Authenticity

Modernization in its broadest sense simply means the replacement of the old by the new. But more specifically, it is usually understood to imply industrialization, urbanization, expansion of (secular) education, greater public participation in government, and the diminution of the legal and social role of ethnic, religious, and other primordial identities. For the Islamic world and the third world generally, all this boils down to imitating the West, namely northern Europe and its American offshoot. When one speaks of modern education in the Islamic world, one is usually speaking of Western-style education, and likewise for modern industry, technology, law, and culture. In other words, *modernization* and *Westernization* have tended to be synonymous, at least since the late nineteenth century.[1]

Modernization in the Middle East has thus generally involved the imitation of the Western powers that have dominated the Islamic world both economically and politically for well over a century. And this has made modernization problematic in a way that it was not in the West—where it was never linked to foreign domination. This is primarily true, however, only of social and cultural modernization.[2]

As all students of Islamic fundamentalism have noted, virtually the entire Islamic world was subjugated by the West during the nineteenth and twentieth centuries. Most of North Africa was conquered by the French, who gave Spain a few crumbs in northern and southern Morocco. The Italians took twenty years (1911–31) to conquer Libya, which they occupied until 1942. The British controlled Egypt from the

1880s to the 1950s. And after the defeat of the Ottoman Empire in World War I, most of the eastern region of the Arab world was divided into British and French mandates, one of which became the modern state of Israel. In Iran, the British and the Russians vied for control until both were supplanted by the United States in 1953. Muslim central Asia was subjugated by Russia. India, with a large Muslim minority and formerly ruled by the Muslim Moghuls, was ruled by the British. And farther east, the British colonized Malaya while the Dutch took Indonesia.

In the decades following World War II, most Muslim countries became legally independent, but they remained economically, politically, and to some extent culturally dependent upon one or more of the industrialized nations of the West—and more recently Japan. The West produces the weapons the Muslims use to wage their wars. The West and Japan produce the cars, buses, and planes that Muslims use to travel, and the televisions, radios, and tape recorders they use for entertainment and information. The West and Japan produce the basic machinery and spare parts without which Muslim factories could not function. And the West provides the aid that enables some Muslim nations with little or no oil to subsist (Egypt being the most graphic example).[3]

As for cultural dependence, throughout most of the Islamic world, Muslims watch "I Love Lucy" and "Dallas" on their televisions and follow the exploits of Clint Eastwood, Burt Reynolds, and Sylvester Stallone in movie theaters. Muslim parents dream of sending their children to study in Europe or the United States so as to ensure them a place in their country's elite. And even in the universities of the Islamic world, the authors of many of the most advanced textbooks are often Westerners, as are some of the professors—who are generally much better paid than their Muslim colleagues.[4]

CULTURAL AUTHENTICITY AND NATIVISM

All this domination by, and dependence upon, the industrialized West has bred considerable resentment in the Middle East, as it has in the third world as a whole. And some scholars have emphasized that the appeal of Islamic movements lies in the desire for cultural authenticity and the rejection of Westernization as a kind of cultural imperialism tied to the economic and political domination of the Islamic world by the West.[5]

Sometimes associated with this explanation of the Islamic resurgence as a quest for cultural authenticity is the notion of nativism as understood by anthropologists. By a nativistic movement, anthropologists usually mean a movement that seeks to revive the ostensibly traditional culture of a dominated society so as to overcome at least some aspects of the domination to which the society in question has been subjected. Such movements typically occur when people feel that their cultural identity, as well as their economic and political autonomy, is threatened by the domination of an alien society. There is also a nativistic dimension to most nationalist movements.[6]

As noted above, nativistic movements are ostensibly intended to revive tradition, the culture of preceding generations. In fact, however, they always involve the reconstruction of tradition in novel (or modern) ways that reflect the influence of the dominant culture they are designed to reject. And phenomena that were traditionally taken for granted (or denigrated) assume new meanings as symbols of cultural identity and defiant rejection of foreign domination. One thinks, for example, of the role of the Afro hairstyle in black "nationalism" in the United States or of the head scarves worn by many educated young women during the Iranian Revolution.[7]

In America, the Afro hairstyle became a symbolic refusal to mimic white culture and a statement of pride in one's blackness. Similarly in Iran, the head scarf (*rusari*) worn by young women in the 1970s became a defiant refusal to imitate Western culture. It came to symbolize rejection of the shah's regime and of Western domination in all its forms. And it became a reaffirmation of the authentic Islamic identity of Iranians. But while the scarf worn by the young Iranian woman was an ideological reaffirmation of the value of Iranian tradition, it was itself a modern innovation. The same is true of the "all-enveloping veils" and gloves worn by young women in the university-based Islamic movements of Egypt. And the same is in fact true of much of what twentieth-century Islamic fundamentalists have to say about Islam.[8]

There is no question but that most of the Islamic movements of the 1970s and 1980s were to various degrees nativistic. This is especially obvious in the writings of Dr. 'Ali Shari'ati, who has been described as "the major ideologue" of the Iranian Revolution.[9] During the five years he spent in France preparing his doctorate at the Sorbonne, Shari'ati was strongly influenced by Frantz Fanon's books on the debilitating cultural and psychological impact of colonialism on the peoples of the third world. During the course of discussing what he sees as the revolutionary role of the prophet Muhammad, Shari'ati cites with approval Fanon's famous exhortation to the third world: "Brothers come on! Let us stop the nauseating and apish imitation of Europe."[10] Shari'ati himself condemns Muslims for imitating Westerners "like monkeys."[11] And he urges them to return to their authentic Islamic identity. This line of reasoning, as well as Shari'ati's emphasis upon the revolutionary character of the pristine Islam of the prophet Muhammad and other early Muslims, had a tremendous impact upon Iranian university students and other Westernized Iranians who sought to return to their "roots."[12]

Shari'ati's writings illustrate another characteristic feature of nativistic movements, namely their tendency to reinterpret the traditional culture they seek to revive in terms of the dominant culture they seek to reject. Like all radical Islamic ideologists, Shari'ati condemns Marxism as a materialistic product of the decadent West. But his own conception of Islam has clearly been affected by the Marxist tradition. For example, he interprets history as a continuous "dialectical" struggle between two types of social order represented by Cain and Abel:

> Now Abel, in my opinion, represents the age of a pasture-based economy, of the primitive socialism that preceded ownership, and Cain represents the system of agriculture, and individual or monopoly ownership. Thereafter a permanent war began so that the whole of history became the stage for a struggle between the party of Cain the killer, and Abel, his victim, or, in other words, the ruler and the ruled.[13]

This is definitely not how the story of Cain and Abel was traditionally understood in the Islamic world.

But even though there was a nativistic dimension to many of the Islamic movements of the late twentieth century, and even though the quest for cultural authenticity was unquestionably a major source of the appeal of such movements to certain social strata (notably the educated young), there remain problems with the nativism-authenticity interpretation of the Islamic resurgence of the late 1970s. First of all, the only people who seek authenticity are those who feel inauthentic. Nothing ever said, written, or done by the Ayatollah Khomeini would suggest that *he* ever suffered any such identity crisis, although he is well aware that the issue of authenticity is extremely important to others. Thus on September 12, 1980, he warned the pilgrims in

Mecca: "Rely on the culture of Islam, resist Western imitation, and stand on your own feet. Attack those intellectuals who are infatuated with the West and the East, and recover your true identity."[14] But Khomeini himself has never been "infatuated with the West or the East" ("the East" refers here to the Soviet Union). And the same is true of most of the more traditional Iranians, notably the ulama and the shopkeepers, who supported and participated in Iran's Islamic revolution along with the secularly educated young.

The nativism and authenticity explanation of the Iranian revolution also leaves us facing some of the same problems posed by the earlier disruptive modernization explanations—notably why was there a successful Islamic revolution only in Iran and only in 1978–79? If Iranian students and university graduates yearned for authenticity, so did those of Egypt, Syria, and all the other Islamic countries strongly affected by Western cultural domination. And the issue of cultural authenticity was, and remains, a major concern of the educated middle classes throughout the third world. But only Iran had a fundamentalist revolution.[15]

ON IRANIAN RESENTMENT OF AMERICAN DOMINATION

Like all third world revolutions of the twentieth century, Iran's revolution of 1978–79 definitely was, among other things, a nationalist uprising directed against foreign domination and a regime perceived as its instrument. One indication of this is the frequency with which Khomeini condemned American domination in 1978–79. On February 18, 1978, in observing the fortieth day of mourning for the martyrs of the January Qum riots, Khomeini declared: "As for America, a signatory to the Declaration of Human Rights, it imposed this shah upon the umma, an appropriate successor to his father Reza Shah. During the period he has ruled, this creature has blatantly transformed Iran into a colony of America. What crimes he has committed in the service of his masters!"[16]

When Khomeini landed at Tehran's airport on February 1, 1979, after over fourteen years of exile, he declared that "our triumph will come when all forms of foreign control have been brought to an end and all roots of the monarchy have been plucked out of the soil of our land."[17] The next day he said that "the people want their army to be independent, not under the orders of American and other foreign advisors."[18] And on September 12, 1979, he told the pilgrims in Mecca that "for more than fifty years, the Pahlavi puppet has dragged our country down, filling the pockets of the foreigners—particularly Britain and America—with the abundant wealth of our land, and awarding what little remained to itself and its agents and hangers-on."[19]

Such condemnation of the shah's subservience to the United States was also among the principal themes of the leaflets and chanted slogans of the revolution. An August 1978 leaflet in Isfahan, where many Vietnam veterans were involved in helicopter maintenance, declared: "The people . . . of Isfahan could see with their own eyes how a filthy foreign minority, with the cooperation of their internal servants, were looting their material and spiritual wealth and resources . . . , and had flooded the city with the prostitutes, the ailing of the Vietnam war and in general the rejects of Western society."[20] And among the principal slogans chanted in the massive marches of December 1978 were "Hang this American king!" "We will destroy Yankee power in Iran!" and "Death to the American dog! Shah held on a leash by the Americans!"[21]

But again although resentment of American domination was among the most conspicuous motives of many of the people who participated in Iran's Islamic revolution, the existence of this resentment does not explain why such a revolution occurred only in Iran and only in 1978–79. Virtually all the Muslim countries have been client states of superpowers since attaining legal independence. After having depended upon Russian aid in the sixties, Egypt was completely dependent upon the United States by the late seventies. If the shah was reviled as an American puppet in Iran, so too were Hasan II in Morocco, Khalid in Saudi Arabia, and Sadat in Egypt, and Syria's al-Asad was sometimes condemned as a stooge of the Russians. But only Iran had an Islamic revolution.[22]

Fundamentalist Islamic ideologists have been articulating resentment of foreign domination for decades, as have most secular ideologists of the Middle East. It will be recalled that the immediate cause of Khomeini's expulsion from Iran in 1964 was his criticism of a law granting diplomatic immunity to American military advisers in Iran, which, he said, reduced Iran to the status of an American colony. Shaul Bakhash notes that in thus criticizing the "status of forces" law of 1964, Khomeini "was echoing sentiments widely shared among the educated and middle classes."[23] And Khomeini continued to condemn the shah's government for its subordination to the United States during the late sixties and early seventies. But the Islamic revolution did not occur until 1978–79.[24]

It is true that the number of Americans working in Iran had grown to over thirty-five thousand in 1978, most of them in Tehran. And it is possible that American influence in Iranian society was more conspicuous and thus more bitterly resented than ever before or than anywhere else in the Islamic world. But even if this assertion were true, which it may well be, it would still not entail an *Islamic* revolution. Iran's leftists and many of its secular social democrats were as critical of American domination as was Khomeini. But they were relatively minor actors in the revolution of 1978–79.[25]

Resentment of foreign domination must be taken into consideration in any attempt to explain why an Islamic revolution occurred only in Iran and only in 1978–79. But like many of the grievances discussed in the previous chapter, such resentment did not, in and of itself, entail a revolution. Foreign domination, like torture, dictatorship, and egregious social inequity, has existed throughout the third world for decades or longer. But only a handful of third world countries have undergone revolutions. And only one has undergone a revolution eventually led by religious scholars demanding a return to a truly Islamic society.

12

Conclusion: Why Only in Iran?

A number of factors combined to transform widespread grievances into an Islamic revolution in Iran—and only in Iran. To begin with, there was the economic crisis of 1976–77 in the wake of the boom engendered by the quadrupling of oil prices in 1973–74. Inflation, sometimes estimated to have been as high as 50 percent from 1975 through 1977, certainly aggravated already existing social tensions. Cynthia Helms, whose husband was the American ambassador to Iran from 1973 to 1977, says that three- and four-bedroom houses in Tehran were being rented for as much as four thousand dollars a month. A bus driver told her, in 1976, that he had been offered over thirty thousand dollars for his house—which consisted of two small rooms heated by a kerosene lamp and an outside toilet. There was no running water in the house, and cooking was done on a small burner "in an outhouse near the toilet."[1]

But inflation alone could not have precipitated the upheaval of 1978–79. Many third world countries have experienced much higher inflation without experiencing revolutions. And the Khomeini regime survived equally high or higher rates of inflation during the early eighties. In fact, although the economic crisis in the mid-seventies did entail severe hardship for many Iranians, it was relatively minor in comparison with the collapse of the Iranian economy after the revolution.[2]

More unsettling than the inflation itself was the government's attempt to curb it by arresting, fining, and generally harassing the bazaaris. (It will be recalled that the bastinadoing of two bazaaris blamed for the high price of sugar sparked one of the early protests of the constitutionalist revolution in 1905.) On top of the various other policies that had hurt the bazaar in previous years, the government's harsh antiprofiteering campaign guaranteed that *once large-scale opposition to the shah emerged,* the bazaaris would support it. Similarly, the 1977 reduction of subsidies to the ulama, although not as crucial as has sometimes been suggested, does appear to have exacerbated the opposition of some ulama to the shah. Given the billions of dollars the government was earning from oil, the government could have dealt with inflation more reasonably without aggravating the hostility of the bazaaris and the ulama—two of the most politically significant segments of Iranian society.

THE CARTER HUMAN RIGHTS POLICY

But the most important *precipitating* cause of the Iranian Revolution was the Carter administration's human rights policy, or more precisely, the Iranian perception of that policy. Revolutions are never simply the inevitable result of widespread discontent. They usually occur only when the ancien régime has been crippled by a specific crisis that renders it incapable of suppressing radical opposition. The Carter human rights policy triggered such a crisis in Iran.[3]

As several scholars and former members of the Carter administration have emphasized, the American government did not in fact *force* the shah to undertake a radical liberalization program. But the shah, like all educated Iranians, never forgot that he owed his throne to the CIA, and he feared that the United States might do to him what it had done to Musaddiq. He thus felt threatened by Carter's emphasis upon human rights and tolerated a certain degree of liberalization that would have been unthinkable a few years earlier. The fact that the shah had cancer may have also encouraged him to undertake some reforms in order to smooth the way for his son's succession. But the human rights rhetoric in Washington was the principal factor.[4]

The degree to which the shah reformed his autocratic regime to please Carter should not be exaggerated. Even in 1977, long before the mass marches of 1978, many of the shah's critics continued to endure various forms of harassment, including imprisonment and physical beating. But some did not. And the fact that at least some secular intellectuals were allowed to criticize the government publicly encour-

aged other opposition forces to articulate their grievances. The grievances were not new. The opportunity to express them publicly was.[5]

Carter transformed Iran's political climate. In the words of Mahdi
Bazargan, "when Carter's human rights drive lifted the hope of the
people, all the built-up pressure exploded."[6] Carter's policy created
hope where before there was none. And, to quote de Tocqueville once
again, "evils which are patiently tolerated when they seem inevitable
become intolerable when once the idea of escape from them is suggested."[7]

Many Iranians, including the shah as well as his supporters and
opponents, assumed that the Carter human rights policy entailed the
dilution of American support for the Pahlavi regime—despite the
Carter administration's repeated public assurances that this was not
the case. This assumption led Iranians to believe that the shah was
more vulnerable than he had been since the early sixties, when the
Kennedy administration had pressured him to reform. And the very
belief that this was so made it so. The aura of invincibility that had
surrounded the shah, *as well as much of the hostility toward him,* was
due in large part to the conviction that he was Washington's man and
that the United States would never tolerate his demise. Once that
conviction was shaken, so were the foundations of the shah's regime.[8]

But although Carter's human rights policy did unquestionably pre-
cipitate the Iranian Revolution, it should be kept in mind that it did
not have a similar impact on all the third world dictatorships supported
by the United States. The Carter administration placed far more pressure on Latin American dictatorships than it did on the shah—in part
at least because of Iran's strategic and economic significance. And of
the various Latin American dictators chastised for their human rights
violations, only Somoza fell. It is true that the Carter administration
crippled Somoza much as it did the shah. But it did not have a similar
impact on Argentina, Brazil, or the other Latin American countries it
criticized for human rights abuses.[9]

Nor did Carter's foreign policy trigger revolutions in South Korea
or the Philippines (where Marcos fell during the second term of a
Republican president who had never pressured him on human rights).
Nor were there revolutions in Jordan, Saudi Arabia, Morocco, or any
of the other authoritarian Middle Eastern regimes supported by the
United States. In other words, the Carter human rights policy did not
entail revolution in all of the United States' client autocracies. And it

would not have sparked one in Iran if the internal political situation in that country had not already been combustible. (The same is true in the case of Nicaragua.)

It is, moreover, essential to view the effect of the Carter policy in its historical context, namely, in the context of the coup of 1953 and the subsequent patron-client relationship between the United States and the shah. If Iranians had not perceived their king to be an American puppet, much of their hostility toward him would not have existed, and a perceived dilution of American support could not have precipitated his overthrow.

In fact, of course, the shah was not always the docile American stooge his critics made him out to be, as he made clear when he pushed for the OPEC price increases in 1973. But the shah's willingness to serve as Washington's policeman in the Persian Gulf and the conspicuous role of over thirty-five thousand Americans at the upper levels of Iran's social, political, and military hierarchies perpetuated the impression that he was indeed a mere puppet whose every move was manipulated by the United States. This naturally outraged a great many Iranians, including those with the greatest ideological and cultural affinities with the United States. Once again, the Carter human rights policy did not create this outrage, only the possibility of its public expression. So although Iranian perceptions of the Carter policy sparked the Iranian Revolution, those perceptions were shaped by a quarter century of American domination and insensitivity to Iranian national pride.[10]

CARTER, THE SHAH, AND THE USE OF FORCE

In addition to the fact that the Carter human rights policy precipitated the revolution, it has also been argued that the United States enabled the revolution to succeed by not supporting the shah more vigorously as opposition to his regime spread during 1978. But the Carter administration did continue to express strong support for the shah throughout most of 1978—much to the dismay of the moderate opposition.[11]

It is true that the American government tried to create a moderate alternative to the crumbling Pahlavi state in the last few months of 1978, but by that time the shah was doomed. It is also true that the conflicting views of the American State Department and the National Security adviser Zbigniew Brzezinski led to some confusion on the part of the shah. The State Department advocated concessions to the moderate opposition while Brzezinski advocated harsh repression before any attempts at compromise. But as Brzezinski observes, "the record does show that the Shah had enough encouragement from Carter and me to have taken—had he wanted to and had he had the will to do so—the tougher line."[12] American policy may have exacerbated the shah's vacillation during the revolution, but it did not entail it.

Those who argue that the American government should have urged the shah to suppress the opposition more brutally often overlook the fact that the opposition *was* brutally suppressed—albeit not as brutally as the Syrian opposition in the early 1980s or the Iranian opposition in June 1963. All scholarly and serious journalistic accounts make clear that troops and police killed thousands of unarmed demonstrators during the course of the revolution. (One of the distinguishing features of the Iranian Revolution was that it consisted essentially of unarmed demonstrations and religious processions until the insurrection of February 1979.)[13]

In fact, one could argue that the shah's forces sometimes erred by responding *too* brutally to the opposition. It will be recalled that during the winter and spring of 1978, the revolution evolved out of a cycle of mourning marches for demonstrators killed by troops and police. Had there been no dead, there would have been no mourning. In other words, if the government forces had used rubber-tipped bullets, tear gas, fire hoses, and other nonlethal devices, they would not have kept creating martyrs to be mourned. We cannot be sure that such tactics would have aborted the revolution, but they might well have—given the central role of martyrdom and mourning in its early phase. Brzezinski notes that the State Department and the U.S. ambassador in Tehran opposed sending the shah's government crowd-control devices in October 1978, apparently for fear of hindering negotiations with the National Front moderates. But by then the revolution had gained so much momentum that such devices would have probably been useless, whereas eight months earlier, when the mourning marches had yet to coalesce into a full-fledged revolution, they might have been invaluable.[14]

The argument that the shah should have suppressed the opposition more brutally overlooks the outrage provoked by the massacre of

"Black Friday" on September 8, 1978. Opposition sources and some foreign journalists claim that troops killed thousands of unarmed demonstrators on this occasion. Whatever the true number of casualties, Black Friday came to assume mythic significance in Iran. It convinced many that the shah was indeed evil incarnate and that compromise with him was henceforth impossible.[15]

The idea that the shah did not use brutal force in attempting to suppress the 1978–79 revolution is an illusion. But he did use force more sparingly than he did in June of 1963 or than did al-Asad in Syria during the early eighties. And it is possible that had the shah's troops slaughtered many times the thousands they did kill, he could have saved his regime—as he did in 1963 and as did al-Asad in 1980 and 1982.

But it would seem that the real flaw in the shah's use of force during the revolution was its inconsistency. For example, on September 4, 1978, there was a massive march in Tehran after prayers celebrating the end of Ramadan, the month of fasting. As the marchers entered the working-class neighborhoods of South Tehran, some of them began chanting "Death to the Shah!" An old woman watching cried "Don't say it, don't say it, they'll kill you!" and she ran away.[16] But when she saw that the nearby soldiers were not shooting, she returned. Then four days later, soldiers shot thousands on Black Friday. (Whether or not this figure is accurate, it became engraved in the popular imagination, as did the idea that the soldiers were actually Israelis because Iranians could not slaughter their own people this way.) In addition to compounding the outrage felt when the shah's troops did shoot, such vacillation between leniency and brutality simply reinforced the impression that the shah was "on the ropes."[17]

The various concessions offered by the shah during 1978 were seen as signs of weakness and even despair, as concessions granted in desperate situations usually are. Moreover, they were not taken seriously by most Iranians, who had heard the shah promise free elections on a number of previous occasions only to find themselves watching the electoral circuses of the past. Had the shah allowed geniunely free elections many years before, when he was at the height of his power, he might well have prevented the revolution by placating the secular intellectuals whose protests started the revolutionary ball rolling in 1977. But concessions by regimes on the verge of collapse rarely save them.[18]

KHOMEINI'S CHARISMA

The shah's regime was crippled in the late seventies by the combined effects of the economic crisis, the Carter human rights policy, and the shah's own weakness and ineptitude (both undoubtedly aggravated by cancer). This situation enabled hitherto submerged discontent to surface. But for such a crisis to engender a full-fledged revolution, there had to be some form of revolutionary leadership and ideology capable of articulating the widely varying grievances of the Iranian people. In Iran, the Ayatollah Khomeini supplied both, with the assistance of some mullahs and many students influenced by Shari'ati.

A basic reason for the unique success of Iran's Islamic revolution was Khomeini's charismatic authority. As has already been noted, the leading mujtahids of Twelver Shi'ism all have such authority in the sense that most Shi'is believe they are the sacred representatives of the messianic hidden imam. So when Khomeini and some other ayatollahs ordered Iranians to oppose the shah in 1978–79, their orders had considerable impact. For many devoutly religious Iranians in the cities, where the religious hierarchy was more firmly established than in the countryside, to oppose a deputy of the hidden imam would have been sinful. This crucial fact induced millions of relatively traditional and normally apolitical Iranians to join the revolution, whereas they would never have done so had the opposition to the shah been led by secular intellectuals or even by Islamic ideologists such as Shari'ati.

Of course, the charismatic authority of the ayatollahs did not suddenly emerge in 1978, any more than did the various grievances already discussed. And charismatic authority had not enabled Khomeini to overthrow the shah in 1963. Nor did it lead to successful Islamic revolutions among the Shi'is of Iraq, Bahrain, or Lebanon. But in the context of Iran's economic and above all political crisis of the late seventies, the charismatic authority of the deputies of the hidden imam was of crucial importance. Without it, the Shi'i ulama could not have overthrown the shah.

One reason for the activation of Khomeini's latent charisma in the late seventies was the impact of Shari'ati's writings among the educated young. The shah had been able to suppress the opposition in 1963 in part because the many secular students and intellectuals opposed to the shah at that time were reluctant to cooperate with Khomeini and the mullahs, whom they viewed as reactionaries. Shari'ati's emphasis upon the revolutionary character of Shi'i Islam and upon the need to return to Islam as a means of regaining cultural authenticity induced university students (whose numbers greatly increased in the 1970s) to join forces with the more traditional mullahs and bazaaris—even though they interpreted Islam quite differently. For these young people, Khomeini came to embody Shari'ati's Islam although Shari'ati certainly did not embody Khomeini's Islam.

In addition to the institutional charismatic authority derived from his position as one of the "sources of imitation" of Twelver Shi'ism, Khomeini also had personal charismatic authority by virtue of his identification with some of the principal archetypes of Shi'i sacred history, notably 'Ali, Husayn, and the hidden imam. He tapped deeply rooted values as well as millenarian expectations. He came to embody the righteousness and courage of Husayn while the shah came to embody the corruption and cruelty of Yazid. And the belief that Khomeini was actually the messianic imam himself, or at least in contact with him, was widespread among less educated urban Iranians. Even for those who did not take such ideas seriously, Khomeini had a mesmerizing messianic aura that was of obvious political utility.[19]

Khomeini became a symbol that had different meanings for different strata of Iranian society. For the Westernized young yearning for cultural authenticity, he *was* cultural authenticity. He was the "real" Iran of the mosque and the bazaar. He was *tradition*—and tradition, or what passes for it, is especially appealing to the alienated young in search of their authentic identity. It tends to become less so when they are forced to live by its rules. Thus many young Iranians who once saw Khomeini as the embodiment of Iranian authenticity now see him as a reactionary despot. Had more people read his writings, the latter facet of the man would have been obvious. But during the revolution, Khomeini the symbol was more important than Khomeini the theorist. What people believed him to be was more important than what he was.[20]

While many university students and other educated Iranians revered Khomeini as a symbol of cultural authenticity, they also revered him as a symbol of Iranian resistance to foreign domination. He articulated the widespread resentment of American domination in all its forms, political as well as cultural. He was the antithesis of the man foisted on Iran by the CIA. (The fact that most Iranian ayatollahs had at least tacitly supported the CIA coup of 1953 was forgotten.)

The more traditional Iranians were less concerned with cultural authenticity, although many also viewed Khomeini as a symbol of resistance to foreign domination. But for such people, Khomeini was above all a deputy of the hidden imam, a godly man, a righteous idol smasher, and the personification of all the traditional values violated by the shah. Whereas such values were extolled by university students because they were authentically Iranian, for more traditional Iranians they were simply God's truth. The university-educated woman might cover her hair to manifest her rejection of Western cultural imperialism and to regain her authentic Iranian identity, but the more traditional woman covered her hair simply because that was the way things ought to be. For the one, Islam was a means to an end; for the other, it was an end in itself. Both could, and did, revere their own Khomeinis. Thus did the imam, like other charismatic leaders before him, become a multifaceted symbol of his people's various discontents.

THE QUESTION OF ORGANIZATION

Those hostile to revolutions tend to attribute them to conspiracies hatched by a handful of cunning villains, whereas revolutionaries themselves often speak of spontaneous revolts of the oppressed that arise from intolerable tyranny, exploitation, and so on. In fact, revolutions inevitably involve both organization and spontaneity. They entail unplanned discontent and crises as well as planned efforts to exploit them.[21]

In the Iranian case, the Ayatollah Khomeini and his mullahs did not plan the revolution of 1978–79. In fact, Khomeini seems to have been as surprised by it, at least initially, as Lenin was by the February revolution of 1917. Khomeini did not plan the Carter human rights policy or the shah's cancer. He did not organize the predominantly secular protests of 1977 or even most of the religious processions early in 1978. Many of his ulama supporters in Iran at this time were in prison. Some of his closest associates reportedly even tried to prevent protests after the publication of the infamous article vilifying Khomeini in January 1978. But thousands of religious students, mullahs, and bazaaris nevertheless staged a huge demonstration in Qum on January 9, during which at least nine people were killed. This demonstration started the cycle of martyrdom and mourning that evolved into Iran's Islamic revolution. Khomeini did not write the article that triggered all this turmoil, nor did he induce Iran's leading newspaper to publish it. The shah's own bureaucrats took care of that.[22]

Obviously demonstrations and mourning marches do not occur without some planning, but they are not necessarily part of a well-orchestrated plan to overthrow a government—and even such well-orchestrated plans do not entail success. Khomeini's followers had periodically engaged in protest marches ever since the riots of 1963 without ever seriously threatening the shah. Only the specific social and political situation of the late seventies enabled Khomeini to achieve his goal of an Islamic revolution.

Khomeini's organizing and tactical skills were certainly crucial in the fall of 1978, when his intransigent refusal to endorse any compromises with the shah entailed the downfall of the latter—much as Lenin's intransigence led to the October coup of 1917. But in the early stages of Iran's Islamic revolution, Khomeini was more important as a symbol than as an organizer.[23]

CONCLUSION

The basic grievances of politically conscious Iranians in the late seventies—notably resentment of foreign domination, authoritarian rule, and the violation of traditional values—existed elsewhere in the Middle East. But the Sunni fundamentalist movements were, typically, student and middle-class movements divorced from popular religious sensibility. To a large extent this was also true of the radical wing of Iran's Islamic movement influenced by Shari'ati, which could never have overthrown the shah on its own—even though Khomeini and the mullahs could not have overthrown the shah without it.

Khomeini and the mullahs of Iran were a part of everyday urban religious belief and practice in a way that Sunni fundamentalists were not. And because of his position as deputy of the hidden imam, his history of struggle against the shah and foreign domination, and his identification with some of the principal symbols and values of Shi'i Islam, Khomeini attained a far greater degree of charismatic authority than any other Muslim fundamentalist of the late twentieth century. His messianic aura enabled him to mobilize segments of Iranian (urban) society that had traditionally been apolitical and acquiescent.

Thus was he able to exploit the crisis of the Pahlavi regime in the late seventies.

There are Sunni ulama, notably Hafiz Salama of Egypt, who could seemingly play comparable roles. But they would never be able to command the obedience of a Shi'i ayatollah. Nor would they be able to tap the same millenarian yearning. And they were in fact remarkably ineffective in the late seventies and early eighties despite the tremendous enthusiasm generated by Iran's revolution. It is true that Iran's Islamic movement seemed as impotent in 1977 as do most Sunni movements in the 1980s, and yet by February of 1979, Khomeini was in power. So one cannot assume that the present weakness of the Sunni fundamentalist movements is permanent. But the fact remains that despite decades of effort, none of them has been able to mount a full-fledged revolution. A handful of men with guns can kill a president or seize a mosque. A revolution requires more.

Syria's Sunni fundamentalists did appear to be on the verge of leading an Islamic revolution in the early 1980s. And the Syrian Muslim Brotherhood certainly did articulate widespread grievances, both secular and religious, as did Khomeini in Iran. But even at the height of its campaign against al-Asad, the Brotherhood was relatively weak in Damascus, where many Sunni shopkeepers were doing well. Tehran, on the other hand, was the nerve center of Iran's revolution. Moreover, many of the strikes and demonstrations of March 1980 were actually organized by secular opponents of al-Asad rather than by the Brotherhood itself, which was never able to mobilize the majority of Syrian Sunnis. Khomeini, on the other hand, did eventually mobilize the majority of Iranian Shi'is—in the cities at any rate.

It is also possible that a crucial distinction between Iran and Syria was the greater and/or more effective use of force in the latter country. The shah might have been able to abort the revolution in early 1978 by having his troops use tear gas and other nonlethal weapons so as to avoid creating more martyrs. Or, alternatively, he might have been able to cripple the opposition by the more consistent style of slaughter for which al-Asad is renowned. There is no way of knowing.

But one point is clear. Force can be used to abort revolutions only before they have gained momentum. Once the ancien régime is perceived to be desperately floundering, it is finished. And by the fall of 1978, in the wake of the rage provoked by Black Friday, the shah's regime was finished. By the time Washington began to realize this,

Muhammad Reza Pahlavi was already virtually a prisoner in his own palace. Government had in effect ceased to exist since most civil servants were on strike. The army was still largely intact, but even here there were more and more desertions and even some mutinies. It is not clear to what extent the shah could still count on his troops to fire at huge crowds of unarmed demonstrators led by venerated holy men. (How long could Catholic troops fire at unarmed crowds led by priests?) In the winter of 1978, a more judicious display of force might have saved the Pahlavi regime. But by the fall of 1978, things had gone too far. Structures of authority had been too severely challenged. Patterns of fearful acquiescence had been too badly shaken.[24]

There are those who believe that the primary lesson to be learned from Iran's revolution, insofar as American foreign policy is concerned, is that right-wing dictators should never be pressured to reform. And it is true that such pressure has to be exerted discreetly, and not when a regime is on the verge of being overthrown by Marxists or Muslim fundamentalists. If, however, the politically conscious people of Iran had been able to express themselves freely in the sixties and seventies, many of them would never have joined forces with Khomeini. And if the ruler of Iran had not been perceived as an American flunky, a basic source of the discontent tapped by Khomeini would have been absent.

Discontent does not entail revolution, but revolution does entail discontent, a great deal of it. And like the Marxist revolutions of the third world, Iran's Islamic revolution was, to a large extent, the result of nationalistic resentment of foreign domination. How could politically conscious Iranians *not* resent a king who owed his throne to the CIA? How could any Iranian patriot not despise a king who, in January 1979, told the highest ranking generals of his country to "obey" a visiting American general (Huyser) after he himself had fled to Egypt?[25]

On January 14, 1979, a member of the Iranian National Assembly, which had been a rubber stamp of the shah's since 1953, declared: "Mr. Prime Minister, I must inform you that Iran's national independence is shouldered by the Iranian people and the Iranian Army. It has nothing to do with General Huyser." Commenting on this statement, General Huyser writes, "I didn't like this anti-American feeling within the parliament."[26] But how would General Huyser feel if an

American president who had been put in office by a foreign power had told the Joint Chiefs of Staff to obey a general of that foreign power's air force? Like many of the people who have shaped American foreign policy, General Huyser seems to think that patriotism is a uniquely American sentiment. It is not.

Instead of overthrowing and undermining the Musaddiqs of the third world, the United States should do everything possible to assist them. Such people embody the nationalist sentiments of their politically conscious compatriots as well as many of the values that are basic to American society, certainly much more so than the shahs and the Somozas—not to mention the Khomeinis and the Ortegas. By strengthening them, the United States weakens the appeal of inimical alternatives (such as Marxism and Muslim fundamentalism). Unless American foreign policy becomes more sensitive to the nationalist aspirations of third world peoples, it will continue to strengthen the very forces it is designed to oppose. *That* is the most important lesson American policymakers should have learned from Iran. But they have not.

Notes

1 Organization of Iranian Moslem Students, *The Rise*, 14. (Although this pamphlet was first printed in 1977, the anthology in which it appears was published in 1979.)
2 Khomeini, *Islam and Revolution*, 276.
3 The term *fundamentalist* actually dates only from early twentieth-century American Protestantism. See Falwell, *The Fundamentalist Phenomenon*, 3. But I use it to characterize religious movements of earlier eras as well as other religions. On radicalism in the Puritan Revolution and in the Reformation generally, see McGregor and Reay, *Radical Religion in the English Revolution*, and Williams, *The Radical Reformation*.
4 *al-Jama'a: Majalla Islamiyya*, no. 2 (June–August 1979): 123. (This is a Moroccan review.)
5 Abramov, *Perpetual Dilemma*, 193, 230, 233.
6 Beeman, "Images of the Great Satan"; Ahmad, "Islamic Revival in Pakistan"; West, "The Security Setting," 39.
7 Kepel, *Le prophète et pharaon*; Ansari, "Jamaat-i-Islami"; Bakhash, *The Reign of the Ayatollahs*, 138, 142–43, 220. See also Batatu, "Syria's Muslim Brethren," 14–15, 19; idem, "Shi'i Organizations in Iraq," 179, 191–94, 198–99; Dekmejian, *Islam in Revolution*, 72–73, 113–14, 122–23, 135; Munson, "The Social Base," 267–69, 281; idem, "Islamic Revivalism," 203–18; Shahrani, "Introduction," 44–52.
8 On opposition to foreign domination, compare Khomeini, *Islam and Revolution*, and Maududi, *Fundamentals of Islam*. On private property, compare Shariati, *On the Sociology of Islam*, 98–110; and Abd-Allah, *The Islamic Struggle in Syria*, 163, 221. On Saudi and Iranian support, see

Heikal, *Autumn of Fury,* 116; Ramazani, *Revolutionary Iran,* 32–53; Wright, *Sacred Rage,* 26–36.

9 On fundamentalist condemnation of sectarian and national divisions among Muslims, see al-Banna, *Majmu'at,* 109–10, 209; Khomeini, *Islam and Revolution,* 48–49, 302. On Iranian support for Shi'i movements, see Ramazani, *Revolutionary Iran,* 32–53; Wright, *Sacred Rage,* 26–36, 116–19, 126–27. On Saudi support for Sunni moderates, see any issue of the Saudi-financed magazine *Arabia,* which is published in London.

CHAPTER 2

1 See Munson, "Geertz on Religion."
2 Eliade, *Aspects du mythe,* 9–18.
3 See Oates, *Let the Trumpet Sound,* 79.
4 Quran 2:35–38, 6:84–90, 7:35–36, 54, 11 (Hud).
5 Quran 3:23, 4:44–46, 5:47–50, 13:39, 43:4.
6 Waugh, "The Popular Muhammad"; Ibn Ishaq, *The Life of Muhammad,* xiii.
7 Munson, "Islam and Inequality in Northwest Morocco," 92. In the following chapter we shall see that in Shi'i Islam, the prophet Muhammad's role as intercessor has been largely supplanted by that of Imam Husayn.
8 Quran 96:1–5.
9 Martin, *Islam,* 33; Ibn Ishaq, *The Life of Muhammad,* 106.
10 Quran 80:24–32; Fischer, *Iran,* 289.
11 Quran 80:38–42.
12 Shariati, *The Visage of Muhammad,* 12. For a less radical fundamentalist view of Muhammad, see Qutb, *Ma'alim fi 'l-Tariq,* 25–26.
13 See Boff, *Jesus Christ Liberator.* Radical Islamic activists almost invariably deny that they have been influenced by Marxism. I have heard such activists (who are usually students) assert that if there are similarities between the ideas of Shari'ati and Marx, it is because the latter borrowed some ideas from Islam.
14 Ibn Ishaq, *The Life of Muhammad,* 118–94.
15 Qutb, *Ma'alim fi 'l-Tariq,* 29.
16 Ibid., 32–35; Imam Khomeini, *Islam and Revolution,* 38.
17 Ibn Ishaq, *The Life of Muhammad,* 45–60, 289–311, 370–401. Quran 8:17, 3:152–54. "Badr" was the code name for the crossing of the Suez Canal by Egyptian troops during the 1973 October War.
18 Ibn Ishaq, *The Life of Muhammad,* 546–54; Hodgson, *The Venture of Islam,* 1:202; Qutb, *Ma'alim fi 'l-Tariq,* 14, 30.
19 Qutb, *Ma'alim fi 'l-Tariq,* 157.
20 al-Khumayni, *Durus,* 156–57.
21 Munson, *The House of Si Abd Allah,* 68.
22 Haddad, "The Arab-Israeli Wars," 119; Voll, *Islam,* 7, 88; Dekmejian, *Islam in Revolution,* 9–19.

23 Lewy, *Religion and Revolution*, 76–79.
24 Falwell, *Listen America!*, 18.
25 Munson, *The House of Si Abd Allah*, 69.
26 Quran 2:155–57.
27 Quran 13:11; Shariati, *On the Sociology of Islam*, 50.
28 Watt, "Islamic Conceptions of the Holy War," 150–52; Qutb, *Ma'alim fi 'l-Tariq*, 58; Heikal, *Autumn of Fury*, 221; Khomeini, *Islam and Revolution*, 46; Stillman, *The Jews of Arab Lands*. On the notion of holy war in the Torah-cum-Old Testament, see Aho, *Religious Mythology*, 165–81; Greenspoon, "The Warrior God"; Lind, "Paradigm of Holy War."
29 Qutb, *Ma'alim fi 'l-Tariq*, 58–59, 136; Maududi, *Fundamentals of Islam*, 243–49; Peters, *Islam and Colonialism*, 118.

CHAPTER 3

1 Ervand Abrahamian estimates that about 83 percent of all Iranians are Shi'is. See Abrahamian, "Social Bases of Iranian Politics," 13. Yann Richard estimates that 84 percent of all Iranians are Shi'is and that 88 percent of the world's Muslims are Sunnis. See Richard, *Le Shi'isme en Iran*, 8. Moojan Momen estimates that 88 percent of all Iranians are Shi'is and 90 percent of the world's Muslims (723 million in 1980) are Sunnis. See Momen, *An Introduction to Shi'i Islam*, 282. All such estimates are highly speculative since censuses in the Islamic world do not usually distinguish between Sunni and Shi'i Muslims.
2 On Iraq, see Batatu, *The Old Social Classes*, 40; idem, "Shi'i Organizations in Iraq." On Bahrain, see Bill, "Resurgent Islam," 116, 120; Ramazani, *Revolutionary Iran*, 48–53, 259.
3 Norton, "Shi'ism and Social Protest," 159; Goldberg, "The Shi'i Minority," 230. Some scholars estimate that Twelver Shi'is actually constitute nearly 40 percent of Lebanon's population. See Ajami, *The Vanished Imam*, 189.
4 al-Banna, *Majmu'at*, 207; Qutb, *Ma'alim fi 'l-Tariq*, 14, 30; Khomeini, *Islam and Revolution*, 55–58.
5 al-Banna, *Majmu'at*, 207–11; Khomeini, *Islam and Revolution*, 38.
6 Arjomand, *The Shadow of God*, 35, 38.
7 Sachedina, *Islamic Messianism*, 5.
8 Akhavi, *Religion and Politics*, 231.
9 Ibid.
10 Ibid.
11 Fischer, *Iran*, 6; Kamal, *The Prescribed Prayers*, 40; Khomeini, *A Clarification of Questions*, 196–97; Rentz, "Wahhabism and Saudi Arabia," 64; al-Banna, *Majmu'at*.
12 Fischer, *Iran*, 6, 291.
13 Ibid., 6.
14 Ibid., 177–78; idem, "Imam Khomeini," 164; Arjomand, "Shi'ite Islam and the Revolution in Iran," 307–08; Taheri, *The Spirit of Allah*, 238.

15 Heikal, *Iran: The Untold Story*, 177.
16 Ibn Ishaq, *The Life of Muhammad*, 79, 114.
17 Tabataba'i, *Shi'ite Islam*, 53.
18 Hodgson, *Venture of Islam*, 1:214.
19 *Shorter Encyclopaedia of Islam*, s.v. "Kharidjites."
20 Ibid.
21 Tabataba'i, *Shi'ite Islam*, 192; Khomeini, *Islam and Revolution*, 18.
22 Eickelman, "From Theocracy to Monarchy."
23 Mitchell, *The Society of the Muslim Brothers*, 320.
24 al-Ghannushi, *Maqalat*, 88; Tabataba'i, *Shi'ite Islam*, 195–96; Momen, *An Introduction to Shi'i Islam*, 28.
25 Tabataba'i, Shi'ite Islam, 195–200.
26 Fischer, *Iran*, 20.
27 Ibid., 204.
28 Ayoub, *Redemptive Suffering in Islam*, 142–43, 184; Fernea and Fernea, "Variation in Religious Observance," 391–94.
29 Hegland, "Two Images of Husain," 221–23.
30 Khomeini, *Islam and Revolution*, 242.
31 Akhavi, *Religion and Politics*, 231.
32 Algar, *Religion and State*, 252.
33 Thaiss, "Religious Symbolism and Social Change," 351–52.
34 Ibid., 359–60.
35 Enayat, *Modern Islamic Political Thought*, 25.
36 Tabataba'i, *Shi'ite Islam*, 190–211; Sachedina, *Islamic Messianism*, 3.
37 Sachedina, *Islamic Messianism*, 9–13; Voll, *Islam*, 138; Al-Yassini, *Religion and State*, 124–29. On messianism in Judaism, Christianity, and other religions, see Sharot, *Messianism, Mysticism, and Magic*; Cohn, *The Pursuit of the Millennium*; Thrupp, *Millennial Dreams in Action*; Worsley, *The Trumpet Shall Sound*.
38 Khomeini, *Islam and Revolution*, 326–27.
39 Arjomand, *The Shadow of God*, 34.
40 Ibid., 22–23.
41 Algar, *Religion and State*, 2.

CHAPTER 4

1 Kamal, *The Prescribed Prayers*, 39–40; Khomeini, *A Clarification of Questions*, 196. Both these sources agree that a woman can serve as imam for a group composed exclusively of women, but public prayers are primarily male activities with male imams.
2 For an overview of the ulama, see Keddie, *Scholars, Saints and Sufis*. On Sunni ulama in Morocco, see Eickelman, *Knowledge and Power in Morocco*, and Brown, *People of Salé*.
3 Arjomand, *The Shadow of God*, 78–82, 109.
4 Ibid., 181; Momen, *An Introduction to Shi'i Islam*, 107–08.

5 Momen, *An Introduction to Shi'i Islam*, 108, 114–16.
6 Ibid., 124–25; Arjomand, *The Shadow of God*, 215–17.
7 Fischer, *Iran*, 109–12; Keddie, *Roots of Revolution*, 21.
8 Keddie, "The Roots of the Ulama's Power," 222–24.
9 Eliash, "Some Misconceptions," 13–15.
10 Arjomand, *The Shadow of God*, 247; Binder, "The Proofs of Islam," 118–40. Nikki Keddie notes that the mujtahids appear to be less significant among the Twelver Shi'is of Pakistan and Lebanon than among those of Iran and, less obviously, Iraq (comment on this manuscript, Feb. 27, 1987). I have myself spoken with a Pakistani Twelver Shi'i who had never heard of the terms *mujtahid* or *marja'-i taqlid*. On Lebanon, see Ajami, *The Vanished Imam*; Gilsenan, *Recognizing Islam*; and Norton, "Shi'ism and Social Protest."
11 Fischer, *Iran*, 88.
12 Momen, *An Introduction to Shi'i Islam*, 188, 205.
13 Eliash, "Some Misconceptions," 18–20.
14 Ajami. *The Vanished Imam*, 107; Arjomand, *The Shadow of God*, 247–48; Khomeini, *A Clarification of Questions*, 242.
15 Khomeini, *A Clarification of Questions*, 242, 254.
16 Fischer, *Iran*, 86–87.
17 Mottahedeh, *The Mantle of the Prophet*, 251.
18 On the notion of charismatic authority, see Weber, *Economy and Society*, 215, 241–45, 111–57.
19 Arjomand, *The Shadow of God*, 138.
20 Algar, *Religion and State*, 88.
21 Ibid., 89.
22 Gellner, *Muslim Society*, 1–85.
23 Akhavi, *Religion and Politics*, 21–22; Enayat, *Modern Islamic Political Thought*, 29–30.
24 Gellner, *Saints of the Atlas*, 7–11.
25 See Eickelman, *Moroccan Islam*; Gilsenan, *Recognizing Islam*, 9–11, 62–71, 251–54; Hegland, "Two Images of Husain," 218–35; Mazzaoui, "Shi'ism and Ashura," 230–34; Munson, *The House of Si Abd Allah*, 36–39.
26 Fischer, *Iran*, 87; idem, "Imam Khomeini," 152.
27 Personal communications, Reza Sheikholislami and Bahman Bakhtiari, March 1987.
28 On reformist and fundamentalist opposition to popular Sunni Islam, see Gellner, *Muslim Society*.
29 The anthropological evidence on this score is abundant. See Crapanzano, *The Hamadsha*; Gilsenan, *Recognizing Islam*; Munson, *The House of Si Abd Allah*; Rabinow, *Symbolic Domination*.
30 al-Banna, *Majmu'at*, 228.
31 Arjomand, *The Shadow of God*, 32–34.

32 I have heard fundamentalist students (both Sunni and Shi'i) speak of Sadat, Hasan, and Fahd as "infidels." For the "merchants of oil" statement, see Munson, "Islamic Revivalism," 204.
33 I have heard devoutly religious Muslims from Egypt, Iran, and Morocco characterize militant fundamentalists as "crazy."
34 Bayat, "The Iranian Revolution of 1978–79," 30–42.

CHAPTER 5

1 See Keddie, *Religion and Rebellion in Iran.*
2 Keddie, *Iran: Religion, Politics and Society,* 58.
3 Keddie, *Sayyid Jamal ad-Din al-Afghani*; Kedourie, *Afghani and Abduh.*
4 Keddie, *Roots of Revolution,* 70–73; Abrahamian, *Iran between Two Revolutions,* 81–82.
5 Abrahamian, *Iran between Two Revolutions,* 83.
6 Ibid.; Arjomand, "The Ulama's Traditionalist Opposition," 177.
7 Abrahamian, *Iran between Two Revolutions,* 83–85.
8 Ibid., 85.
9 Bagley, "New Light," 51.
10 Abrahamian, *Iran between Two Revolutions,* 87–92; Browne, *The Persian Revolution,* 355–56, 372–77.
11 Arjomand, "The Ulama's Traditionalist Opposition," 179.
12 Ibid., 180–81; Abrahamian, *Iran between Two Revolutions,* 97.
13 Abrahamian, *Iran between Two Revolutions,* 94–100; Arjomand, "The Ulama's Traditionalist Opposition," 182–84.
14 Arjomand, "The Ulama's Traditionalist Opposition," 184–87.
15 Abrahamian, *Iran between Two Revolutions,* 102–10.
16 Ibid., 112.
17 Cottam, *Nationalism in Iran,* 102–06; Keddie, *Roots of Revolution,* 88.
18 Abrahamian, *Iran between Two Revolutions,* 131.
19 Akhavi, *Religion and Politics,* 29–30; Mardin, "Religion and Politics," 142–43.
20 Abrahamian, *Iran between Two Revolutions,* 134. For Khomeini's contention that monarchies are contrary to Islam, see Khomeini, *Islam and Revolution,* 31, 47, 200, 202.
21 Elwell-Sutton, "Reza Shah the Great," 37; Katouzian, *The Political Economy,* 91.
22 Akhavi, *Religion and Politics,* 32–59.
23 Katouzian, *The Political Economy,* 126.
24 Baraheni, *The Crowned Cannibals,* 52.
25 Akhavi, *Religion and Politics,* 44.
26 Fischer, *Iran,* 98–99.
27 Abrahamian, *Iran between Two Revolutions,* 135–65.
28 Avery, *Modern Iran,* 330.

29 Keddie, *Roots of Revolution*, 114–17; Lenczowski, *Russia and the West*, 176, 263–74.

30 Lenczowski, *Russia and the West*, 216–23, 286–312.

31 Akhavi, *Religion and Politics*, 63.

32 Ibid., 63–64; Richard, "Ayatollah Kashani," 120. Akhavi says this conference took place in 1949, but Richard says that he is mistaken and that it was actually 1950.

33 Kazemi, "The *Fada'iyan-e Islam*," 162–65; Richard, "Ayatollah Kashani," 109–10.

34 Abrahamian, *Iran between Two Revolutions*, 250–61.

35 Ibid., 276; Akhavi, *Religion and Politics*, 69–71.

36 This and the following quotations are from Cottam, *Nationalism in Iran*, 212–13.

37 Ibid., 212–16. See Roosevelt, *Countercoup*.

38 Abrahamian, *Iran between Two Revolutions*, 270–80, 320–21.

39 Ibid., 279–80, 324–25; Cottam, *Nationalism in Iran*, 225–26.

40 Akhavi, *Religion and Politics*, 69; Cottam, *Nationalism in Iran*, 155; Richard, "Ayatollah Kashani," 116; Roosevelt, *Countercoup*, 71.

41 On parallels between the Musaddiq period and the constitutional revolution, see Abrahamian, *Iran between Two Revolutions*, 100–07, 275–78. On the loyalty of some ulama to Musaddiq after his split with Kashani, see Akhavi, *Religion and Politics*, 69; Richard "Ayatollah Kashani," 117.

42 Keddie, *Roots of Revolution*, 134–41.

43 Abrahamian, *Iran between Two Revolutions*, 419–21; Keddie, *Roots of Revolution*, 144; Akhavi, *Religion and Politics*, 72–90.

44 Cottam, *Nationalism in Iran*, 297–307; Katouzian, *The Political Economy*, 213–17.

45 Cottam, *Nationalism in Iran*, 306–07; Zonis, *The Political Elite of Iran*, 72–77.

46 Keddie, *Roots of Revolution*, 156, 158–59; Floor, "The Revolutionary Character," 77–88; Tabari, "The Role of the Clergy," 66–67.

47 al-Khumayni, *Durus*, 52–59; Khomeini, *Islam and Revolution*, 177–80; Zonis, *The Political Elite of Iran*, 45.

48 Taheri, *The Spirit of Allah*, 143.

49 Katouzian, *The Political Economy*, 228; Tabari, "The Role of the Clergy," 69–70.

50 Keddie, *Roots of Revolution*, 158; al-Khumayni, *Durus*, 51.

51 Zonis, *The Political Elite of Iran*, 45.

52 al-Khumayni, *Durus*, 106.

53 Ibid., 107.

54 Keddie, *Roots of Revolution*, 159.

55 Ibid., 159–60; Akhavi, *Religion and Politics*, 161–62.

56 Akhavi, *Religion and Politics*, 110–16; Richard, "Modern Iranian Political Thought," 213–15.

57 Akhavi, *Religion and Politics*, 143–58; 231–33; Sachedina, "Ali Shariati,"

58 Abrahamian, "The Guerrilla Movement in Iran," 10.

59 Abrahamian, *Iran between Two Revolutions*, 489–95.

60 On the economic crisis, see Graham, *Iran*; Pesaran, "Economic Development," 31–34.

61 Zabih, *Iran's Revolutionary Upheaval*, 49.

62 I have often heard this view expressed by both Marxist and radical Islamic Iranian students.

63 Graham, *Iran*, 256.

64 Abrahamian, *Iran between Two Revolutions*, 503–05; Behrang, *Iran*, 38–43; Balta and Rulleau, *L'Iran insurgé*, 22–23; Fischer, *Iran*, 192–93.

65 Taheri, *The Spirit of Allah*, 182–83.

66 Ibid.; personal communication from Bahman Bakhtiari, April 1987.

67 Pahlavi, *Answer to History*, 152–53.

68 Abrahamian, *Iran between Two Revolutions*, 505; Fischer, *Iran*, 194; Taheri, *The Spirit of Allah*, 200–01. Taheri claims that the article was actually a letter to the editor. But, in a comment on this manuscript, Bahman Bakhtiari assures me that he is mistaken.

69 Taheri, *The Spirit of Allah*, 201.

70 Keddie, *Roots of Revolution*, 243.

71 Fischer, *Iran*, 195; Sheikholislami, "From Religious Accommodation to Religious Revolution," 229.

72 Behrang, *Iran*, 50–51; Fischer, *Iran*, 195.

73 Fischer, *Iran*, 195–96.

74 Ibid., 197; Balta and Rulleau, *L'Iran insurgé*, 26; Green, *Revolution in Iran*, 96.

75 Fischer, *Iran*, 198.

76 Ibid., 198–99; Berges, "Eyewitness Report from Martyrs' Square," 197–200.

77 Behrang, *Iran*, 50–54. The question of the social composition of the shah's opposition is discussed in chapter 9.

78 Abrahamian, *Iran between Two Revolutions*, 517–18; Fischer, *Iran*, 199–201; Green, *Revolution in Iran*, 104–27; Taheri, *The Spirit of Allah*, 233–34. Taheri claims that middle- and upper-class Iranians sent $2.6 billion abroad in the last three months of 1978 on the basis of an estimate of the Central Bank of Iran made in February 1979. Bakhash, also using figures from the Central Bank, says that over $4 billion in savings were transferred out of Iran between September 1978 and January 1979. See Bakhash, *The Reign of the Ayatollahs*, 176.

79 Green, *Revolution in Iran*, 103–04.

80 Abrahamian, *Iran between Two Revolutions*, 521; Balta and Rulleau, *L'Iran insurgé*, 57.

81 Balta and Rulleau, *L'Iran insurgé*, 57–63; Brière and Blanchet, *Iran*, 104–07; Fischer, *Iran*, 205.

82 Balta and Rulleau, *L'Iran insurgé*, 61–62; Brière and Blanchet, 106; Fischer, *Iran*, 205. For other slogans, see Bakhash, "Sermons, Revolutionary Pamphleteering and Mobilisation" and Taheri, *The Spirit of Allah*, 321–22.

83 Fischer, *Iran*, 207, 211–12; Green, *Revolution in Iran*, 134–41; Keddie, *Roots of Revolution*, 253. On American attempts to arrange a compromise with National Front moderates, see Sick, *All Fall Down*; Sullivan, *Mission to Iran*. Seats on the jumbo jet bringing Khomeini back to Iran were sold to reporters to finance the flight. See Rubin, *Paved with Good Intentions*, 248.

84 Abrahamian, *Iran between Two Revolutions*, 527–29; Balta and Rulleau, *L'Iran insurgé*, 89–96; Mottahedeh, *The Mantle of the Prophet*, 12.

85 I have spoken with many Iranian intellectuals who strongly supported the revolution on the assumption that Khomeini would withdraw from the political arena once the shah had been overthrown. And Khomeini and his aides led Western reporters as well as Westernized Iranians to believe that he would do just that. See Sciolino, "Iran's Durable Revolution," 894.

86 The unraveling of the revolutionary coalition and the fate of the opposition to the Khomeini regime are well described in Bakhash, *The Reign of the Ayatollahs*; Hiro, *Iran under the Ayatollahs*; and Zabih, *Iran since the Revolution*. The opposition of mujtahids and other ulama to Khomeini's concept of Islamic government is described in Akhavi, "Clerical Politics since 1979," and Momen, *An Introduction to Shi'i Islam*, 291, 295–99.

87 See Bakhash, *The Reign of the Ayatollahs*.

CHAPTER 6

1 Rentz, "Wahhabism and Saudi Arabia," 55–57.

2 Ibid., 61–63.

3 Philby, *Sa'udi Arabia*, 274.

4 Ibid., 4, 261–62; Habib, *Ibn Sa'ud's Warriors*, 21–22, 50–51; Kostiner, "On Instruments and Their Designers," 299.

5 Philby, *Arabian Jubilee*, 89. Some of those who threw stones at the procession may have been non-Ikhwan pilgrims from the Najd, where the puritanical Wahhabi ethos had much deeper roots than it did in the more cosmopolitan Hijaz, where Mecca, Madina, and the port of Jidda are situated.

6 Habib, *Ibn Sa'ud's Warriors*, 122.

7 Layish, "'Ulama' and Politics," 47.

8 Ibid., 47; Habib, *Ibn Sa'ud's Warriors*, 123.

9 Glubb, *War in the Desert*, 193; Habib, *Ibn Sa'ud's Warriors*, 125–26.

10 Glubb, *War in the Desert*, 266, 281–96, 341.

11 Safran, *Saudi Arabia*, 60.

12 Lackner, *A House Built on Sand*, 96–98; Buchan, "Secular and Religious Opposition," 112–13.

13 Lackner, *A House Built on Sand,* 90–95, 98–106; Buchan, "Secular and Religious Opposition," 116; Dhaouadi and Ibrahim, "Documents," 68–69.

14 Lacey, *The Kingdom,* 368–71; Holden and Johns, *The House of Saud,* 261–62. For a slightly different version of the attack on the television station, see Huyette, *Political Adaptation in Sa'udi Arabia,* 74.

15 Buchan, "The Return of the Ikhwan," 511–26; Lacey, *The Kingdom,* 481–83.

16 Buchan, "The Return of the Ikhwan," 518; idem, "Secular and Religious Opposition," 122; Holden and Johns, *The House of Saud,* 262; Al-Yassini, *Religion and State,* 125.

17 Buchan, "The Return of the Ikhwan," 513, 522–23; Lacey, *The Kingdom,* 478; Layish, "*'Ulama'* and Politics," 50–51; Mortimer, *Faith and Power,* 182; al-Yassini, *Religion and State,* 125.

18 Lacey, *The Kingdom,* 487.

19 Buchan, "The Return of the Ikhwan," 525–26; Holden and Johns, *The House of Saud,* 527–28; al-Yassini, *Religion and State,* 124–25.

20 Wright, *Sacred Rage,* 148–49.

21 Ibid., 149; Holden and Johns, *The House of Saud,* 528.

22 Buchan, "Secular and Religious Opposition," 119. In speaking of the Shi'is of Saudi Arabia, I refer exclusively to Twelver Shi'is. There are also other less significant Shi'i minorities (Isma'ilis and Zaidis) in Saudi Arabia.

23 Buchan, "The Return of the Ikhwan," 525; Goldberg, "The Shi'i Minority," 239–41.

24 There are no reliable published census data for Saudi Arabia. Three economists who have studied the Saudi labor force estimate that in 1980 there were about 5.5 million Saudi citizens and 2.5 million foreign workers. See Sirageldin, Sherbiny, and Sirageldin, *Saudis in Transition,* 32. Jacob Goldberg estimates a (citizen?) population of 6 million in the early eighties, with about 6 percent Shi'is. See Goldberg, "The Shi'i Minority," 230. Ghassane Salameh estimates 4 million to 4.5 million Saudi citizens in 1980, including some 200,000 Shi'is (4–5 percent). See Salameh, "Political Power," 13. Estimates of the percentage of Shi'is in ARAMCO's work force also vary. Goldberg states that "during the 1970s it was estimated that over 25 percent of the workers in the oil fields were Shi'is" (p. 237). But a few pages later, he writes that in 1979, "seven thousand of ARAMCO's Saudi workers (35 percent of the local work force) were Shi'is" (p. 242). The earlier statement could refer to the foreign as well as the Saudi work force. But James Piscatori says that Shi'is constitute 35 percent of ARAMCO's work force as a whole. See Piscatori, "Ideological Politics in Sa'udi Arabia," 67. R. K. Ramazani writes that "the Shias are concentrated in the oil-rich al-Hasa Province, where they constitute between 40 and 60 percent of the work force in the nation's vital oil industry." See Ramazani, *Revolutionary Iran,* 39. James Bill contends that al-Hasa Province is 55 to 60 percent Shi'i. See Bill, "Resurgent Islam," 120. The sources of these various esti-

mates are not given. But it would appear that at least 35 percent of AR-AMCO's work force is Shi'i.

25 Philby, *Sa'udi Arabia,* 93.
26 Ibid., 96–97; Goldberg, "The Shi'i Minority," 236–37; Habib, "Ibn Sa'ud's Warriors," 122–24.
27 Goldberg, "The Shi'i Minority," 238–41; Holden and Johns, *The House of Saud,* 531.
28 Goldberg, "The Shi'i Minority," 243–45; Quandt, *Saudi Arabia in the 1980s,* 39–40, 96–97.
29 Al-Yassini, *Religion and State,* 123. See also Dhaouadi and Ibrahim, "Documents," 60–71. Iranian pilgrims to Mecca have repeatedly distributed such tracts.
30 Quandt, *Saudi Arabia in the 1980s,* 39–40; Wright, *Sacred Rage,* 156–60, 171; al-Yassini, *Religion and State,* 123.
31 Kay, "Social Change," 177–82; Salameh, "Political Power," 18–19; Holden and Johns, *The House of Saud,* 519, 530.
32 Heller and Safran, "The New Middle Class"; Holden and Johns, *The House of Saud,* 530, 534–38.

CHAPTER 7

1 See Hourani, *Arabic Thought*; Keddie, *Sayyid Jamal ad-Din 'al-Afghani'*; Kedourie, *Afghani and Abduh*; Kerr, *Islamic Reform*; Safran, *Egypt.*
2 Safran, *Egypt,* 73–84, 101.
3 Berque, *Egypt,* 284, 304–21; Deeb, "The 1919 Popular Uprising."
4 Al-Banna, *Majmu'at,* 225. For al-Banna's life and the first two decades of the Brotherhood's existence, see Mitchell, *The Society,* 1–71.
5 Mitchell, *The Society,* 65–67, 72, 274–90, 328–30.
6 Ibid., 151, 153, 160–61; Vatikiotis, *Nasser and His Generation,* 15, 53.
7 Kepel, *Le prophète et pharaon,* 34–37.
8 Carré and Michaud, *Les frères musulmans,* 107–08; El Guindi, "Veiling Infitah," 467; Marsot, *A Short History,* 126.
9 Dekmejian, *Islam in Revolution,* 85–86.
10 Heikal, *Autumn of Fury,* 5, 205–06; Hinnebusch, "Children of the Elite," 546; Kepel, *Le prophète et pharaon,* 109–14; Marsot, *A Short History,* 136; Al-Mashat, "Egyptian Attitudes," 398–99.
11 Kepel, *Le prophète et pharaon,* 29; Sivan, *Radical Islam,* 144–45.
12 Kepel, *Le prophète et pharaon,* 106–08, 124; Sivan, *Radical Islam,* 139.
13 Ibrahim, "Anatomy," 425, 427, 435–40.
14 Ibid., 427, 436–40, 442, 450.
15 *al-Ahram,* May 9, 1982, 1, 6–7; May 10, 1982, 1, 6–7; Ansari, "The Islamic Militants," 133; *al-Jumhuriyya,* May 9, 1982,, 1, 5, 9–10; Kepel, *Le prophète et pharaon,* 204. See also Jansen, *The Neglected Duty.*
16 *al-Ahram,* May 9, 1982, 7; Ansari, "Islamic Militants," 126–30; Brière and Carré, *Islam, guerre à l'occident?,* 66–67.

17 Ansari, "Islamic Militants," 125, 135, 137–41; idem, "Sectarian Conflict, 406–07; Gaffney, "From University Campus to Mosque"; Kepel, *Le prophète et pharaon*, 165–82, 198–99.
18 Kepel, *Muslim Extremism in Egypt*, 241–50; *al-Sharq al-Awsat*, December 18, 1986, 1.
19 *Jeune Afrique*, no. 1372 (April 22, 1987): 17; Kepel, *Muslim Extremism in Egypt*, 247.
20 Kepel, *Muslim Extremism in Egypt*, 251–55.
21 Ansari, "The Islamic Militants," 143.
22 *al-Muslimun*, July 20–26, 1985, 1, 3; Kepel, *Muslim Extremism in Egypt*, 255.
23 *al-Muslimun*, July 20–26, 1985, 3; Kepel, *Muslim Extremism in Egypt*, 256.
24 *al-Sharq al-Awsat*, Nov. 29, 1985, 3.
25 Gaffney, "From University Campus to Mosque." On demonstrations by militant Islamic university students in the 1980s, see *al-Sharq al-Awsat*, Dec. 30, 1985; Jan. 12, 1986; April 2 and 5, 1986; Nov. 13, 21, and 25, 1986; Dec. 9 and 29, 1986, 1; Jan. 7, 1987; March 2 and 19, 1987.
26 On Egypt's economic crisis, see Waterbury, *Egypt*.

CHAPTER 8

 1 See Tibawi, *A Modern History of Syria*.
 2 Batatu, "Syria's Muslim Brethren," 17.
 3 Ibid., 14–19; Abd-Allah, *The Islamic Struggle*, 88–103.
 4 Petran, *Syria*, 89–91.
 5 Van Dam, *The Struggle for Power*, 15.
 6 Batatu, "Some Observations," 333–34; idem, "Syria's Muslim Brethren," 13–19; Drysdale, "The Asad Regime," 7.
 7 Petran, *Syria*, 174–75; Rabinovich, *Syria under the Ba'th*, 109–11; Tibawi, *A Modern History of Syria*, 415–16.
 8 Petran, *Syria*, 175–76; Rabinovich, *Syria under the Ba'th*, 111–17.
 9 Hinnebusch, "The Islamic Movement," 158–59; Petran, *Syria*, 177–79.
10 Carré and Michaud, *Les frères musulmans*, 133.
11 Lewis, "The Return of Islam," 25; Petran, *Syria*, 197–98.
12 Abd-Allah, *The Islamic Struggle*, 58–63; Petran, *Syria*, 199–201.
13 Abd-Allah, "The Islamic Struggle," 101–08.
14 Ibid., 105.
15 Ibid., 104–07; Sivan, *Radical Islam*, 45, 82, 114.
16 Van Dam, *The Struggle for Power*, 56–63, 83–94.
17 Picard, "La Syrie de 1946 à 1979," 168–71, 179.
18 Carré and Michaud, *Les frères musulmans*, 134; Raymond A. Hinnebusch, "The Islamic Movement," 161–62; Humphreys, "Islam and Political Values," 301.
19 Sivan, *Radical Islam*, 53.
20 For the Brotherhood's view of the 'Alawis as heretics, see Abd-Allah, *The*

Islamic Struggle, 42–48. On al-Asad's efforts to portray himself and the 'Alawis as good Muslims, see Batatu, "Some Observations," 335; Drysdale, "The Asad Regime," 8. On the hostility of some Sunni ulama toward al-Asad, see Abd-Allah, *The Islamic Struggle*, 111, 122–27; Sivan, *Radical Islam*, 54.

21 Abd-Allah, *The Islamic Struggle*, 108–09; Batatu, "Syria's Muslim Brethren," 20; Drysdale, "The Asad Regime," 8.

22 Abd-Allah, *The Islamic Struggle*, 58–63, 70–79.

23 Batatu, "Syria's Muslim Brethren," 20; Carré and Michaud, *Les frères musulmans*, 135; Drysdale, "The Asad Regime," 5–8; Hinnebusch, "The Islamic Movement," 162–64; Reed, "Dateline Syria," 176–77. Reed speaks of "some 60" cadets killed.

24 Carré and Michaud, *Les frères musulmans*, 136–37; Hinnebusch, "The Islamic Movement," 163–64.

25 Carré and Michaud, *Les frères musulmans*, 136, 142; Reed, "Dateline Syria," 177.

26 Abd-Allah, *The Islamic Struggle*, 111–13; Carré and Michaud, *Les frères musulmans*, 141–43; Drysdale, "The Asad Regime," 8; Hinnebusch, "The Islamic Movement," 164; Mortimer, *Faith and Power*, 267; Reed, "Dateline Syria," 181–82.

27 Carré and Michaud, *Les frères musulmans*, 145–46; Drysdale, "The Asad Regime," 8; Michaud, "The Importance of Bodyguards," 30; Reed, "Dateline Syria," 176.

28 Carré and Michaud, *Les frères musulmans*, 146–51; Drysdale, "The Asad Regime," 8; Michaud, "The Importance of Bodyguards," 30.

29 Abd-Allah, *The Islamic Struggle*, 114–17, 189; Carré and Michaud, *Les frères musulmans*, 151.

30 Abd-Allah, *The Islamic Struggle*, 191–93; Carré and Michaud, *Les frères musulmans*, 160; Lawson, "Social Bases," 24.

31 Drysdale, "The Asad Regime," 10.

32 Abd-Allah, *The Islamic Struggle*, 192–93; Carré and Michaud, *Les frères musulmans*, 159–60; Drysdale, "The Asad Regime," 9–10, 36.

33 *Jeune Afrique*, no. 1368 (March 25, 1987): 20.

34 Abd-Allah, *The Islamic Struggle*, 179–87, 194.

35 Ibid., 9–16, 179–87, 194. For the "American surrogate" view of Saudi Arabia, see pp. 65, 69, and 71 of Abd-Allah's book.

36 See Hirschfeld, "The Odd Couple."

37 Abd-Allah, *The Islamic Struggle*, 194–95; Carré and Michaud, *Les frères musulmans*, 160; Drysdale, "The Asad Regime," 9.

38 Abd-Allah, *The Islamic Struggle*, 195.

39 Sadowski, "Cadres, Guns, and Money," 4.

CHAPTER 9

1 Mannheim, *Essays on Sociology*, 74–77.

2 On Iran, see Fischer, *Iran*, 194–202. On Saudi Arabia, see Buchan, "Sec-

ular and Religious Opposition," 123. On Egypt, see Ibrahim, "Anatomy," 438–40. On Syria, see Batatu, "Syria's Muslim Brethren," 15. On the fact that Islamic militant students often study engineering and other applied scientific fields, see Abrahamian, *Iran between Two Revolutions*, 481, 492; Ibrahim, "Anatomy," 439–40; Sivan, *Radical Islam*, 119.

3 On the alienation of students by bullying tactics, see Abdalla, *The Student Movement*, 227–28, and Gaffney, "From University Campus to Mosque." On apolitical Islamic revivalists, see El Guindi, "The Emerging Islamic Order," 62.

4 On conflicts between Muslim fundamentalists and secular leftists, see Abdalla, *The Islamic Movement*, 193; Munson, "The Social Base," 271. I have myself observed heated debates between fundamentalist and Marxist students from Iran. On the apolitical "silent majority," see Abdalla, *The Student Movement*, 222, 232.

5 Abrahamian, *Iran between Two Revolutions*, 481, 489–92; Fischer, "Islam and the Revolt," 112–13.

6 Ibrahim, "Anatomy," 439. On the new middle class, see Halpern, *The Politics of Social Change*, 51–78.

7 Abdalla, *The Student Movement*, 223; Allman, *Social Mobility*, 78–79.

8 Abdalla, *The Student Movement*, 232.

9 Davis, "Ideology," 140–43; Mitchell, *The Society*, 328–30.

10 Mitchell, *The Society*, 330.

11 On middle-aged reformists elsewhere, see Batatu, "Syria's Muslim Brethren," 20; Richard, "Modern Iranian Political Thought," 213; Toprak, "Politicisation of Islam," 129–31.

12 Fischer, "Islam and the Revolt," 112–13. On Syria, see Batatu, "Syria's Muslim Brethren," 20. On Pakistan, see Sayeed, *Politics in Pakistan*, 157–61.

13 Ansari, "Sectarian Conflict," 415; Heikal, *Autumn of Fury*, 242–52; Ibrahim, "Anatomy," 439–40; Kepel, *Le prophète et pharaon*, 195–204.

14 Kepel, *Le prophète et pharaon*, 208. See *al-Jumhuriyya*, May 9, 1982, 5, 9, 10; and *Time*, October 15, 1984, 67.

15 Davis, "Ideology," 142–43; Mitchell, *The Society*, 328–30. Merchants and artisans are never mentioned in discussions of the social bases of Islamic movements in Morocco, Saudi Arabia, and Tunisia. See Buchan, "Secular and Religious Opposition"; Hermassi, "La société tunisienne," 41–44; Munson, "Morocco."

16 Abrahamian, *Iran between Two Revolutions*, 474.

17 Sivan, *Radical Islam*, 53.

18 Ibid., 13–14, 50–56, 83, 104–05.

19 Ibid. On Salama, see Ansari, "The Islamic Militants," 143, and *al-Muslimun*, July 20–26, 1985, 1, 3. On Shaykh Habbanaka, see Batatu, "Syria's Muslim Brethren," 19, and Hinnebusch, "The Islamic Movement," 151.

20 Abrahamian, *Iran between Two Revolutions*, 510; Ladan Boroumand, "Les

ouvriers," 61. Professor Bahman Bakhtiari has a number of documents indicating that strikes in the fall of 1978 were usually initiated by management personnel. Professor Reza Sheikholislami has stressed the same point (conversation with the author, April 1987).

21 Munson, *The House of Si Abd Allah*, 68, 260; idem, "Islamic Revivalism," 204.

22 The anomic migrant hypothesis is endorsed in the following works, all of which are otherwise excellent: Abrahamian, *Iran between Two Revolutions*, 535; Davis, "Ideology," 137, 144; Keddie, *Roots of Revolution*, 246. The hypothesis's inadequacy is demonstrated in the following works: Abu-Lughod, "Migrant Adjustment"; Kazemi, *Poverty and Revolution*; Nelson, *Access to Power*; Perlman, *The Myth of Marginality*.

23 Ibrahim, "Anatomy," 438–39.

24 Abu-Lughod, "Migrant Adjustment"; Ansari, "The Islamic Militants," 132; Kepel, *Le prophète et pharaon*, 208–12; Rugh, *Family in Contemporary Egypt*; Wikan, *Life among the Poor in Cairo*.

25 Bauer, "Poor Women and Social Consciousness," 161; Kazemi, *Poverty and Revolution*, 2, 71, 88, 94–96.

26 Bauer, "Poor Women and Social Consciousness," 161.

27 Kazemi, *Poverty and Revolution*, 95–96. On the nonrevolutionary character of the urban poor generally, see Huntington, *Political Order in Changing Societies*, 288, and Nelson, *Access to Power*, 12, 111, 135.

28 Ashraf and Banuazizi, "The State," 25; Beck, *The Qashqa'i of Iran*, 296–301; Goodell, *The Elementary Structures*, 343; Hegland, "Imam Khomeini's Village," 519–20, 563, 566, 843; Hooglund, *Land and Revolution*, 139–48.

29 On Egypt, see Heikal, *Autumn of Fury*, 242–55; *al-Sharq al-Awsat*, Dec. 5, 1986, 1; Dec. 11, 1986, 1; Dec. 12, 1986, 1. On Tunisia, see Munson, "Islamic Revivalism," 212. On Iran, see Green, *Revolution in Iran*, 119, 140–41, 144; Huyser, *Mission to Tehran*, 181, 187–88, 200, 217, 244. Green's eyewitness accounts suggest that General Huyser's estimate of a desertion rate of only a hundred a day in January 1979 is somewhat low.

30 See chapter 4.

31 Ashraf and Banuazizi, "The State," 25, 35–36. On Khomeini's appeal, see Fischer, "Imam Khomeini." Mary Hegland stresses that it was only when the shah seemed doomed—in late 1978—that many people came out in support of the revolution (comment on this manuscript). See also Hegland, "Imam Khomeini's Village," 651–55. Bahman Bakhtiari, Mary Hegland, and Reza Sheikholislami have all noted, in conversations with the author, that the religious hierarchy in Iran was much less significant in rural areas than in the cities. See also Hooglund, *Land and Revolution*, 149.

CHAPTER 10

1 On activists in engineering and other applied sciences, see Abrahamian, *Iran between Two Revolutions,* 492; Ibrahim, "Anatomy," 439–40; Sivan, *Radical Islam,* 119.
2 Khomeini, *Islam and Revolution,* 39.
3 Karimi, "Economic Policies and Structural Changes."
4 Habib, *Ibn Sa'ud's Warriors,* 122.
5 On the Quran and the telephone, see Philby, *Sa'udi Arabia,* 305.
6 Lerner, "Modernization—Social Aspects"; Nash, *Unfinished Agenda.*
7 al-Banna, *Majmu'at,* 223; Khomeini, *Islam and Revolution,* 29–30, 38; Qutb, *Ma'alim fi 'l-Tariq,* 35, 49.
8 al-Banna, *Majmu'at,* 193–95.
9 On condemnation of vices, see Khomeini, *Islam and Revolution,* 171–72, 183, 191; Maududi, *Fundamentals of Islam,* 245–46. On Islamic Republic, see Tabari and Yeganeh, *In the Shadow of Islam,* 96, 233, 235.
10 Ervand Abrahamian, "Structural Causes," 25–26.
11 It will be recalled that the Muslim Brotherhood was founded in 1928.
12 Keddie, "Comment on Skocpol," 288–89; Najmabadi, "Iran's Turn to Islam," 206. The drastic secularizing reforms of Ataturk in Turkey and Bourguiba in Tunisia provoked widespread resentment but nothing remotely resembling a revolution. See Salem, *Habib Bourguiba,* and Toprak, *Islam and Political Development.*
13 See Huntington, *Political Order in Changing Societies,* 49–50, and Olson, "Rapid Growth," 529–52. For a critique of such arguments, see Tilly, "Does Modernization Breed Revolution?"
14 World Bank, *World Tables,* 2nd ed., 107, 109, 227. On Iraq's Islamic movement, see Batatu, "Shi'i Organizations in Iraq."
15 See Nelson, *Access to Power,* and Perlman, *The Myth of Marginality.*
16 World Bank, *World Development Report 1983,* 190–91.
17 See Munson, *The House of Si Abd Allah.*
18 Huntington, *Political Order in Changing Societies,* 47–48, 278–81, 288–91, 369–73; Lipset, *Student Politics.*
19 World Bank, *World Development Report 1983,* 196–97.
20 Huntington, *Political Order in Changing Societies,* 4–5, 56–57, 461; Green, *Revolution in Iran,* xi–xiii, 149.
21 For an excellent case study of how ostensibly free elections in the Middle East are often conducted, see Eickelman, "Royal Authority and Religious Legitimacy."
22 Afkhami, *The Iranian Revolution,* 23; Hoveyda, *The Fall of the Shah,* 84–85; Pahlavi, *Answer to History,* 155; Ledeen and Lewis, *Debacle,* 100–01.
23 Akhavi, *Religion and Politics,* 38–59; Keddie, "Comment on Skocpol," 288–89.
24 Abrahamian, "Structural Causes," 25–26; Moshiri, *The State,* 75–76.

25 Bashiriyeh, *The State and Revolution*, 92–96. The usual figures given are 8,000 jailed, 23,000 banned from their hometowns, and 250,000 fined. See Bakhash, *Reign of the Ayatollahs*, 13; Green, *Revolution in Iran*, 42.

26 Bashiriyeh, *The State and Revolution*, 92–96; Keddie, *Roots of Revolution*, 246; Green, *Revolution in Iran*, 42.

27 Cited in Davies, "Toward a Theory of Revolution," 178.

28 Ibid.; Hetherington, "Industrialization and Revolution in Iran."

29 On workers in Europe, see Munson, *The House of Si Abd Allah*, 103–07. On women, see Mernissi, *Beyond the Veil*.

30 Aya, "Theories of Revolution Reconsidered," 54–57; Olson, "Rapid Growth," 536–41.

31 On Iran, see Looney, *Economic Origins*, 4–5. On collapse of oil prices, see Farid and Sirriyeh, *The Decline*, and Hunter, "The Gulf Economic Crisis."

CHAPTER 11

1 Huntington, *Political Order in Changing Societies*, 32.

2 Marsden, *Fundamentalism and American Culture*, 227.

3 Although *dependence* is a useful label with which to describe the relationship of most third world countries to the industrialized world (including the Soviet Union), *dependency theory* is considerably less useful when it comes to explaining this relationship. The term *dependence* is used here descriptively as it is in Weinbaum, "Dependent Development," which focuses on the American-Egyptian relationship.

4 Green, *Revolution in Iran*, 25–26, 32, 37.

5 Ajami, *The Arab Predicament*, 7; Arjomand, "Introduction," 19; Cudsi and Dessouki, "Introduction," 7; Kramer, *Political Islam*, 21, 42, 45.

6 Linton, "Nativistic Movements"; Mühlmann, *Messianismes révolutionnaires du tiers monde*, 14–16.

7 Geertz, *Islam Observed*, 61–62; Linton, "Nativistic Movements," 231; Mühlmann, *Messianismes révolutionnaires du tiers monde*, 14–16. For a more general discussion of the ideologization of tradition, see Mannheim, *Essays on Sociology*, 94–115. On the head scarf, see Betteridge, "To Veil," 117.

8 Betteridge, "To Veil"; El Guindi, "Veiling Infitah."

9 Algar, *The Islamic Revolution in Iran*, 36.

10 Shariati, *The Visage of Muhammad*, 26.

11 Shariati, *One Followed by an Eternity*, 2.

12 Fischer, *Iran*, 183.

13 Shariati, *On the Sociology of Islam*, 98. The very fact that Shari'ati focuses on the Cain and Abel story is probably a reflection of his awareness of its central role in Western culture, since it is of minor significance in the popular Islamic imagination.

14 Khomeini, *Islam and Revolution*, 304.

15 Al-Banna had bemoaned mimicry of the West and Muslim self-hatred in the 1940s. See *Majmu'at*, 221. And the quest for authenticity has led to the ideologization of many religions other than Islam. See, for example, Ashby, *Modern Trends in Islam*, 33–36, 91–115, and Lewy, *Religion and Revolution*, 277–345, 467–78.

16 al-Khumayni, *Durus*, 280; Khomeini, *Islam and Revolution*, 215. On the nationalist character of third world revolutions, see Huntington, *Political Order in Changing Societies*, 304–08. On the nationalist character of Iran's revolution, see, for example, Abrahamian, *Iran between Two Revolutions*, 532, and Arjomand, "Iran's Islamic Revolution," 388.

17 Khomeini, *Islam and Revolution*, 252.

18 Ibid., 260.

19 Ibid., 303.

20 Bakhash, "Sermons," 184.

21 Brière and Blanchet, *Iran*, 106; Fischer, *Iran*, 205.

22 On Egyptian resentment of the country's dependence on the United States under Sadat, see Heikal, *Autumn of Fury*, 69, 74–81, 86–89, 175. On Syrian resentment of al-Asad's dependence on the Soviet Union, see Carré and Michaud, *Les frères musulmans*, picture facing 145. I have often heard Moroccan intellectuals ridicule King Hasan II as a puppet of the United States. For a similar view of the Saudi kings, see Abd-Allah, *The Islamic Struggle*, 65, 71.

23 Bakhash, *Reign of the Ayatollahs*, 34–35. See Khomeini, *Islam and Revolution*, 182; al-Khumayni, *Durus*, 115.

24 See Khomeini, *Islam and Revolution*, 189, 191–92, 195–98, 209–10.

25 Gary Sick, who was on the National Security Council staff from 1976 through 1981, says that there were 41,000 Americans in Iran in 1978. See Sick, *All Fall Down*, 59. William Sullivan, the American ambassador to Iran from June 1977 to April 1979, speaks of 35,000 Americans living in Tehran in 1977. Sullivan, *Mission to Iran*, 28. Jerrold Green, who was in Iran during the revolution, gives a good picture of Iranian resentment of the American presence. See Green, *Revolution in Iran*, 25–26, 32, 36–37.

CHAPTER 12

1 Helms, *An Ambassador's Wife in Iran*, 172. On inflation, see Looney, *Economic Origins*, 2.

2 Karimi, "Economic Policies"; Pesaran, "Economic Development"; Rouleau, "Khomeini's Iran"; World Bank, *World Development Report 1985*, 175. On Latin America, see Hirschman, *Essays in Trespassing*, 177–207. On Turkey, see Ahmad, "Military Intervention," 11, 23; Yalpat, "Turkey's Economy under the Generals," 16, 19. Turkey did have a coup in 1980, but not a revolution.

3 Keddie, *Roots of Revolution*, 231; Moshiri, *The State*, 119; Skocpol, *States and Social Revolutions*, 47.

4 Cottam, "Goodbye to America's Shah," 12–13; Green, *Revolution in Iran,* 62; Keddie, *Roots of Revolution,* 231; Rubin, *Paved with Good Intentions,* 193; Sick, "Washington's Encounter," 128.

5 Green, *Revolution in Iran,* 62; Richards, "Carter's Human Rights Policy," 97–99.

6 Cited in Zabih, *Iran's Revolutionary Upheaval,* 49.

7 Davies, "Toward a Theory of Revolution," 178.

8 Cottam, "American Policy," 286; Sick, *All Fall Down,* 31, 52.

9 Rubin, *Paved with Good Intentions,* 193; Sick, "Washington's Encounter," 128; Tarr, "Human Rights," 69–70, 75–76.

10 Chubin, "Local Soil, Foreign Plants"; Moshiri, *The State,* 123; Ramazani, "Who Lost America?" I have often heard Iranian students opposed to the shah argue that the United States deliberately encouraged him to push for the OPEC price increases so that he would have more money to spend on American weaponry. Conversely, I have heard pro-shah Iranians claim that the United States deliberately engineered the 1978–79 revolution to punish the shah for his role in the 1973 oil price increases.

11 Cottam, "Goodbye to America's Shah," 12–13.

12 The quotation is from Brzezinski, *Power and Principle,* 356. For more on American policy at the end of 1978, see pp. 354–98 of Brzezinski's book, as well as Pahlavi, *Answer to History,* 164–65; Sick, *All Fall Down*; Sullivan, *Mission to Iran.*

13 Abrahamian, *Iran between Two Revolutions,* 496–529; Balta and Rulleau, *L'Iran insurgé,* 24–95; Fischer, *Iran,* 192–213; Green, *Revolution in Iran,* 84–142; Keddie, *Roots of Revolution,* 242–58.

14 Brzezinski, *Power and Principle,* 355, 362. Michael Ledeen and William Lewis claim that the United States blocked Iranian requests for tear gas canisters for nearly a year and never supplied the rubber-tipped bullets requested by the Iranians, who eventually obtained them from the British. See Ledeen and Lewis, *Debacle,* 146–47. The shah does not mention these facts in his indictment of American policy during the revolution. See Pahlavi, *Answer to History.*

15 Abrahamian, *Iran between Two Revolutions,* 516; Balta and Rulleau, *L'Iran insurgé,* 31; Nobari, *Iran Erupts,* 189–215.

16 Fischer, 198–99.

17 Green, *Revolution in Iran,* 64, 86.

18 Pahlavi, *Answer to History,* 149.

19 On charismatic authority, see Weber, *Economy and Society,* 215, 241–45, 1111–57; Willner, *The Spellbinders*; Worsley, *The Trumpet Shall Sound,* ix–xviii. On Khomeini's charismatic authority and messianic aura, see Arjomand, "Shi'ite Islam," 307–08; Fischer, "Becoming Mollah," 108–13. A young Iranian woman once told Professor Bahman Bakhtiari that she hated what Khomeini had done to Iran, but he had a hypnotic effect on her whenever she saw him on television (Bakhtiari, conversation with the author, April 1987).

20 This is based on conversations with Professors Bahman Bakhtiari and Reza Sheikholislami and with dozens of Iranian students. While teaching at the University of California at Santa Barbara in 1980–81, I discovered that most of my Iranian students had never read any of Khomeini's writings until taking courses with me. This was especially surprising in the case of an intelligent young woman who was one of the principal leaders of the Iranian Islamic organization at UCSB.

21 Brinton, *The Anatomy of Revolution*, 79–83.

22 Bakhash, *The Reign of the Ayatollahs*, 45; Conquest, *V. I. Lenin*, 77–79; Green, "Countermobilization in the Iranian Revolution," 131, 136–37; Taheri, *The Spirit of Allah*, 200–01. Taheri claims that, at Khomeini's orders, the Ayatollah Mutahhari organized a small "council" of ulama to lead the opposition to Khomeini in late 1977 or early 1978 (pp. 184–86, 190, 197). I have seen no other references to such a council at this early date and three specialists in Iranian political history have warned me not to rely on Taheri's account. At any rate, Taheri himself notes that Mutahhari and his associates were unable to prevent the Qum demonstration of January 9, 1978, and he observes that "there were to be many more occasions when the central leadership proved too cautious for the rank and file" (p. 201).

23 Abrahamian, *Iran between Two Revolutions*, 519–20; Conquest, *V. I. Lenin*, 87–88; Green, "Countermobilization in the Iranian Revolution," 131, 136–37.

24 Green, *Revolution in Iran*, 97, 119, 140–41, 144.

25 Huyser, *Mission to Tehran*, 131–32, 134, 234. On nationalism and revolution, see Huntington, *Political Order in Changing Societies*, 304–08.

26 Huyser, *Mission to Tehran*, 110.

Bibliography

The Arabic definite article *al-* is ignored for the purpose of alphabetization, except where authors have incorporated some form of it into the Western version of their name, as in *El Guindi*.

SOURCES IN ARABIC

al-Banna, Hasan. *Majmu'at Rasa'il al-Imam al-Shahid Hasan al-Banna* (The collected epistles of the martyred Imam Hasan al-Banna). Beirut: Dar al-Andalus, 1965.

al-Ghannushi, Rashid. *Maqalat* (Essays). Paris: Dar al-Karawan li'l-taba'a wa 'l-nashr wa'l-tawzi' bi Baris, 1984.

al-Khumayni, al-Imam. *Durus fi 'l-Jihad wa 'l-Rafd* (Lessons in holy war and rejection). Beirut: n.p., 1978.

Qutb, Sayyid. *Ma'alim fi 'l-Tariq* (Milestones on the path). Beirut: Dar al-Qur'an al-karim, 1978.

SOURCES IN WESTERN LANGUAGES

Abdalla, Ahmed. *The Student Movement and National Politics in Egypt, 1923–1973*. London: Al Saqi Books, 1985.

Abd-Allah, Umar F. *The Islamic Struggle in Syria*. Berkeley: Mizan Press, 1983.

Abrahamian, Ervand. "Social Bases of Iranian Politics: The Tudeh Party 1941–53." Ph.D. diss., Columbia University, 1969.

159

————. "The Guerrilla Movement in Iran, 1963–1977." *MERIP Reports,* no. 86 (1980): 3–21.

————. "Structural Causes of the Iranian Revolution." *MERIP Reports,* no. 87 (1980): 21–26. (Reprinted in Goldstone, *Revolutions.*)

————. *Iran between Two Revolutions.* Princeton University Press, 1982.

Abramov, S. Zalman. *Perpetual Dilemma: Jewish Religion in the Jewish State.* Cranbury, N.J.: Associated University Presses, 1978.

Abu-Lughod, Janet. "Migrant Adjustment to City Life: The Egyptian Case." *American Journal of Sociology* 47 (1961): 22–32.

Afkhami, Gholam R. *The Iranian Revolution: Thanatos on a National Scale.* Washington, D.C.: Middle East Institute, 1985.

Ahmad, Feroz. "Military Intervention and the Crisis in Turkey." *MERIP Reports,* no. 93 (1981): 5–24.

Ahmad, Mumtaz. "Islamic Revival in Pakistan." In *Islam in the Contemporary World,* edited by Cyriac Pullapilly. Notre Dame: Cross Roads Books, 1980.

————. "Class, Power and Religion: Some Aspects of Islamic Fundamentalism in Pakistan." Paper presented at the Conference on Islamic Revival, Center for Middle Eastern Studies, University of Chicago, May 1980.

Aho, James. *Religious Mythology and the Art of War: Comparative Religious Symbolisms of Military Violence.* Westport, Conn.: Greenwood Press, 1981.

Ajami, Fouad. *The Arab Predicament: Arab Political Thought and Practice since 1967.* Cambridge: Cambridge University Press, 1981.

————. *The Vanished Imam: Musa al Sadr and the Shia of Lebanon.* Ithaca: Cornell University Press, 1986.

Akhavi, Shahrough. *Religion and Politics in Contemporary Iran: Clergy-State Relations in the Pahlavi Period.* Albany: State University of New York Press, 1980.

————. "Clerical Politics in Iran since 1979." In Keddie and Hooglund, *The Iranian Revolution and the Islamic Republic.*

————. "Elite Factionalism in the Islamic Republic of Iran." *Middle East Journal* 41 (Spring 1987): 181–201.

Algar, Hamid. *Religion and State in Iran, 1785–1906.* Berkeley and Los Angeles: University of California Press, 1969.

————. *The Islamic Revolution in Iran.* Edited by Kalim Siddiqui. London: Open Press and Muslim Institute, 1980.

————. "Introduction by the Translator." In Khomeini, *Islam and Revolution.*

Allman, James. *Social Mobility, Education and Development in Tunisia.* Leiden: E. J. Brill, 1979.

Anderson, Lisa. "Qaddafi's Islam." In Esposito, *Voices of Resurgent Islam.*

Ansari, Hamied N. "The Islamic Militants in Egyptian Politics." *International Journal of Middle East Studies* 16 (March 1984): 123–44.

———. "Sectarian Conflict in Egypt and the Political Expediency of Islam." *Middle East Journal* 38 (Summer 1984): 397–418.

———. *Egypt: The Stalled Society.* Albany: State University of New York Press, 1986.

Ansari, Javed. "Jamaat-i-Islami and the Politics of Pakistan." *Arabia,* December 1985, 64–65.

Arjomand, Said Amir. "The Ulama's Traditionalist Opposition to Parliamentarianism." *Middle Eastern Studies* 17 (April 1981): 174–90.

———. "Shi'ite Islam and the Revolution in Iran." *Government and Opposition* 16 (Summer 1981): 293–316.

———. *The Shadow of God and the Hidden Imam: Religion, Political Order, and Societal Change in Shi'ite Iran from the Beginning to 1890.* Chicago: University of Chicago Press, 1984.

———. "Introduction: Social Movements in the Contemporary Near and Middle East." In Arjomand, *From Nationalism to Revolutionary Islam.*

———. "Traditionalism in Twentieth-century Iran." In Arjomand, *From Nationalism to Revolutionary Islam.*

———. "Iran's Islamic Revolution in Comparative Perspective." *World Politics* 38 (April 1986): 383–414.

Arjomand, Said Amir, ed. *From Nationalism to Revolutionary Islam.* Albany: New York State University Press, 1984.

Ashby, Philip H. *Modern Trends in Hinduism.* New York: Columbia University Press, 1974.

Ashraf, Ahmad, and Ali Banuazizi. "The State, Classes and Modes of Mobilization in the Iranian Revolution." *State, Culture and Society* 1 (1985): 3–40.

Aya, Rod. "Theories of Revolution Reconsidered." *Theory and Society* 8 (1979): 39–99.

Ayoub, Mahmoud. *Redemptive Suffering in Islam: A Study of the Devotional Aspects of 'Ashura in Twelver Shi'ism.* The Hague: Mouton, 1978.

Ayubi, Nazih N. M. "The Politics of Militant Islamic Movements in the Middle East." *Journal of International Affairs* 36 (1982–83): 271–83.

Bagley, F. R. C. "New Light on the Iranian Constitutional Movement." In *Qajar Iran: Political, Social and Cultural Change,* edited by Edmund

Bosworth and Carole Hillenbrand. Edinburgh: Edinburgh University Press, 1983.

Bakhash, Shaul. *The Reign of the Ayatollahs: Iran and the Islamic Revolution.* New York: Basic Books, 1984.

———. "Sermons, Revolutionary Pamphleteering and Mobilisation: Iran, 1978." In Arjomand, *From Nationalism to Revolutionary Islam.*

Balta, Paul and Claudine Rulleau. *L'Iran insurgé.* Paris: Sindbad, 1979.

Baraheni, Reza. *The Crowned Cannibals: Writings on Repression in Iran.* New York: Vintage Books, 1977.

Bashiriyeh, Hossein. *The State and Revolution in Iran, 1962–1982.* New York: St. Martin's Press, 1984.

Batatu, Hanna. *The Old Social Classes and the Revolutionary Movements of Iraq.* Princeton: Princeton University Press, 1978.

———. "Some Observations on the Social Roots of Syria's Ruling Military Group and the Causes for Its Dominance." *Middle East Journal,* no. 35 (1981): 331–44.

———. "Syria's Muslim Brethren." *MERIP Reports,* no. 110 (1982): 12–20.

———. "Shi'i Organizations in Iraq: al-Da'wah al-Islamiyah and al-Mujahidin." In Cole and Keddie, *Shi'ism and Social Protest.*

Bauer, Janet. "Poor Women and Social Consciousness in Iran." In Nashat, *Women and Revolution in Iran.*

Beck, Lois. *The Qashqa'i of Iran.* New Haven: Yale University Press, 1986.

Beeman, William O. "Images of the Great Satan: Representations of the United States in the Iranian Revolution." In Keddie, *Religion and Politics in Iran.*

Behrang [Pseudonym for a group of French and Iranian Marxists]. *Iran: Le maillon faible.* Paris: François Maspéro, 1979.

Berges, Yves-Guy. "Eyewitness Report from Martyrs' Square." In Nobari, *Iran Erupts.*

Berque, Jacques. *Egypt: Imperialism and Revolution.* Translated by Jean Stewart. New York: Praeger, 1972.

Betteridge, Anne. "To Veil or Not to Veil: A Matter of Protest or Policy." In Nashat, *Women and Revolution in Iran.*

Bill, James A. "Resurgent Islam in the Persian Gulf." *Foreign Affairs* 63 (Fall 1984): 108–27.

Binder, Leonard. *Religion and Politics in Pakistan.* Berkeley and Los Angeles: University of California Press, 1961.

———. "The Proofs of Islam: Religion and Politics in Iran." In *Arabic and Islamic Studies in Honor of Hamilton Gibb,* edited by George Makdisi. Leiden: E. J. Brill, 1965.

Boff, Leonardo. *Jesus Christ Liberator.* Maryknoll, N.Y.: Orbis Books, 1978.

Boroumand, Ladan. "Les ouvriers, l'ingénieur et les militantes khomeinistes: Entretien dans une usine au lendemain de la révolution." *Peuples Méditerranéens* 8 (July–September 1979): 59–76.

Brière, Claire, and Pierre Blanchet. *Iran: La révolution au nom de Dieu.* Paris: Editions du Seuil, 1979.

Brinton, Crane. *The Anatomy of Revolution.* Rev. ed. New York: Vintage Books, 1965.

Brown, Kenneth. *People of Salé: Tradition and Change in a Moroccan City, 1830–1930.* Cambridge: Harvard University Press, 1976.

Browne, Edward G. *The Persian Revolution of 1905–1909.* Cambridge: Cambridge University Press, 1910.

Brzezinski, Zbigniew. *Power and Principle: Memoirs of the National Security Advisor, 1977–1981.* New York: Farrar, Straus & Giroux, 1983.

Buchan, James. "The Return of the Ikhwan." In Holden and Johns, *The House of Saud.*

———. "Secular and Religious Opposition in Saudi Arabia." In Niblock, *State, Economy and Society in Saudi Arabia.*

Carré, Olivier, and Gérard Michaud. *Les frères musulmans (1928–1982).* Paris: Editions Gallimard/Julliard, 1983.

Carré, Olivier, and Michel Seurat. "L'utopie islamiste au Moyen-Orient arabe et particulièrement en Egypte et en Syrie." In *L'Islam et l'état dans le monde d'aujourd'hui,* edited by Olivier Carré. Paris: Presses Universitaires de France, 1982.

Chubin, Shahram. "Local Soil, Foreign Plants." *Foreign Policy,* no. 34 (1979): 20–23.

Cohn, Norman. *The Pursuit of the Millennium.* Rev. ed. New York: Oxford University Press, 1970.

Cole, Juan R. I., and Nikki R. Keddie, eds. *Shi'ism and Social Protest.* New Haven: Yale University Press, 1986.

Conquest, Robert. *V. I. Lenin.* New York: Viking Press, 1972

Cottam, Richard W. *Nationalism in Iran.* Pittsburgh: University of Pittsburgh Press, 1964.

———. "Goodbye to America's Shah." *Foreign Policy,* no. 34 (1979): 3–14.

———. "American Policy and the Iranian Crisis." *Iranian Studies* (special issue) 13, nos. 1–4 (1980): 279–305.

Crapanzano, Vincent. *The Hamadsha: A Study in Moroccan Ethnopsychiatry.* Berkeley and Los Angeles: University of California Press, 1973.

Cudsi, Alexander S., and Ali E. Hillal Dessouki. Introduction to *Islam and Power,* edited by Alexander S. Cudsi and Ali E. Hillal Dessouki. Baltimore: Johns Hopkins University Press, 1981.

Curtis, Michael, ed. *Religion and Politics in the Middle East.* Boulder, Colo.: Westview Press, 1981.

Davies, James C. "Toward a Theory of Revolution." in *Why Revolution? Theories and Analyses,* edited by Clifford T. Paynton and Robert Blackey. Cambridge: Schenkman, 1971.

Davis, Eric. "Ideology, Social Class and Islamic Radicalism in Modern Egypt." In Arjomand, *From Nationalism to Revolutionary Islam.*

Deeb, Marius. "The 1919 Popular Uprising: A Genesis of Egyptian Nationalism." *Canadian Review of Studies in Nationalism* 1 (1973): 106–19.

Dekmejian, R. Hrair. *Islam in Revolution: Fundamentalism in the Arab World.* Syracuse: Syracuse University Press, 1985.

Dessouki, Ali E. Hillal, ed. *The Islamic Resurgence in the Arab World.* New York: Praeger, 1982.

Dhaouadi, Zouhaier, and Amr Ibrahim. "Documents: Arabie Seoudite." *Peuples Méditerranéens,* no. 21 (1982): 60–71.

Drysdale, Alasdair. "The Asad Regime and Its Troubles." *MERIP Reports,* no. 110 (1982): 3–11.

Eickelman, Dale F. *Moroccan Islam: Tradition and Society in a Pilgrimage Center.* Austin: University of Texas Press, 1976.

———. *Knowledge and Power in Morocco: The Education of a Twentieth-Century Notable.* Princeton: Princeton University Press, 1985.

———. "From Theocracy to Monarchy: Authority and Legitimacy in Inner Oman, 1935–1957." *International Journal of Middle East Studies* 17 (February 1985): 3–24.

———. "Royal Authority and Religious Legitimacy: Morocco's Elections, 1960–1984." In *The Frailty of Authority.* Political Anthropology 5, edited by Myron J. Aronoff. New Brunswick, N.J.: Transaction Books, 1986.

El Guindi, Fadwa. "Veiling Infitah with Muslim Ethic: Egypt's Contemporary Islamic Movement." *Social Problems* 28 (1981): 465–85.

———. "The Emerging Islamic Order: The Case of Egypt's Contemporary Islamic Movement." In *Political Behavior in the Arab States,* edited by Tawfic E. Farah. Boulder, Colo.: Westview Press, 1983.

Eliade, Mircea. *Aspects du mythe.* Paris: Gallimard, 1963.

Eliash, Joseph. "Misconceptions Regarding the Juridical Status of the Iranian 'Ulama.'" *International Journal of Middle East Studies* 10 (1979): 118–40.

Elwell-Sutton, L. P. "Reza Shah the Great: Founder of the Pahlavi Dynasty." In *Iran under the Pahlavis,* edited by George Lenczowski. Stanford: Hoover Institution Press, 1978.

Enayat, Hamid. *Modern Islamic Political Thought.* Austin: University of Texas Press, 1982.

Esposito, John L., ed. *Voices of Resurgent Islam.* New York: Oxford University Press, 1983.

———. *Islam and Politics.* Syracuse: Syracuse University Press, 1984.

Falwell, Jerry. *Listen America!* Garden City, N.Y.: Doubleday, 1980.

Falwell, Jerry, ed. *The Fundamentalist Phenomenon: The Resurgence of Conservative Christianity.* Garden City, N.Y.: Doubleday, 1981.

Farid, Abdel Majid, and Hussein Sirriyeh, eds. *The Decline of Arab Oil Revenues.* London: Croom Helm, 1986.

Fernea, Robert A., and Elizabeth W. Fernea. "Variation in Religious Observance among Islamic Women." In Keddie, *Scholars, Saints and Sufis.*

Fischer, Michael M. J. *Iran: From Religious Dispute to Revolution.* Cambridge: Harvard University Press, 1980.

———. "Becoming Mollah: Reflections on Iranian Clerics in a Revolutionary Age." *Iranian Studies* (special issue) 13, nos. 1–4 (1980): 83–117.

———. "Islam and the Revolt of the Petite Bourgeoisie." *Daedalus* 111 (Winter 1982): 101–25.

———. "Imam Khomeini: Four Levels of Understanding." In Esposito, *Voices of Resurgent Islam.*

Floor, William F. "Revolutionary Character of the Ulama: Wishful Thinking or Reality?" In Keddie, *Religion and Politics in Iran.*

Gaffney, Patrick D. "From University Campus to Mosque and Town: Islamic Movements in Contemporary Egypt." Paper presented at the annual meeting of the Middle East Studies Association, Boston, November 1986.

Geertz, Clifford. *Islam Observed: Religious Development in Morocco and Indonesia.* New Haven: Yale University Press, 1968.

Gellner, Ernest. *Saints of the Atlas.* Chicago: University of Chicago Press, 1969.

———. *Muslim Society.* Cambridge: Cambridge University Press, 1981.

Gilsenan, Michael. *Recognizing Islam: Religion and Society in the Modern Arab World.* New York: Pantheon Books, 1982.

Glubb, Sir John Bagot. *War in the Desert.* New York: W. W. Norton, 1961.

Goldberg, Jacob. "The Shi'i Minority in Saudi Arabia." In Cole and Keddie, *Shi'ism and Social Protest.*

Goldstone, Jack A., ed. *Revolutions: Theoretical, Comparative, and Historical Studies.* New York: Harcourt Brace Jovanovich, 1986.

Goodell, Grace E. *The Elementary Structures of Political Life: Rural Development in Pahlavi Iran.* New York: Oxford Universtiy Press, 1986.

Graham, Robert. *Iran: The Illusion of Power.* New York: St. Martin's Press, 1979.

Green, Jerrold D. *Revolution in Iran: The Politics of Countermobilization.* New York: Praeger, 1982.

―――. "Countermobilization in the Iranian Revolution." In Goldstone, *Revolutions.*

Greenspan, Leonard. "The Warrior God, or God, the Divine Warrior." In *Religion and Politics,* edited by Peter H. Merkl and Ninian Smart. New York: New York University Press, 1983.

Habib, John S. *Ibn Sa'ud's Warriors of Islam: The Ikhwan of Najd and Their Role in the Creation of the Sa'udi Kingdom 1910–1930.* Leiden: E. J. Brill, 1978.

Haddad, Yvonne Y. "The Arab-Israeli Wars, Nasserism and the Affirmation of Islamic Identity." In *Islam and Development: Religion and Sociopolitical Change,* edited by John L. Esposito. Syracuse: Syracuse University Press, 1980.

Halpern, Manfred. *The Politics of Social Change in the Middle East and North Africa.* Princeton: Princeton University Press, 1963.

Hegland, Mary. "Two Images of Husain: Accommodation and Revolution in an Iranian Village." In Keddie, *Religion and Politics in Iran.*

―――. "Imam Khomaini's Village: Recruitment to Revolution." Ph.D. diss., State University of New York at Binghamton, 1986.

Heikal, Mohamed. *Iran: The Untold Story.* New York: Pantheon Books, 1982.

―――. *Autumn of Fury: The Assassination of Sadat.* New York: Random House, 1983.

Heller, Mark, and Nadav Safran. *The New Middle Class and Regime Stability in Saudi Arabia.* Harvard Middle East Papers, modern series, no. 3. Cambridge: Center for Middle Eastern Studies, Harvard University, 1985.

Helms, Cynthia. *An Ambassador's Wife in Iran.* New York: Dodd, Mead & Co., 1981.

Hermassi, Mohamed Elbaki. "La société tunisienne au miroir islamiste." *Maghreb-Machrek,* no. 103 (1984): 39–56.

Hetherington, Norris S. "Industrialization and Revolution in Iran: Forced Progress or Unmet Expectation?" *Middle East Journal* 36 (1982): 362–73.

Hinnebusch, Raymond A. "The Islamic Movement in Syria: Sectarian Conflict and Urban Rebellion in an Authoritarian-Populist Regime." In Dessouki, *Islamic Resurgence in the Arab World.*

———. "Children of the Elite: Political Attitudes of the Westernized Bourgeoisie in Egypt." *Middle East Journal* 36 (1982): 535–61.

Hiro, Dilip. *Iran under the Ayatollahs.* London: Routledge & Kegan Paul, 1985.

Hirschfeld, Yair. "The Odd Couple: Ba'thist Syria and Khomeini's Iran." In *Syria under Assad: Domestic Constraints and Regional Risks,* edited by Moshe Ma'oz and Avner Yaniv. New York: St. Martin's Press, 1986.

Hirshman, Albert O. *Essays in Trespassing: Economics to Politics and Beyond.* New York: Cambridge University Press, 1981.

Hodgson, Marshall. *The Venture of Islam: Conscience and History in a World Civilization.* Vol. 1. Chicago: University of Chicago Press, 1974.

Holden, David, and Richard Johns. *The House of Saud: The Rise and Rule of the Most Powerful Dynasty in the Arab World.* New York: Holt, Rinehart & Winston, 1982 (with one chapter by James Buchan).

Hooglund, Eric. "Rural Participation in the Revolution." *MERIP Reports,* no. 87 (1980): 3–6.

———. *Land and Revolution in Iran, 1960–1980.* Austin: University of Texas Press, 1982.

Hoveyda, Fereydoun. *The Fall of the Shah.* Translated by Roger Liddell. New York: Simon & Schuster, 1980.

Humphreys, R. Stephen. "Islam and Political Values in Saudi Arabia, Egypt, and Syria." In Curtis, *Religion and Politics in the Middle East.*

Hunter, Shireen T. "The Gulf Economic Crisis and Its Social and Political Consequences." *Middle East Journal* 40 (Autumn 1986): 593–613.

Hunter, Shireen T., ed. *The Politics of Islamic Revivalism.* Bloomington: Indiana University Press, forthcoming.

Huntington, Samuel P. *Political Order in Changing Societies.* New Haven: Yale University Press, 1968.

Huyette, Summer Scott. *Political Adaptation in Sa'udi Arabia: A Study of the Council of Ministers.* Boulder, Colo.: Westview Press, 1985.

Huyser, General Robert E. *Mission to Tehran.* New York: Harper & Row, 1986.

Ibn Ishaq, Muhammad. *The Life of Muhammad.* Translated and edited by Alfred Guillaume. London: Oxford University Press, 1955.

Ibrahim, Saad Eddin. "Anatomy of Egypt's Militant Islamic Groups: Methodological Note and Preliminary Findings." *International Journal of Middle East Studies* 12 (1980): 423–53.

Jansen, Johannes J. G. *The Neglected Duty: The Creed of Sadat's Assassins and Islamic Resurgence in the Middle East.* New York: Macmillan, 1986.

Kamal, Abdul Aziz. *The Prescribed Prayers.* 3rd ed. Lahore: Islamic Publications, 1978.

Karimi, Setareh. "Economic Policies and Structural Changes since the Revolution." In Keddie and Hooglund, *The Iranian Revolution and the Islamic Republic.*

Katouzian, Homa. *The Political Economy of Modern Iran: Despotism and Pseudo-Modernism, 1926–1979.* New York: New York University Press, 1981.

Kay, Shirley. "Social Change in Modern Saudi Arabia." In Niblock, *State, Society and Economy in Saudi Arabia.*

Kazemi, Farhad. *Poverty and Revolution in Iran: The Migrant Poor, Urban Marginality and Politics.* New York: New York University Press, 1980.

———. "The *Fada'iyan-e Islam*: Fanaticism, Politics and Terror." In Arjomand, *From Nationalism to Revolutionary Islam.*

Keddie, Nikki R. *Sayyid Jamal ad-Din 'al-Afghani': A Political Biography.* Berkeley and Los Angeles: University of California Press, 1972.

———. "The Roots of the Ulama's Power in Modern Iran." In Keddie, *Scholars, Saints and Sufis.*

———. *Iran: Religion, Politics and Society.* London: Frank Cass, 1980.

———. *Roots of Revolution: An Interpretive History of Modern Iran.* New Haven: Yale University Press, 1981 (with one chapter by Yann Richard).

———. "Comments on Skocpol." *Theory and Society* 11 (1982): 285–92.

Keddie, Nikki R., ed. *Scholars, Saints and Sufis: Muslim Religious Institutions Since 1500.* Berkeley and Los Angeles: University of California Press, 1972.

———. *Religion and Politics in Iran: From Quietism to Revolution.* New Haven: Yale University Press, 1982.

Keddie, Nikki R., and Eric Hooglund, eds. *The Iranian Revolution and the Islamic Republic.* New ed. Syracuse: Syracuse University Press, 1986. (This contains some papers not included in the earlier version of this book published by the Middle East Institute in 1982.)

Kedourie, Elie. *Afghani and Abduh: An Essay on Religious Unbelief and Political Activism in Modern Iran.* London: Frank Cass, 1966.

Kepel, Gilles. *Le prophète et pharaon: Les mouvements islamistes dans l'Egypte contemporaine.* Paris: Editions La Découverte, 1984.

———. *Muslim Extremism in Egypt: The Prophet and Pharaoh.* Translated by Jon Rothschild. Berkeley and Los Angeles: University of California Press, 1986. (This translation includes an afterword covering the years 1981 through 1985.)

Khomeini, Ruh Allah. *Islam and Revolution: Writings and Declarations of Imam Khomeini.* Translated and edited by Hamid Algar. Berkeley: Mizan Press, 1981.

———. *A Clarification of Questions.* Translated by J. Borujerdi. Boulder, Colo.: Westview Press, 1984.

Kostiner, Joseph. "On Instruments and Their Designers: The Ikhwan of Najd and the Emergence of the Saudi State." *Middle Eastern Studies* 21 (1985): 298–323.

Kramer, Martin. *Political Islam.* Beverly Hills: Sage Publications, 1980.

Lacey, Robert. *The Kingdom: Arabia and the House of Sa'ud.* New York: Harcourt Brace Jovanovich, 1981.

Lackner, Helen. *A House Built on Sand: A Political Economy of Saudi Arabia.* London: Ithaca Press, 1978.

Lapidus, Ira M. *Contemporary Islamic Movements in Historical Perspective.* Policy Papers in International Affairs, no. 18. Berkeley: University of California, Institute of International Studies, 1983.

Lawrence, Bruce B. "Muslim Fundamentalist Movements: Reflections toward a New Approach." In *The Islamic Impulse,* edited by Barbara F. Stowasser. London: Croom Helm, 1987.

Lawson, Fred H. "Social Bases for the Hamah Revolt." *MERIP Reports,* no. 110 (1982): 24–28.

Layish, Aaron. "'*Ulama*' and Politics in Saudi Arabia." In *Islam and Politics in the Modern Middle East,* edited by Metin Heper and Raphael Israeli. New York: St. Martin's Press, 1984.

Ledeen, Michael, and William Lewis. *Debacle: The American Failure in Iran.* New York: Alfred A. Knopf, 1981.

Lenczowski, George. *Russia and the West in Iran, 1914–1948: A Study in Big-Power Rivalry.* Ithaca: Cornell University Press, 1949.

Lerner, Daniel. "Modernization—Social Aspects." In *Encyclopedia of the Social Sciences,* edited by David L. Sills. New York: Macmillan and Free Press, 1968.

Lewis, Bernard. "The Return of Islam" In Curtis, *Religion and Politics in the Middle East.*

Lewy, Guenter. *Religion and Revolution.* New York: Oxford University Press, 1974.

Lind, Millard C. "Paradigm of Holy War in the Old Testament." *Biblical Research* 16 (1971): 16–31.

Linton, Ralph. "Nativistic Movements." *American Anthropologist* 45 (1943): 230–40.

Lipset, Seymour Martin, ed. *Student Politics.* New York: Basic Books, 1969.

Looney, Robert E. *Economic Origins of the Iranian Revolution.* New York: Pergamon Press, 1982.

Mannheim, Karl. *Essays on Sociology and Social Psychology.* Edited by Paul Kecskemeti. London: Routledge & Kegan Paul, 1953.

Mardin, Serif. "Bediüzzaman Said Nursi (1873–1960): The Shaping of a Vocation." In *Religious Organization and Religious Experience,* edited by John Davis. London: Academic Press, 1982.

———. "Religion and Politics in Modern Turkey." In Piscatori, *Islam and the Political Process.*

Marsden, George. *Fundamentalism and American Culture: The Shaping of Twentieth Century Evangelicalism, 1870–1925.* New York: Oxford University Press, 1980.

Marsot, Afaf Lufti al-Sayyid. *A Short History of Modern Egypt.* New York: Cambridge University Press, 1985.

Martin, Richard C. *Islam: A Cultural Perspective.* Englewood Cliffs, N.J: Prentice-Hall, 1982.

Martin, Richard C., ed. *Approaches to Islam in Religious Studies.* Tucson: University of Arizona Press, 1985.

Al-Mashat, Abdul-Monem. "Egyptian Attitudes toward the Peace Process: Views of an 'Alert Elite.'" *Middle East Journal* 37 (Summer 1983): 394–411.

Maududi, S. Abul A'la. *Fundamentals of Islam.* 2nd ed. Lahore: Islamic Publications, 1976.

Mazzaoui, Michel M. "Shi'ism and Ashura in South Lebanon." In *Ta'ziyeh: Ritual and Drama in Iran,* edited by Peter Chelkowski. New York: New York University Press, 1979.

Mernissi, Fatima. *Beyond the Veil: Male-Female Dynamics in a Modern Muslim Society.* Cambridge: Schenkman, 1975.

Michaud, Gerard. "The Importance of Bodyguards." *MERIP Reports,* no. 110 (1982): 29–31.

Mitchell, Richard P. *The Society of the Muslim Brothers.* London: Oxford University Press, 1969.

Momen, Moojan. *An Introduction to Shi'i Islam: The History and Doctrines of Twelver Shi'ism.* New Haven: Yale University Press, 1985.

Mortimer, Edward. *Faith and Power: The Politics of Islam.* New York: Vintage Books, 1982.

Moshiri, Farrokh. *The State and Social Revolution in Iran: A Theoretical Perspective.* New York: Peter Lang, 1985.

Mottahedeh, Roy. *The Mantle of the Prophet: Religion and Politics in Iran.* New York: Simon & Schuster, 1985.

Mühlmann, Wilhelm E. *Messianismes révolutionnaires du tiers monde.* Translated by Jean Baudrillard. Paris: Gallimard, 1968.

Munson, Henry, Jr. "Islam and Inequality in Northwest Morocco." Ph.D. diss., University of Chicago, 1980.

————. "Geertz on Religion: The Theory and the Practice." *Religion* 14 (1986): 19–32.

————. "The Social Base of Islamic Militancy in Morocco." *Middle East Journal* 40 (1986): 267–84.

————. "Islamic Revivalism in Morocco and Tunisia." *Muslim World* 76 (1986): 203–18.

————. "Morocco." In Hunter, *The Politics of Islamic Revivalism.*

Munson, Henry, Jr., ed. and trans. *The House of Si Abd Allah: The Oral History of a Moroccan Family.* New Haven: Yale University Press, 1984. (This book was also recorded by Munson.)

Nagata, Judith. *The Reflowering of Malaysian Islam: Modern Religious Radicals and Their Roots.* Vancouver: University of British Columbia Press, 1984.

Najmabadi, Afsaneh. "Iran's Turn to Islam: From Modernism to a Moral Order." *Middle East Journal* 41 (1987): 202–17. (See also her works under the pseudonym Azar Tabari.)

Nash, Manning. "Fundamentalist Islam: Reservoir for Turbulence." *Journal of Asian and African Studies* 19 (1984): 73–79.

————. *Unfinished Agenda: The Dynamics of Modernization in the Developing Nations.* Boulder, Colo.: Westview Press, 1984.

Nashat, Guity, ed. *Women and Revolution in Iran.* Boulder, Colo.: Westview Press, 1983.

Nelson, Joan M. *Access to Power: Politics and the Urban Poor in Developing Nations.* Princeton: Princeton University Press, 1979.

Niblock, Tim, ed. *State, Society and Economy in Saudi Arabia.* New York: St. Martin's Press, 1982.

Nobari, Ali-Reza, ed. *Iran Erupts.* Stanford: Iran-America Documentation Group, 1978.

Norton, Augustus Richard. "Harakat Amal (the Movement of Hope)." In *Religion and Politics.* Political Anthropology 3, edited by Myron J. Aronoff. New Brunswick, N.J.: Transaction Books, 1984.

————. "Shi'ism and Social Protest in Lebanon." In Cole and Keddie, *Shi'ism and Social Protest.*

Oates, Stephen B. *Let the Trumpet Sound: The Life of Martin Luther King, Jr.* New York: Harper & Row, 1982.

Olson, Mancur, Jr. "Rapid Growth as a Destabilizing Force." *Journal of Economic History* 23 (1963): 529–52.

Organization of Iranian Moslem Students. *The Rise (English Defense Publication) and Leaflets in English: Compiled Documents of the O.I.M.S., September 1976 to April 1979.* Wilmette, Ill.: O.I.M.S.

Pahlavi, Mohammad Reza, the Shah of Iran. *Answer to History.* Briarcliff Manor, N.Y.: Stein & Day, 1980.

Perlman, Janice E. *The Myth of Marginality: Urban Poverty and Politics in Rio de Janeiro.* Berkeley and Los Angeles: University of California Press, 1976.

Pesaran, M. H. "Economic Development and Revolutionary Upheavals in Iran." In *Iran: A Revolution in Turmoil,* edited by Haleh Afshar. Albany: State University of New York Press, 1985.

Peters, Rudolph. *Islam and Colonialism: The Doctrine of Jihad in Modern History.* The Hague: Mouton, 1979.

Petran, Tabitha. *Syria.* London: Ernest Benn, 1972.

Philby, Harry St. John. *Arabian Jubilee.* London: Robert Hale, 1952.

———. *Sa'udi Arabia.* London: Ernest Benn, 1955.

Picard, Elisabeth. "La Syrie de 1946 à 1979." In *La Syrie d'aujourd'hui,* edited by André Raymond. Paris: Editions du CNRS, 1980.

Pipes, Daniel. *In the Path of God: Islam and Political Power.* New York: Basic Books, 1983.

Piscatori, James P., ed. *Islam in the Political Process.* New York: Cambridge University Press, 1983.

———. "Ideological Politics in Sa'udi Arabia." In Piscatori, *Islam in the Political Process.*

Quandt, William B. *Saudi Arabia in the 1980s: Foreign Policy, Security, and Oil.* Washington: Brookings Institution, 1981.

Rabinovitch, Itamar. *Syria under the Ba'th, 1963–1966: The Army-Party Symbiosis.* New York: Halsted Press, 1972.

Rabinow, Paul. *Symbolic Domination: Cultural Form and Historical Change in Morocco.* Chicago: University of Chicago Press, 1975.

Ramazani, R. K. "Who Lost America? The Case of Iran." *Middle East Journal* 36 (1982): 5–21.

———. *Revolutionary Iran: Challenge and Response in the Middle East.* Baltimore: Johns Hopkins University Press, 1986.

Reed, Stanley F., III. "Dateline Syria: Fin de Regime?" *Foreign Policy,* no. 39 (1980): 176–90.

Rentz, George. "Wahhabism and Saudi Arabia." In *The Arabian Peninsula: Society and Politics,* edited by Derek Hopwood. Totowa, N.J.: Rowman & Littlefield, 1972.

Richard, Yann. *Le Shi'isme en Iran: Iman et révolution.* Paris: Maisonneuve, 1980.

――――. "Contemporary Shi'i Thought." In Keddie, *Roots of Revolution.*

――――. "Ayatollah Kashani: Precursor of the Islamic Republic?" In Keddie, *Religion and Politics in Iran.*

Richards, Helmut. "Carter's Human Rights Policy and the Pahlavi Dictatorship." In Nobari, *Iran Erupts.*

Roosevelt, Kermit. *Countercoup: The Struggle for the Control of Iran.* New York: McGraw-Hill, 1979.

Rouleau, Eric. "Khomeini's Iran." *Foreign Affairs* 59 (1980): 1–20.

Rubin, Barry. *Paved with Good Intentions: The American Experience and Iran.* New York: Oxford University Press, 1980.

Rugh, Andrea B. *Family in Contemporary Egypt.* Syracuse: Syracuse University Press, 1984.

Sachedina, Abdulaziz Abdulhussein. *Islamic Messianism: The Idea of the Mahdi in Twelver Shi'ism.* Albany: State University of New York Press, 1981.

Sadowski, Yahya M. "Cadres, Guns and Money: The Eighth Regional Congress of the Syrian Ba'th." *MERIP Reports,* no. 134 (1985): 3–8.

Safran, Nadav. *Egypt in Search of Political Community: An Analysis of the Intellectual and Political Evolution of Egypt, 1804–1952.* Cambridge: Harvard University Press, 1961.

――――. *Saudi Arabia: The Ceaseless Quest for Security.* Cambridge: Harvard University Press, Belknap Press, 1985.

Salameh, Ghassan. "Political Power and the Saudi State." *MERIP Reports,* no. 91 (1980): 5–22.

Salem, Norma. *Habib Bourguiba, Islam and the Creation of Tunisia.* London: Croom Helm, 1984.

Sayeed, Khalid B. *Politics in Pakistan: The Nature and Direction of Change.* New York: Praeger, 1980.

Sciolino, Elaine. "Iran's Durable Revolution." *Foreign Affairs* 61 (1982–83): 893–920.

Shahrani, M. Nazif. "Introduction: Marxist 'Revolution' and Islamic Resistance in Afghanistan." In Shahrani and Canfield, *Revolutions and Rebellions in Afghanistan.*

Shahrani, M. Nazif, and Robert L. Canfield, eds. *Revolutions and Rebellions in Afghanistan: Anthropological Perspectives.* Berkeley: Institute of International Studies, University of California, 1984.

Shariati, Ali. *On the Sociology of Islam.* Translated and edited by Hamid Algar. Berkeley: Mizan Press, 1979.
———. *The Visage of Muhammad.* Translated by A. A. Sachedina. Houston: Free Islamic Literatures, 1979.
———. *One Followed by an Eternity of Zeroes.* Translated by Ali Ashgar Ghassemy. Houston: Free Islamic Literatures, 1980.
Sharot, Stephen. *Messianism, Mysticism, and Magic: A Sociological Analysis of Jewish Religious Movements.* Chapel Hill: University of North Carolina Press, 1982.
Sheikholislami, Reza. "From Religious Accommodation to Religious Revolution: The Transformation of Shi'ism in Iran." In *The State, Religion, and Ethnic Politics: Afghanistan, Iran, and Pakistan,* edited by Ali Banuazizi and Myron Weiner. Syracuse: Syracuse University Press, 1986.
Sick, Gary. "Washington's Encounter with the Iranian Revolution." In *The Iranian Revolution and the Islamic Republic: Proceedings of a Conference,* edited by Nikki R. Keddie and Eric Hooglund. Washington, D.C.: Middle East Institute, 1982. (A revised version of this work was published by Syracuse University Press in 1986.)
———. *All Fall Down: America's Tragic Encounter with Iran.* New York: Random House, 1985.
Sirageldin, Ismail A., Naiem A. Sherbiny, and M. Ismail Sirageldin. *Saudis in Transition: The Challenges of a Changing Labor Market.* New York: Oxford University Press for the World Bank, 1984.
Sivan, Emmanuel. *Radical Islam: Medieval Theology and Modern Politics.* New Haven: Yale University Press, 1985.
Skocpol, Theda. *States and Social Revolutions: A Comparative Analysis of France, Russia and China.* New York: Cambridge University Press, 1979.
Stillman, Norman A. *The Jews of Arab Lands: A History and Source Book.* Philadelphia: Jewish Publication Society of America, 1979.
Sullivan, William. *Mission to Iran.* New York: W. W. Norton, 1981.
Tabari, Azar. "The Role of the Clergy in Modern Iranian Politics." In Keddie, *Religion and Politics in Modern Iran.* (Azar Tabari is the former pseudonym of Afsaneh Najmabadi.)
Tabari, Azar, and Nahid Yeganeh, eds. *In the Shadow of Islam: The Women's Movement in Iran.* London: Zed Press, 1982.
Tabataba'i, 'Allamah Sayyid Muhammad Hossein. *Shi'ite Islam.* Translated and edited by Seyyed Hossein Nasr. Albany: State University of New York Press, 1975.
Taheri, Amir. *The Spirit of Allah: Khomeini and the Islamic Revolution.* Bethesda: Adler & Adler, 1986.

Tarr, Cedric W., Jr. "Human Rights and Arms Transfer Policy." In *Global Human Rights: Public Policies, Comparative Measures, and NGO Strategies,* edited by Ved P. Nanda, James R. Scaritt, and George Shepherd, Jr. Boulder, Colo.: Westview Press, 1981.

Thaiss, Gustav. "Religious Symbolism and Social Change." In Keddie, *Scholars, Saints and Sufis.*

Thrupp, Sylvia, ed. *Millennial Dreams in Action: Studies in Religious Revolutionary Movements.* New York: Schocken Books, 1970.

Tibawi, A. L. *A Modern History of Syria, including Lebanon and Palestine.* New York: St. Martin's Press, 1969.

Tilly, Charles. "Does Modernization Breed Revolution?" *Comparative Politics* 5 (1973): 425–47.

Toprak, Binnaz. *Islam and Political Development in Turkey.* Leiden: E. J. Brill, 1981.

———. "Politicisation of Islam in a Secular State: The National Salvation Party in Turkey." In Arjomand, *From Nationalism to Revolutionary Islam.*

Van Dam, Nikolaos. *The Struggle for Power in Syria: Sectarianism, Regionalism and Tribalism in Politics, 1961–1976.* New York: St. Martin's Press, 1979.

Vatikiotis, P. J. *Nasser and His Generation.* New York: St. Martin's Press, 1978.

Voll, John Obert. *Islam: Continuity and Change in the Modern World.* Boulder, Colo.: Westview Press, 1982.

Waterbury, John. *The Egypt of Nasser and Sadat: The Political Economy of Two Regimes.* Princeton: Princeton University Press, 1983.

Watt, W. Montgomery. "Islamic Conceptions of the Holy War." In *The Holy War,* edited by Thomas Patrick Murphy. Columbus: Ohio State University Press, 1976.

Waugh, Earle H. "The Popular Muhammad: Models in the Interpretation of an Islamic Paradigm." In Martin, *Approaches to Islam.*

Weber, Max. *Economy and Society: An Outline of Interpretive Sociology.* Edited by Guenther Roth and Claus Wittich. New York: Bedminster Press, 1968.

Weinbaum, Marvin G. "Dependent Development and U.S. Economic Aid to Egypt." *International Journal of Middle East Studies* 18 (May 1986): 119–34.

West, Francis J., Jr. "The Security Setting." In *U.S. Foreign Assistance: Investment or Folly?* edited by John Wilhelm and Gerry Feinstein. New York: Praeger, 1984.

Wikan, Unni. *Life among the Poor in Cairo*. Translated by Ann Henning. New York: Tavistock, 1980.

Williams, George Hunston. *The Radical Reformation*. Philadelphia: Westminster Press, 1962.

Willner, Ann Ruth. *The Spellbinders: Charismatic Political Leadership*. New Haven: Yale University Press, 1984.

World Bank. *World Tables*. 2nd ed. Baltimore: Johns Hopkins University Press, 1980.

———. *World Development Report 1983*. New York: Oxford University Press, 1983.

———. *World Development Report 1985*. New York: Oxford University Press, 1985.

Worsley, Peter. *The Trumpet Shall Sound: A Study of "Cargo" Cults in Melanesia*. 2nd ed. New York: Schocken Books, 1968.

Wright, Robin. *Sacred Rage: The Crusade of Modern Islam*. New York: Linden Press, 1985.

Yalpat, Altan. "The Economy." *MERIP Reports*, no. 122 (1984): 16–24.

Al-Yassini, Ayman. *Religion and State in the Kingdom of Saudi Arabia*. Boulder, Colo.: Westview Press, 1985.

Zabih, Sepehr. *Iran's Revolutionary Upheaval: An Interpretive Essay*. San Francisco: Alchemy Books, 1979.

———. *Iran since the Revolution*. Baltimore: Johns Hopkins University Press, 1982.

Zonis, Marvin. *The Political Elite of Iran*. Princeton: Princeton University Press, 1971.

Index